Scars of Conquest/
Masks of Resistance

Scars of Conquest/ Masks of Resistance

The Invention of Cultural Identities in African, African-American, and Caribbean Drama

TEJUMOLA OLANIYAN

New York   Oxford
OXFORD UNIVERSITY PRESS
1995

Oxford University Press

Oxford   New York
Athens   Auckland   Bangkok   Bombay
Calcutta   Capetown   Dar es Salaam   Delhi
Florence   Hong Kong   Istanbul   Karachi
Kuala Lumpur   Madras   Madrid   Melbourne
Mexico City   Nairobi   Paris   Singapore
Taipei   Tokyo   Toronto

and associated companies in
Berlin   Ibadan

Copyright © 1995 by Tejumola Olaniyan

Published by Oxford University Press, Inc.,
198 Madison Avenue, New York, New York 10016

Oxford is a registered trademark of Oxford University Press

Library of Congress Cataloging-in-Publication Data
Olaniyan, Tejumola.
Scars of conquest/masks of resistance : the invention of cultural identities in African,
African-American, and Caribbean drama/Tejumola Olaniyan.
p. cm.   Includes bibliographical references (p.) and index.
ISBN 0-19-509405-0.—ISBN 0-19-509406-9 (pbk.)
1. American drama—Afro-American authors—History and criticism
2. Baraka, Imamu Amiri, 1934– —Criticism and interpretation.   3. Shange, Ntozake—
Criticism and interpretation.   4. Afro-Americans in literature.   5. Walcott, Derek—Dramatic works.
6. Soyinka, Wole—Dramatic works.   7. Caribbean Area—In literature.
8. Africa—In literature.   9. Blacks in literature.   I. Title.
PS338.N4043   1995
809.2'008996073—dc20   94-33238

A portion of an earlier and abbreviated version of chapter 5 appeared in *Imagination, Emblems and Expression: Essays on Latin American, Caribbean, and Continental Culture and Identity*, edited by Helen Ryan-Ranson, copyright 1993 by The Popular Press.

Balboa/The Liar from *Dead Lecturer/Three Books* by Amiri Baraka. Reprinted by permission of Sterling Lord Literistic, Inc. Copyright © 1975 by Amiri Baraka.

"Note on Commercial Theatre" from *Selected Poems* by Langston Hughes. Reprinted by permission of Harold Ober Associates Incorporated. Copyright © 1959 by Langston Hughes.

Reprinted with permission of Simon & Schuster and Reed Consumer Books Ltd. from *for colored girls who have considered suicide when the rainbow is enuf* by Ntozake Shange. Copyright © 1975, 1976, 1977 by Ntozake Shange.

Sassafrass, Cypress & Indigo by Ntozake Shange, Copyright © 1982 by Ntozake Shange, St. Martin's Press, Inc., New York, NY and Methuen London.

"Letter to a Feminist Friend" by Molara Ogundip-Leslie from *Women in Nigeria Today* by Felix Mthali, published by Zed Books, London. Reprinted by permission of the publisher.

Excerpts from *Collected Poems 1948–1984* by Derek Walcott. Copyright © 1986 by Dereck Walcott. Reprinted by permission of Farrar, Straus & Giroux, Inc. and Faber & Faber.

Excerpts from *Dream on Monkey Mountain* by Derek Walcott. Copyright © 1970 by Derek Walcott. Reprinted by permission of Farrar, Straus & Giroux.

1 3 5 7 9 8 6 4 2

Printed in the United States of America
on acid-free paper

For Oyedun and 'Joko
in memoriam

Acknowledgments

This study has benefited from a great deal of support, both intellectual and material. I am highly indebted to my very good friends and former teachers Timothy Murray, Biodun Jeyifo, and Henry L. Gates, Jr., for their unending encouragement and intellectual succor and challenge. Always with great and meticulous care, they read versions of this work and offered useful critical insights. They were part of the general stimulating environment at Cornell University to which I am indebted more than I can acknowledge. The members of the Marxist Literary Group and Colonialism reading group provided a highly supportive atmosphere at the initial stages of this work.

Friendly as well as professional backing at various times came from Laura Brown, Walter Cohen, Satya P. Mohanty, David Bathrick, Kwame A. Appiah, and Tom Lodge.

The ambitious scope of the work in bridging the Atlantic would have remained a mere wish without a generous two-year fellowship from the Carter G. Woodson Institute for Afro-American and African Studies at the University of Virginia. A substantial part of the work was written during my tenure in this highly congenial milieu. I am deeply grateful for the unflagging support of the staff of the institute, especially Gail Shirley, administrative assistant, Mary Rose, programmer, William E. Jackson, associate director for research, and Armstead Robinson, director. The presence of other fellows, especially Terry Epperson, Mieko Nishida, Marianne Ferme, and Michele Wagner, conspired to make my stay at the institute rewarding. Deborah E. McDowell, attentive friend and colleague, read and offerred valuable comments on the manuscript.

Further work on the project was carried out during my tenure as a Rockefeller Residency fellow at Northwestern University's Institute for Advanced Study and Research in the African Humanities. In all respects, I found the institute an ideal working environment. I am grateful to the staff, especially David William Cohen, Ivan Karp (preceptor for 1991/ 92), Akbar Virmani, Roseanne Mark, Linda Kerr, and Sandra Collins, for their friendship and for supplying resources necessary for productive intellectual inquiry. I thank my unrelenting critical sparring partners, members of the Northwestern University-University of Chicago Red Lion Seminar, as well as my co-fellows Kofi Agovi, Adam Ashforth, Misty Bastian, Tim Burke, Nahum Chandler, Paulla Ebron, Abdullai Ibrahim, Cory Kratz, and Alan Waters. Sandra L. Richards, Margaret T. Drewal, Ralph Austen, Jean Comaroff, William Murphy, Catherine Bledsoe, and Olufemi Taiwo also contributed to the fruitful time I had in Evanston/Chicago.

Friends and former colleagues at the Obafemi Awolowo University and the University of Ibadan, Nigeria, kept up their interest and assistance throughout the writing. I am grateful to Femi Osofisan, Reuben Abati, Dele Layiwola, and Awam Amkpa.

For Wole Soyinka, it is, once again, thanks—for many things, besides his believing in me and his encouragement of this project. In spite of her busy schedule of lectures and performances, Ntozake Shange faithfully kept promises and returned phone calls—I am ashamed to admit that I was in fact amazed by this.

At the University of the West Indies, Mona Campus, Jamaica, I received assistance in various ways from Harclyde Walcott, director, Creative Arts Centre; Elizabeth Wilson, then chairperson, French Department; Rex Nettleford; Mervin Morris, who helped so much in spite of his absence when I was there; and the staff of the West Indian Collection of the UWI Library. Special thanks to Carolyn Allen, who made many needed connections for me and guided me through the exciting Kingston theater scene. The Sistren Theatre Collective allowed me to attend some of its workshops and gave me access to its video library. I thank all the sisters, especially Beverly Hanson and Honor Ford-Smith, with whom I had extended interviews. Ruby Burthon of the National Library of Jamaica tirelessly tracked down reviews of past productions. At the UWI Saint Augustine Campus, Trinidad, I enjoyed the superb hospitality of the Aiyejinas, the family of my former teacher and friend, Funso Aiyejina. Rawle Gibbons, director of the Creative Arts Centre, granted me an interview and took me round theaters in Port-of-Spain. This work would have been much poorer without the support of these individuals and institutions.

I am greatly indebted to Liz Maguire, Colby Stong, and Elda Rotor at Oxford University Press for their unflagging assistance and understanding. A portion of an earlier and abbreviated version of Chapter 5 appeared in *Imagination, Emblems and Expression: Essays on Latin American, Caribbean, and Continental Culture and Identity,* edited by Helen Ryan-Ranson of the Popular Press. I also acknowledge the University of Virginia Small Grants Committee for its assistance in defraying permission expenses.

The closest supervision of this work comes from Mojisola Olaniyan—who also did the initial word-processing—and the "train." It is difficult to admit but there just are times when an intellectual activity needs—demands—unappeasable disruption. It is a great treasure indeed to have at hand those who know when and how to do so constructively.

Contents

Introduction   3

I   Contingent "Origins"

1. Agones: The Constitution of a Practice   11

    A Colonialist Discourse   12
    A Counterhegemonic Discourse   18
    A Post-Afrocentric Discourse   26

2. Difference, Differently   29

    The Expressive and the Performative   30
    Cultural Identity as Articulation   35
    Genre   37
    Language   38

II   Inventing Cultural Identities

*3. Wole Soyinka: "Race Retrieval" and Cultural
Self-Apprehension*   43

    Assimilative Wisdom and Period Dialectics   45
    History as Mythopoeic Resource   49
    The Cultural, the Political   58

4. *LeRoi Jones/Amiri Baraka: The Motion of History*   67

    The Violence of Naming   67
    The Protean Essence   69

5. *Derek Walcott: Islands of History at a Rendezvous
   with a Muse*   93

    History as Culture: The Romance of Adam   97
    Toward Inflammatory Dreams (for the New World Black) 104
    Author as Text and Character   109
    Coherent Deformation and Its Context   111

6. *Ntozake Shange: The Vengeance of Difference, or
   The Gender of Black Cultural Identity*   116

    Combat Breathing   120
    "A Layin on of Hands"   128

7. *Subjectivities and Institutions*   139

    Notes   143
    Bibliography   171
    Index   191

Scars of Conquest/
Masks of Resistance

Introduction

Ralph Ellison once said that "it is not culture which binds the peoples who are of partially African origin now scattered throughout the world, but an identity of passions."[1] With repetitive urgency, Wole Soyinka, the Nigerian poet and playwright and Nobel laureate, never ceases to emphasize the cultural particularity of his dramaturgy: its source in the "African worldview." The South African Black Consciousness theater, both in its early days and in its later offshoots, was preoccupied with self-definition as a cultural arm of the struggle against apartheid. The late 1960s and early 1970s black activist theater in the United States flaunted new myths, songs, symbols, and values, presenting itself as a "post-American form" categorically asserting African-American cultural autonomy. Caribbean dramatists have been no less preoccupied with defining an identifiable cultural matrix for their work. Derek Walcott, St. Lucian poet and dramatist, another Nobelist, after facing a series of dead-ends—the impossibility of being Marlowe's heir in spite of his mastery of Western forms, the difficulties of an unproblematic look to Africa for succor, and the new Caribbean nation-states' corruption of viable folk forms—finally settles for "using old names anew," a strategy he sees as apt for the "hybrid" West Indies. This study investigates this dominant preoccupation with the refashioning of the cultural self in the drama of English-speaking peoples of African origin cross-culturally and cross-continentally. The euphoria over political decolonization in the erstwhile colonies subsided quickly to the sobering realization of unabated *cultural* imperialism,[2] and African-American writers have never considered their cultural Americanness unproblematic.

In reading this agonistic condition and one of its effects, specifically the constitution of a practice known as " 'African' "[3] or "black" drama and theater, I find rewarding the concept of *discourse*. "Discourse" is not only "a violence that we do to things . . . a practice that we impose upon them,"[4] as Foucault says, but also a violence, a practice that we do to and impose on human beings; "the complexes of signs and practices which organize social existence and social reproduction."[5] To speak of discourse is to speak against the given and the inevitable and to emphasize instead the enormous transformational *work* involved in the construction of social phenomena, and hence their overdetermined and contingent existence. Since discourse is not monologic but multiple and most often dispersed and contradictory,[6] the realm of the social is replete with agones, scars, and masks both offensive and defensive—incessant battles for the framing and definition of "reality." "Engaged with the realities of power," Richard Terdiman writes, "human communities use words not in contemplation but in *competition*."[7] The competing discursive practices that constitute the social are not equal in their effects. Some exercise effects of supremacy though never complete hegemony, while others are consigned to querulous subordination.

What I discover in a close examination of the transcontinental "passions"—the all-consuming quest for the manufacture of postimperial dramatic subjectivity—is the conflictual interaction of three discursive formations: a hegemonic, colonialist, *Eurocentric* discourse distinguished by its prejudiced representation of black cultural forms; an anticolonialjist, *Afrocentric* counterdiscourse preoccupied with subverting the Eurocentric and registering cultural autonomy; and a budding, liminal, interstitial discourse that aims at once to be both anticolonialist and *post-Afrocentric*.[8] The post-Afrocentric's great strength is a singular insistence on unscrambling and supplanting the excessive Manichaeism that both constitutes the Eurocentric and undermines the subversive potential of the Afrocentric, while affirming instead the foundational premise of an irreversible imbrication of histories, and therefore of cultures and cultural forms. I devote Chapter 1 to excavating these contingent, overdetermined origins of the project of inventing a black dramatic voice self-consciously embedded in a cultural matrix.

The prime animating question of the three discursive complexes is how to *think difference*. I suggest that inscribed in them, implicitly or explicitly, are two conceptual paradigms of cultural identity and difference: the *expressive*, with its rigid claims and oftentimes unexamined ethnocentric biases; and the *performative*, a self-critical model that conceives identity as open, interculturally negotiable, and always in the making—a *process*. Even some of the assumptions of the performative, I find, need revisioning, which leads me to propose an enabling performative identity as "articulation," not only nonessentialist in its insistence on an abrasion of histories but also emphasizing, as an articulated structure, interactional levels of subordination and the exercise of power within, between, and among cultures and cultural forms, structured as they are, in dominance. I substantiate my suggestion in detail in Chapter 2, also examining its implications for approaching perhaps the two most intractable dilemmas of the anti-Eurocentric discourses (both Afrocentric and post-Afrocentric), genre and language.

The dramatists I examine in the next chapters propose, in general, the performative identity, though not before or without some vacillation or submission to the conservative norms of the expressive. Soyinka's proposition of an African worldview has often been disdained as purist. But his vista does not exclude the European experience, which he has in fact actively and creatively appropriated. His famous theory of African tragedy, "The Fourth Stage," is inconceivable as it is without Nietzsche and ancient Greek mythology, yet this is elicited largely from the features of deities in (his) Yoruba cosmology. Fundamentalist Afrocentric critics, on the other hand, have condemned this composite, describing Soyinka as an agent of Western cultural imperialism. I insist that the ambiguities of Soyinka's performative aesthetics lie elsewhere, for instance, in his apprehension and utilization of difference. While his plays repeatedly present characters whose antagonisms are fueled by class or gender frictions, his critical essays insistently question the appropriateness of class or gender considerations in the formulation of African cultural identity. With Europe, difference is affirmed, but "internally" it is questioned.

An ambiguity of a different sort is evinced in Walcott's works. His suggestion of a nodal "mulatto" aesthetics recognizes not only the leading influence of African-derived cultural forms but also other contributory streams that make up the Caribbean. He has faced charges of Eurocentrism but again, as in the case of Soyinka, a superb mastery of Western forms seems to be a main catalyst for the accusations. The productive manner to engage Walcott, I argue, is to question his opposition, in defining the context of possibility of a hybrid style and cultural identity, between history as culture and history as politics. As if these are absolutes, he privileges the former and condemns the latter, thereby freezing their identities—an overreaction to the proponents of political commitment in art whose cost hangs spectrally on his performative dramaturgy.

Baraka is the least ambiguous but the most *dramatic*: from a romantic rebellion against bourgeois norms to an expressive, particularist cultural nationalism to an equally restrictive, doctrinaire Marxism and now to an open Marxism-feminism. It is a mark of Baraka's enduring performative outlook that he has never ceased self-reexamination. From seeking exclusively black dramaturgic forms, he has turned to diverse directions for inspiration, including film. Against the stereotype of Baraka that we all know too well, I argue that the nodal point of his artistic practice is *change*—the open and the tentative—what cannot not be privileged in fashioning an African-American difference: an eloquent prescription for a ceaselessly harried and harrassed identity.

If it has not been too difficult for these writers to propose a difference, an identity, alert to Western cultural domination, it has been quite a problem for them to conceive of one that would *also* recognize, and find noncoercive ways of negotiating, the fact that inscribed in difference is a repetition without an end. So far, the most profound and articulate nemesis of the discourse of black cultural identity has been gender and its contingencies. Hence my critique of the three leading dramatists proceeds through a detailed consideration of the feminist artist Ntozake Shange, who is also engaged in the same struggle but in ways that interrogate, extend, and re-vision the work of the other three.

My choice of dramatists for examination is guided by the *extent, consistency,* and *complexity* of engagement with the historic issue of black–white encounter in general and the impact of Euro-American cultural hegemony on black cultural identity in particular. By coincidence, my choices also happen to be leading playwrights in their respective regions. The evident cross-continental, cross-cultural bent is meant not to propose a sameness of black cultures across space or time or to so much affirm an identity of "race" as to also, *simultaneously*—and perhaps more importantly—underscore, as Ellison put it, an "identity of passions." The diversity in choice of playwrights affords us an interesting view of how similar passions due to comparable sociohistorical experiences are played out differently across cultures diverse but not completely alien to one another.

My emphasis is on the literary artists, the "intellectuals." But they constitute by no means the only group sensitive to, or preoccupied with, questions of Western cultural imperialism and black cultural identity. There are vibrant traditions of popular theater, especially in Africa and the Caribbean, that are also engaged with like issues.[9] Their formulations of cultural difference are equally worthy of close attention and even serious comparison with those of the literary dramatists. For one thing, it is not always the case that there is or will be a congruence of views between "professional" intellectuals and popular culture producers on the representation of common experience or history.[10] Such a comparison is a promising area for exploration but it is beyond the scope of this book.

Some notes are in order on the title of this study. "Scar" and "mask" conceptually delineate the dual-voiced character of the project of black cultural identity; a balance of historical subjection, with all its underlying originary violence, on the one hand, and a bold assertion of subjectivity on the other. We lose sight of the relational character of black difference if we ignore this dialectical formulation. "Invention" is simultaneously a key category of dramatic/theatrical production and a suggestive epistemological foothold into certain social processes. Thus "inventing cultural identities" does not refer simply to the *cultural self-*definitions evident in black dramatic practice but also to the fact that subjectivity as such is inaccessible to us except through staging, representation, performance, invention, *work*—self-autonomy is never absolute and the space of the subject is always a contingent one; the notion of a subject original and central to all the elaborate processes of knowing, especially as has been constructed for the Western liberal Subject, is precisely what the existence of the subordinate discourses—Afrocentric and post-Afrocentric—give the lie to.[11]

The materials mobilized toward this study also require some discussion. In investigating propositions of a "distinctively culturally situated black dramatic *practice*" ("practice" understood as social process whose multifaceted parts resist any arbitrary hierarchical or puritanical categorization), I have had to pay close attention to many sources, beyond dramatic texts and/or performances. In this work, a writer's dramatic text, theoretical reflections, poetry and fiction where appropriate, and biographical details, as well as reviews of other writers, critical reception of the writer's work, and the general discursive context of the writer's practice, are all considered crucial to the task at hand. They not only yield crucial insights into the formation, consolidation, and diffusion of aesthetic practices and attendant ideological attitudes, but they also constitute important elements of the repertoire of dramatic/theatrical memory. Hence my attention to the materials, conventionally thought to be "primary" or "secondary" or "tertiary," critically interact with, embed, determine, and point to one another in a relentlessly *open* manner. This, in my view, is the kind of attention due to social practices. But enough of these foyer and ticket-counter introductions, let us enter the theater and let the *show* begin. . . .

I
Contingent "Origins"

1

Agones: The Constitution of a Practice

The historicity of contemporary black (African, African-American, and Caribbean) dramatic practice is unintelligible outside the agonistic interactions among three main competing, more-or-less coherent discursive formations: the hegemonic, colonialist *Eurocentric*; the counter-hegemonic, anticolonialist *Afrocentric*; and an *emerging post-Afrocentric*, which subverts both the Eurocentric and the Afrocentric while refining and advancing the aims of the latter.[1] The emphasis here is on the sociality of the discourses as concrete practices within contested and contestable spaces. For instance, the Eurocentric discourse on black drama is thinkable only within the materiality of the rise of Europe, the conquest and enslavement of African peoples, colonialism, neocolonialism, and ongoing aggressive capitalist imperialism. The numerous slave rebellions, emancipation, the massive wave of decolonization followed by the anguish of arrested decolonization—so well described by Edward Said[2]— and the contemporary general assaults on the authority of Western culture form the substance and condition of possibility of the two anti-Eurocentric discourses. In emphasizing this historicity, what I intend is nothing less than an account of the social foundations of an aesthetic form, of the invention of a culturally situated "black" dramatic theory and practice. The account is also, in its own way, an aspect of the story of how the West was won and of the resistance of the victims to making this winning a zero-sum.

In illustrating the discourses, I will focus on significant junctures and representative cases, rather than on an accumulation of data. This means that a lot will be left out, given the vastness of the field. The main point of this study does not depend, however, on an encyclopedic exemplification of the various formations but rather on the adequacy of the adopted methodology: to yield valuable insights even with skeletal instantiations.

A Colonialist Discourse

> There is a fact: White men consider themselves superior to black men.
>
> Frantz Fanon[3]

> There is first affirmed the existence of human groups having no culture; then of a hierarchy of cultures; and finally, the concept of cultural relativity.
>
> Frantz Fanon[4]

> . . . what, then, is at work, if not desire and power?
>
> Michel Foucault[5]

The Eurocentric discourse on black drama rests on a number of settled assumptions, practices, and "critical" orthodoxies. The ruling norm here is the implacable inferiorization of black cultures and cultural forms. It is asserted or implied that blacks have no indigenous traditions of drama. Where it is conceded that blacks may indeed have dramatic traditions, a hierarchy is erected in which, compared with Europe and Asia, these traditions are found to be merely "proto-dramatic" or "quasi-dramatic," forms in a state of developmental arrest in terms of style, aesthetic canons, formalization of technique, and mode of historical transmission. Closely related is the claim that if there is indeed a "properly dramatic" black tradition, then—like "education," Christianity, and so on—it is obviously another great advantage of the Africa–Europe encounter. In other words, these properly dramatic black traditions are but mere derivatives of Western forms and traditions.[6]

In the larger symbolic realm, beyond debates about the identity of a cultural form, what is at stake is nothing less than the black's capacity for culture. This should surprise none, for the founding "regime of truth" of the "prehistory" of this discourse is constituted by the subjectivist racist discourse of such names with enormous social and symbolic "capital"[7] such as Hegel, Jefferson, Hume, Kant, Frobenius, Freud, Gobineau, Tempels, Levy-Bruhl, and a host of other participating "fellows"[8]—explorers, colonial administrators, missionaries, ethnologists, and so on.[9] And "a great array of bayonets and cannons,"[10] Fanon writes, facilitated its dominance. I will examine this formation's claims in some detail through two performance traditions of critical significance to the constitution of black drama in Africa-America and the Caribbean, black-face minstrelsy and the Trinidad Carnival; and the scholarly debate on the presence or absence of "drama" in Africa.

The blackface minstrelsy, which numerous critics and scholars consider the first quintessentially American theatrical entertainment, flourished roughly between the early nineteenth century and the 1920s.[11] White performers in "blacked-up" faces, elaborate makeup, and costume grotesquely represent what they consider black "peculiarities," to the hilarity and delight of their equally white audiences. Troupes proliferated with the form's increasing popularity. Blackface minstrelsy was by no means the first instance of white impersonation of blacks on the American stage. Preceding it—even overlapping with it—was the tradition of nineteenth-century melodramas and farces in which "white low comics and supernumeraries typically played black characters . . . [v]ariously called such zany names as Cusha, Pompey, Cincinatus, Sam, Juba, Cato, and the inevitable Sambo . . . [and] merely functioned as one-line comic domestics."[12] But it was minstrelsy, wholly devoted, as a group announced in 1834, to the performance of the "oddities, peculiarities, eccentricities, and comicalities of that Sable Genus of Humanity" that caught on, arrested the national imagination for over half a century, and commanded extensive acclaim and adoration "from the White House to the California gold fields, from New Orleans to New England, from riverboats and saloons to 2500–seat theaters."[13]

With comic grotesquery as the informing principle of representation, minstrelsy emphasized "black" physical features, manners, dances, speech, music, religion, dress, and so on, in a most sensational and exaggerated form. Embellished by wigs, burnt cork, and carmine, minstrels performed weird body contortions, slapstick gags, jokes, and burlesque skits. In all this the model is the southern plantation slave, represented in a study as "the folk-figure of a simple, somewhat rustic character, instinctively humorous, irrationally credulous, gifted in song and dance, interesting in spontaneous frolic, endowed with artless philosophy."[14] The theatrical representations elaborate this sketch into the black as lazy and shiftless, afflicted with a peculiar appetite for watermelon, which is devoured in an equally peculiar manner, a cavernous mouth coming in handy, which, on other occasions, shapes itself into unmatchably funny and slavishly broad grins, or as a funnel for a glass too many of cheap gin, or yet as witness to atrocious incapacities such as twisted pronunciations, meaningless long words, and incomprehensible jabberings. With the honored predilection for the choice mixture in costume of the most violent and flashy colors, the black becomes a vain, grotesque, "feeble-mindedness" in human form. "Throughout the life of blackface minstrelsy as a popular form, " Jeyifo writes, "it projected one composite, undifferentiated image of blacks: that of *Sambo*, the overgrown child of great näiveté and obtuseness, often given to impudence but basically of affecting good humor and simplicity."[15]

Perhaps more than any discursive complex, blackface minstrelsy contributed significantly to the establishment of a particular kind of American perception of blacks and their cultural difference, and the evolution of enduring negative stereotypes. It is only too obvious that "Sambo was ultimately intended to subordinate a minority group."[16] For instance, though black inferiorization was the norm of the shows, in the early years skits were sometimes interspersed with occasional swipes at the brutality and inhumanity of the sponsoring context, slavery, though not necessarily out of any principled abhorrence of the system or sympathy for the slaves. However, when the early 1850s crisis set in, threatening the stability of the Union and institutionalized white privilege, the negative representations of slavery "virtually disappeared, leaving only contrasting caricatures of contented slaves and unhappy free Negroes."[17] This dominating apparatus was so powerful that when freedom came, the black troupes that emerged were forced by circumstances—of a highly commercialized enterprise controlled and patronized by whites—to take up wholesale the performance formats and standard repertoire of the white companies, including the blackened face, widened mouth, and all those outward markers set up to signify a feeble mind. Very few contexts could boast of so blatant a circumscription of a dominated group's self-representation. Yet if we ignore or devalue this problematic, multivocal black participation in a discourse designed for their subjection, we would be overlooking one of the origins of an *authentic* African-American theatrical subjectivity.

For the better part of the first few decades of this century, black theatrical presence on the American stage simply refused to excise its conceptual moorings from the minstrelsy, from the early black musicals to the white-controlled, "radical" Federal Theater units.[18] Even post-1960s black theater, with its generally more self-conscious attitude to the formal determinants of its practice, cannot pretend to have escaped minstrelsy's shadow. When Ntozake Shange attempted to exorcise this ghost in 1979 in her *spell #7*, she realized painfully that "the minstrel may be 'banned' as racist/ but the minstrel is more powerful in his deformities than our alleged rejection of him," hence after performance every night, "we wd be grandly applauded."[19]

It is interesting to compare the blackface minstrelsy, in terms of growth and influence, with what appears to be its West Indian version, the Trinidadian *camboulay*. Thanks to such factors as the numerical superiority of the slaves and the peculiarities of West Indian slavery (the phenomenon of absentee landlords, for instance), camboulay never developed into an extensive, highly packaged commercialized form or exercised such an enduring dominative influence as its American counterpart. The other important factor was that camboulay was never cut off from its secure, ceremonial location within a specific, ephemeral, time-delineated cultural occasion/form, the carnival.

A typical fare of preabolition (1834) Trinidad carnival, camboulay was almost a parallel development with minstrelsy. It featured the "pillars of society"—the white planter aristocrats and overseers—caricaturing their slaves and performing slave dances and songs, to the rhythm of "African drums." Errol Hill in *The Trinidad Carnival* cites a correspondent—a retired planter—in the *Port-of-Spain Gazette* of March 19, 1881, on this form:

> At the time carnival flourished, the elite of society was masked or disguised. The favorite costume of the ladies was the graceful and costly "mulatress" of the period, while gentlemen adopted that of the garden Negro, in Creole, *negue jadin*, or black field slave. At carnival time our mothers and grandmothers have even danced the *belair* to the African drum whose sounds did not offend their dainty ears, and our fathers and grandfathers danced the *bamboula*, the *ghouba*, and the *calinda* . . . sometimes also the *negue jadin* united in bands would proceed on evenings to the *cannes brulees*. Their splendid march with torches through the town streets imitated what actually took place in the estates when a plantation was on fire. In such cases laborers on neighboring estates were conducted there alternately, day and night, to assist in grinding the burned canes before they went sour; thus the *cannes brulees*.[20]

Introduced to the region by the whites, the Trinidad carnival was for long kept up and sanitized against the participation of other racial groups. A strictly hierarchical society, the recognized distinctions were, in order of importance, "Whites, Free Persons of Colour, Indians and Slaves." Permission for non-white participation in the revelries, of course, followed this hierarchy, as a former police chief, L. M. Fraser, reported in 1881:

> The Free Persons of Colour were subjected to very stringent Regulations and although not forbidden to mask, were yet compelled to keep to themselves and never presumed to join in the amusements of the privileged class. The Indians kept entirely aloof, and the slaves except as onlookers, or by special favour when required to take part, had no share in the Carnival which was confined exclusively to the upper class of the community.[21]

As long as the status quo remained, the available newspapers—veritable mirrors of ruling class opinion—supported the carnival with elaborate reports and "flattering praise for the glitter and the merrymaking escapades of the upper-class maskers." However, following emancipation in 1834—and then the abolition of compulsory apprenticeship in 1838—when the former slaves and other lower-class elements practically appropriated the carnival, the tone of these papers changed dramatically, becoming "antipathetic and hostile." The upper-class whites withdrew from the carnival. In Fraser's view, Carnival became a "disorderly amusement for the lower classes." As early as the very first year of freedom, a paper lamented the "deficiency of elegant bustle, which was to be seen during the Carnival week of olden times." In 1838 it was a "wretched buffoonery" which can only "brutalize the faculty of the lower order of our population."[22] The campaign for its abolition, ultimately unsuccessful, continued throughout the century.

Camboulay passed on to the former slaves, who staged it with great devotion, complete with the black makeup and costume, just as in black participation in blackfaced minstrelsy—a representation of a representation. Unlike minstrelsy, however, what was caricatured in camboulay was not the slaves' so-called peculiarities but their response to a particularly agonizing moment of forced labor. This accounted, perhaps, for the ex-slaves' prompt and passionate appropriation of the form. The *Port-of-Spain Gazette* certainly grasped the power and subversive potential of such passionate enactments when it described a performance in 1858 as little more than "the hooting of a parcel of semi-savages . . . exhibiting hellish scenes and the most demoniacal representations of the days of slavery as they were forty years ago."[23] Decades, even over a century later, we still hear echoes of this description in the representations of black West Indian performance forms by scholars such as Martha W. Beckwith, Richardson Wright, and Ivy Baxter.[24]

While the former slaves, appropriating Carnival with their own forms, insisted on connectedness of histories by their cultural eclecticism, the whites violently clung to difference and purism, even at the cost of giving up and labeling inferior a form they had evidently enjoyed so much. The dominant white attitude to carnival did not begin to change to tolerance until the late teens and early twenties of this century. But even if this were otherwise, the influence of this form was bound to be profound on contemporary Caribbean drama.

The colonialist Eurocentric discourse on continental African performance forms is similarly fixated with conceptual purism. Here the emphasis is largely on a critical definition of what constitutes "drama" in Africa. Ruth Finnegan's influential work, *Oral Literature in Africa*, published in 1970, is singular in this regard. Her chapter "Drama" still remains for many the canonical survey. Her opening lines alone reveal her unconfessed limitations and restrictive methodology:

> How far one can speak of indigenous drama in Africa is not an easy question. In this it differs from previous topics [treated in the book] like, say, panegyric, political poetry, or prose narratives, for there it was easy to discover African analogies to the familiar European forms.[25]

Only if Africa could supply indigenous "analogies to the familiar European forms" would it be established as a continent with drama. Yet it is not difficult to contend that her proposition still leaves a space of freedom, a leeway, if only "analogy" were interpreted with some vision and creativity, away from the anesthesia of thesaurus and dictionary entries. Shunning this path, Finnegan keeps looking for European drama on the African continent: "what . . . *we* normally regard as drama"; what "*we* are accustomed [to]." The "definition" of drama she proposes, in all its pedantic formalism, is designed to achieve little else if not failure:

> It is clearly necessary to reach at least some rough agreement about what is to count as "drama". Rather than produce a verbal definition, it seems better to point to the various elements which tend to come together in what, in the wide sense, we normally regard as drama. Most important is the idea of enactment, of representation through actors who imitate persons and events. This is also usually associated with other elements, appearing to a greater or lesser degree at different times or places: linguistic content; plot; the represented interaction of several characters; specialized scenery, etc.; often music; and—of particular importance in most African performances—dance. Now it is very seldom in Africa that all these elements of drama come together in a single performance.

Her—undeniably productive—failure prepares and authorizes her thesis, even against acknowledged contrary evidence: "Though some writers have very positively affirmed the existence of native African drama, it would perhaps be truer to say that in Africa, in contrast to Western Europe and Asia, drama is not typically a wide-spread or a developed form."[26]

In the long passage that follows, let me direct attention to Finnegan's important newfound lack in African drama, "tragedy" (the highest and most civilized art, thanks to Aristotle), and to the redoubtable performance of discursive violence especially in the consistent attribution of difference as fault and, toward the end, the visitation of a clear haziness of vision and failure of scholarship upon supposed inadequacies of the phenomenon under study:

> We go further and add that what dramatic or quasi- dramatic performances can be discovered never seem to involve tragedy in the normal sense. The events and characters are depicted as comedy, and treated more or less realistically, even cynically. Though costumes and masks are sometimes important, there is no evidence of specialized scenery or of buildings or sites specifically designed for theatrical performances. The players are sometimes skilled experts or belong to artistic associations such as the *Ekine* Society, but there is no tradition of *professional* actors. The audience, finally, is sometimes a "pure" audience in the sense that it appreciates without itself taking part directly; but, with the significance of the dance and the absence of the "proscenium barrier," there is often a tendency to greater audience participation than is typical of most recent Western drama. We can also make other negative points. Little direct light is thrown on the question of the origin of drama by a study of African dramatic forms— except possibly in the vague sense that it might be said to enlarge our general view of the possibilities of drama, or of certain elements in drama. Similarly it adds little support to the kind of tragic archetypes and of rituals ultimately referable to *The Golden Bough.*[27]

When a few years later E. T. Kirby begins his essay "Indigenous African Theatre" thus: "It is true, as Ruth Finnegan has observed . . . ,"[28] he testifies to the epidemic of a new narcissistic theoretical canon.

It is important to understand Finnegan's concept of difference, given her insistence that Africans in Africa produce European drama. To the extent that we are all the same, her work becomes unnecessary. If it is difference that enables her project, then her insistence on its erasure becomes paradoxical. But we must not assume that this illogicality lacks any logic, or that it thus self-destructs in the realm of power. Difference here is not erased but whipped into conformity and delimited in a *hierarchy*.[29] It is interesting then to note that Ibadan, where Finnegan stayed for a time while working on her book, and where she signed the preface, is one of the main centers of the still vibrant Yoruba traveling theater "movement," with a recorded tradition going back to the late 1590s.[30] Apparently this theater refused to provide Finnegan with "analogies to the familiar European forms."

We can say only that black drama or lack of it that appears in Eurocentric discourse is, as Edward Said writes of the Orient in *Orientalism*, "a system of representations framed by a whole set of forces" that brings it into the orbit of Western consciousness and empire.[31] It has little to do with a supposed original model, though Eurocentrism never ceases to claim dispassionate investigation, "scientificity," "realism," and "truth." Nor is the power, efficacy, and value of Eurocentrism as an apparatus of domination in any way dependent on the closeness of its representations to the presumed "real." Amilcar Cabral shows best this apparatus of domination in its broadest ramifications:

> The practice of imperialist rule—its affirmation or negation—demanded (and still demands) a more or less accurate knowledge of the society it rules and of the historical reality (. . . economic, social, and cultural) in the middle of which it exists. This knowledge is necessarily exposed in terms of comparison with the dominating subject and with its own historical reality. Such a knowledge is a vital necessity in the practice of imperialist rule which results in the confrontation, mostly violent, between two identities which are totally dissimilar in their historical elements and contradictory in their different functions. The search for such a knowledge contributed to a general enrichment of human and social knowledge in spite of the fact that it was one- sided, subjective, and very often unjust.[32]

A Counterhegemonic Discourse

> There is a fact: White men consider themselves superior to black men.
> There is another fact: Black men want to prove to white men, at all costs, the richness of their thought, the equal value of their intellect.
>
> Frantz Fanon

> You've taken my blues and gone—
> You sing 'em on Broadway

And you sing 'em in Hollywood Bowl,
You mixed 'em up with symphonies
And you fixed 'em
So they don't sound like me.
Yep, you done taken my blues and gone.
You also took my spirituals and gone.
You put me in *Macbeth* and *Carmen Jones*
And in all kinds of *Swing Mikados*
And in everything but what's about me—
But someday somebody'll
Stand up and talk about me,
And write about me—
Black and beautiful—
And sing about me,
And put on plays about me!
I reckon it'll be
Me myself!
Yes, it'll be me!

Langston Hughes[33]

Our aim was to give vent to our talent and to prove to everybody who was willing to look, to watch, to listen, that we were as good at drama as anybody else had been or could be. The door was opened a tiny bit to us and, as always, the Black man, when faced with an open door, no matter how small the wedge might be, eased in.

Clarence Muse[34]

If it is the horizon of hope of every dominant discursive practice to be hegemonic, that is, to achieve the plenitude and immediacy of a fully operational "habitus"[35] so that it passes itself off as natural and becomes unconscious of its own construction—*genesis amnesia* in Bourdieu's phrase—it is the characteristic feature of counterdiscourses to insistently question this eloquent certitude and to emphasize instead the necessarily contingent status of the dominant. The claim of the dominant to seamlessly account for all experience is embarrassed by a force and passion that is not only disconcerting, but also negative. And this force is guaranteed, paradoxically, by an "internal necessity" that defines dominant discourses:

[N]ot only are they unable to admit difference, in a sense they are incapable of imagining it. This is so for a simple reason. Once imagined, even so that it might be proscribed, difference acquires a phantom but fundamental existence. If it is countenanced at all, its legitimation, its inclusion within the canons of the orthodox, has to that extent begun. Thus even the work of proscribing it must be proscribed."[36]

The task of proscription again discloses the fiction of inevitability and intrinsic self-evidence, and thus authorizes a counterdiscursive space, a space that is opened in a "structural limitation of social control," for no discourse is capable of hegemony with a totalitarian completeness. This is where we must locate the great value of counterdiscourses: as counterhegemonic practices, they are "the emergent principle of history's dynamism . . . the force which ensures the flow of social time," for "situated as other [they] have the capacity to *situate*: to relativize the authority and stability of a dominant system of utterances which cannot even countenance their existence. They read that which cannot read them all."[37]

In this capacity, however, lies a problematic feature of counterdiscourses: their deep and intricate relations with the dominant. They share the same ground with the dominant and thus run the risk of a fixation with the restrictive binary logics of the latter and of recycling its epistemological premises. It is not surprising then that many counterdiscourses are easily incorporated by the dominant.

In its multiplex manifestations, the anticolonialist, anti-Eurocentric counterdiscourse on black drama evinces these strengths as well as weaknesses. In its insistence on privileging the presence, point of view, and self-determination of Africans, continental or diasporan, this discourse has earned for itself the label "Afrocentric."[38]

The unevenness of this discourse demands concrete specification. Deeply inscribed in it is an unresolved tension between the imperatives of its counterhegemonic practice and the reality of an absence or underdevelopment of counterhegemonic infrastructures. Thus it is often the rule rather than the exception that many Afrocentric formulations unwittingly borrow supporting props, albeit in an inverted and most often subversive form, from the colonialist Eurocentric epistemology. We are led then to the formation's greatest strength and distinguishing hallmark: its *relativism*, the basis on which it challenges Eurocentric epistemological dominance by proposing different rationalities: there are different rules for what constitutes "drama" in different societies; European drama is not *the* norm. Trying to escape *a surrender to the logics of hegemonic representations*, it substitutes *a quest for different representations*. Let us briefly explore the significant traces of this pan-African formation.

In her famous 1895 lecture "The Value of Race Literature," Victoria Earle Matthews insisted that "[n]ever was the outlook for Race Literature brighter" in spite of the "appalling evil" of "oppressive legislation, aided by grossly inhuman customs" being suffered by the African-American. She thus advertised an agenda that, with rare singleness of purpose, would occupy the "race" for the better part of the twentieth century, a "recipe" for an escape from the clutches of minstrelsy.[39] Against the widespread "perverted and indifferent translations of those prejudiced against us," Matthews called for counterrepresentations, "thoughtful counter-irritants": a "Race Literature" that will not only emphasize "our history and individuality as a people" but also "suggest to the world the wrong and contempt with which the lion viewed the picture that the hunter and the famous painter besides, had drawn of the King of the Forest." She argued, though, that Race Literature does not mean "thoughtless praise of ourselves," a warning that presages later famous engagements with Negritude such as that of Wole Soyinka or Paulin Hountondji, or Cabral's own proposition of a liberating attitude to African cultural materials.[40]

One of the new talents mentioned by Matthews as hope for the literature of struggle was none other than W. E. B. Du Bois, who had just then obtained his Ph.D. at Harvard. Du Bois was to later play a prominent role in bringing to national prominence the problem of the representation of difference in American culture not only through his organizational acumen-his management of the National Association for the Advancement of Colored People (NAACP)—but also through his writings focusing on the politics of the production and circulation of cultural discourses and their attendant subjectivities. "The Negro in Art: How Shall He Be Portrayed?" took the form of a national debate as the Harlem Renaissance was just beginning. Du Bois subsequently put forward an idea for a theatrical counterdiscourse, elaborating its four fundamental principles: *About us, By us, For us,* and *Near us,* principles that directly challenged the reigning fashion of "Negro Theater" written and packaged by whites, and also the idea of audience and related theatrical success defined merely commercially, within the asphyxiating parameters of Broadway. With this manifesto also came Du Bois's *formal* preference for the pageant, a large-scale, large-cast theatrical event with diffused plot and dispersed climaxes, a form that simulates traditional African festivals and is at odds with the hegemonic tradition of the "well-made play." The Little Theatre Movement housed in Harlem, as well as the *Crisis* playwrighting contests, were designed to give institutional sanctions to the new theatrical practice.[41] The ultimate aim, Du Bois said, echoing a widespread conception at the time, was "a real folk-play movement of American Negroes."[42]

The "real folk" formulation is not unproblematic, to say the least.[43] Not even the age's most eloquent, and perhaps most influential formulation, Langston Hughes's "The Negro Artist and the Racial Mountain," is able to totally distance itself from the classical anthropological tone in its valorization of the vital and close-to-earth "low-down folks," and the matching condemnation of the pretentious, "standardized" culture of the black middle class.[44] A set of attributes the Eurocentric imagination attached to black culture—earthy, *natural*: a classical romantic whip against the *mechanistic* dominant white culture—is uncritically appropriated by the black (middle-class) intellectual and foisted on the black lower class. This twist is clearer in Alain Locke's understanding of the folk form and his investment of "Negro life" as its "authentic atmosphere": "The drama that will refine and entertain, that may even captivate us before long, is likely to be uncurdled, almost naive reflection of the poetry and

folk feeling of a people who have after all a different soul and tempera-
ment from that of the smug, unimaginative industrialist and the self-
righteous and inhibited Puritan."[45] This is another version of Negritude's
canonical nostrum expressed by Léopold Sédar Senghor: emotion is completely Negro as reason is Greek.[46]

But Locke was still able to envison a strikingly different dramatic practice, though he did not live to see it happen:

> Negro dramatic art must not only be liberated from the handicaps of external
> disparagement, but from its self- imposed limitation. It must more and more
> have the courage to be original, to break with established dramatic convention
> of all sorts. It must have the courage to develop its own idiom, to pour itself
> into new moulds; in short, to be experimental.[47]

Such iconoclastic experimentation did surface, decades later, with the
great cultural ferment of the 1960s known as the Black Arts Movement.
Unlike the previous eras preoccupied largely with a neutralization of the
"negative images of the race" while remaining essentially grounded
within the same aesthetic structure and vision that produced the lamented
images in the first place, the new dispensation made that received structure and vision constant targets of interrogation. The movement had a
variable character, for its interrogations did not always translate to enabling propositions. Thus it was that within a generally (racially) self-
critical movement, we also had full-blown what was the hidden prop of
the valorization of a supposedly "folk" black culture from Du Bois to
Locke: the reification of culture known as *cultural nationalism*.[48] In spite
of this, we could still say of the movement that never in the tradition was
there such an irruption so simultaneously inward—an uncompromising
critique of black culture itself—and outward—a re-visioning of the relationship with the larger social structure, in both national *and* international dimensions.[49]

The first anthology of the movement, *Black Fire*, edited by Amiri
Baraka and Larry Neal, appeared in 1968, containing essays, poetry, fiction, and short plays. It was, however, the *Drama Review* special issue
on black theater of the same year, edited by Ed Bullins, that immediately
became the movement's unofficial manifesto. Together with *Black Expression* (1969) and *The Black Aesthetic* (1971), these anthologies codified
the movement's central concern, the development of an anti-Eurocentric,
anti-imperialist theatrical-cultural practice known as the "black aesthetic."[50] LeRoi Jones/Amiri Baraka, unarguably the one in the
movement in whom the consciousness explosion of the times received its
most complex expression, articulated the informing operational canons
of this aesthetic:

> I would like to . . . say that my conception of art, black art, is that it has to be
> collective, it has to be functional, it has to be committed and that actually, if
> it's not stemming from conscious nationalism, then at this time it's invalid.
> When I say collective, that it comes from the collective experience of black

people, when I say committed, it has to be committed to change, revolutionary change. When I say functional, it has to have a function to the lives of black people.[51]

In these terms, the new black theater literally defined itself away from the mainstream American theater. "Collective" pushes this theater from the norm of formalized entertainment symbolized by Broadway to a non-play event characteristic of communal rituals and religious occasions. "Committed" underscores consciousness grasped as transitory, continually transforming itself in response—"functional"—to the perceived needs, hopes, and aspirations of black people. The task, properly perceived, is a quest for form, suggested by Baraka as *post-white* or *post-American form.*

These largely didactic expositions interspersed with vague rhetorical intimations of formal specificity later gave way to more sustained explorations of a distinctive difference for the black theatrical event built on re-visioned African-American and African performance forms.[52] The dramatic achievements are equally varied, from ideological vociferations and agitprop pieces to some form of modified realism to expansive rituals—the latter the most favored as the truly Afrocentric and anti-Western form. Kimberly W. Benston suggestively traces this path as "a curve which moves dialectically from quasi-naturalism and overt rage against Euro-American institutions toward the shaping of uniquely Afro-American mythologies and symbolisms, flexibility of dramatic form, and participatory theatre within the black community," from *mimesis* to *methexis:*

> Spiritually and technically, this movement is one from *mimesis*, or representation of an action, to *methexis*, or communal "helping-out" of the action by all assembled. It is a process that could be described alternatively as a shift from *drama*—the spectacle observed—to *ritual*—the event which dissolves traditional divisions between actor and spectator, between self and other. Through this process, the Black beholder is theoretically transformed from a detached individual whose private consciousness the playwright sought to reform, to a participatory member of tribal or, in this case, national ceremony which affirms a shared vision.[53]

Although a similar graph could be plotted for the late 1960s South African Black Consciousness Movement (BCM) theater—a parallel to the African-American cultural renaissance—no comparable body of theoretical elaborations was produced.[54] A "Theatre Council" planned by the South African Students Organization (SASO, the core body within BCM) to appropriate "poetry, music, drama, fine arts and films" as weapons in the anti-apartheid struggle did little to detail strategies toward achieving the stated objective.[55] What was repeated most often by the theater groups was the "conscientization" (consciousness-raising) and revolutionary functions relevent black cultural forms must perform.[56]

The groups in practice cared little for specifically indigenous or non-

Eurocentric forms but mixed forms at will, combining elements of realism and nonrealism; barriers between performers and the audience were observed or ignored as seen fit; fiery, direct polemical speeches were not uncommon; and many groups were well-known for multimedia shows, integrating song, film projection, recitation, and chant. Kavanagh comments on this harried eclecticism:

> To a large extent, such a form emerged organically from the relation of the audience to the performers. This was not a commercial theatre. The actors were not hired. They were angry members of a wronged community talking directly to others of that community about their common oppression. Artifice and the traditional embellishments of bourgeois realist or avant-garde theatre were not only unnecessary but would have interposed themselves damagingly between the performers and their audience.[57]

Recent black and racially mixed South African drama not only show elements of this form but are far more assured in the appropriation of indigenous formal structures fashioned in the context of anti-apartheid struggle. Take, for instance, the prevalence of small casts whose members play multiple roles, simultaneously constructing and deconstructing—a pragmatic response by the most social of the arts to an environment hostile to even elementary forms of human assembly. Athol Fugard, who popularized this form, called it "two-hander" dramaturgy.[58]

On their own part, Afrocentric scholars of African drama engaged the all-important question of taxonomy, debunking colonialist, "universal" standards of measurement and classification and proposing instead different sets of criteria informed by the indigenous traditions for the appreciation of the traditions' performance forms. What the Eurocentric discourse denigrated as "predrama" became validly dramatic. And to the colonialist charge of a lack of historical consciousness due to an absence of written records, the unequivocal anticolonialist answer was that orality is an equally valid medium of historical transmission of cultural forms and their varied developmental patterns. This validation of orality also served to link the past with the present and thereby deny the colonialist claim of an absolute historical break in African culture due to colonialism (such that African theatrical forms today are theorized to be only derivatives of Western sources). This outline closely approximates the position differently articulated, explicitly or otherwise, and with varying degrees of sophistication, by theorists and critics such as Adedeji, Ossie Enekwe, Mineke Schipper, Bakary Traore, Oyin Ogunba, Oyekan Owomoyela, Kacke Gotrick, and Wole Soyinka. Among these are to be found systematic answers to the charges of the Eurocentric discourse. It is instructive that Soyinka's famous theoretical essay on African tragedy, "The Fourth Stage"—to which I will return in detail in the chapter on Soyinka—got no mention in Finnegan and only a footnote reference, within a different emphasis, in Graham-White, for years the American "authority" on African drama. Also ignored was the work of Adedeji on the Alarinjo, Yoruba professional theater since the late 1500s.[59]

To take a representative argument here: against the colonialist dismissal of African festivals as the " 'spontaneous' inartistic expression" of primitive tribes, Soyinka suggested that the festivals be seen as constituting "in themselves *pure theatre* at its most prodigal and resourceful . . . the most stirring expressions of man's instinct and need for drama at its most comprehensive and community-involving." In one sweeping move, he turned a Eurocentric canon on its head: "instead of considering festivals from one point of view only—that of providing, in a primitive form, the ingredients of drama—we may even begin examining the opposite point of view: that contemporary drama, as we experience it today, is a contraction of drama, necessitated by the the productive order of society in other directions."[60]

This last intervention has a close bearing on the ongoing debate in the Caribbean regarding the dramatic relevance—as an authentic and indigenous form—of carnival, the region's most popular cultural form. Derek Walcott, the area's leading dramatist, even while dramaturgically utilizing carnival forms, nevertheless once launched a withering attack at the suggestion, describing carnival as simply "theatrical" and not "theater," and as "the art of the brochure"—to underscore its corruption and commercialization by the state. He argued that "[c]arnival was as meaningless as the art of the actor confined to mimicry. And now the intellectuals, courting and fearing the mass, found values in it that they had formerly despised. They apotheosised the folk form, insisting that calypsos were poems. Their programme, for all its pretext to change, was a manual for stasis. . . ."[61]

Walcott's position directly challenged that of Errol Hill, who sees carnival as a great cultural resource from which an indigenous drama can be fashioned. In *Trinidad Carnival*, he analyzed in meticulous detail the "dramatic elements" of carnival and concluded that much of carnival's material is suited to the theater. Its creative appropriation promises an end to the eyesore in which "[p]lays written by native authors are about Trinidadians or West Indians and are set in Trinidad or the West Indies. But the form of these plays is European inspired, and their manner of presentation is European." The carnival, in short, is the "mandate" for a national theater.[62]

While Walcott may be right on the commercialization of carnival, this is a different argument from declaring it as dramatic or nondramatic. And there is just no reason why calypsos cannot be "poems," if only the gospel of poetry "according to Milton" would be dropped. The irony here is that in spite of their apparent disagreements, Walcott and Hill are drawing from the same unexamined assumptions borrowed from the ruling discourse. Hill aims to defend the "dramatic" potential of carnival but he takes for granted the unproblematic universal translatability of "drama," in spite of his consistently articulated disagreements with the structure of "Euro-American" theater. If indeed, as he insists, these— the structures of Euro-American theater—should no longer be privileged because they are inapplicable to the West Indies, then his analyses point to only one result: carnival is authentic, full-fledged drama, Soyinka's own argument about African festivals. Yet Hill never makes this point. On what basis then is carnival not "drama" but its potential?

The Afrocentric discourse, basically binarist in its strategies, must not blandly be dismissed. This is the insight dispersed throughout Fanon's works, in his simultaneous justification and critique of Negritude. Also, Chinua Achebe reputedly once said, against Sartre's famous stricture on Negritude (that it is an antiracist racism), that an antiracist racism can be an important antidote to white racism.[63] I anchor, then, with this incisive point from Jonathan Dollimore:

> Jacques Derrida reminds us that binary oppositions are "a violent hierarchy" where one of the two terms forcefully governs the other. A crucial stage in their deconstruction involves an overturning, an inversion "which brings low what is high." The political effect of ignoring this stage, of trying to jump beyond the hierarchy into a world quite free of it is simply to leave it intact in the only world we have. Both the reversal of authentic/inauthentic opposition . . . and the subversion of authenticity itself . . . are different aspects of overturning in Derrida's sense. Moreover they are stages in a *process* of resistance. . . . [64]

A Post-Afrocentric Discourse

> There is a fact: White men consider themselves superior to black men.
> There is another fact: Black men want to prove to white men at all costs, the richness of their thought, the equal value of their intellect.
> How do we extricate ourselves?
>
> When someone else strives and strains to prove to me that black men are as intelligent as white men, I say that intelligence has never saved anyone; and that is true, for, if . . . intelligence [is] invoked to proclaim the equality of men, [it has] also been employed to justify the extermination of men.
>
> Frantz Fanon[65]

Fanon's question and challenge define the space of an *emerging* discourse that tries at once to be both anticolonialist and post-Afrocentric. Its great distinguishing feature and strength is a more or less singular insistence on working through the excessive manichaeism of the Eurocentric and Afrocentric discourses and affirming instead the more difficult foundational premise of an irreversible imbrication of histories. I say this premise is "more difficult" because it displaces and is incompatible with the easy, smug satisfaction of a binary apprehension. What it suggests is an agonistic terrain, proposed as *shared* but from which a distinct identity must nevertheless be forged, for the sharing is in grossly unequal terms. It is thus a zone of the most complex, challenging, and dynamic conceptions of difference; a zone of endless critical questioning, as Fanon indicates:

> Sartre begins *Orphee Noir* thus: "What then did you expect when you unbound the gag that had muted those black mouths? That they would chant your praises? Did you think that when those heads that our fathers had forcibly bowed down to the ground were raised again, you would find adoration in their eyes?" I do not know; but I say that he who looks into my eyes for anything but a perpetual question will have to lose his sight; neither recognition nor hate.[66]

What the "perpetual questioning" subverts is the *culturalist* notion of difference that animates *both* the Eurocentric and Afrocentric discourses—the fixation of one upon white = civilized—black = barbaric opposition and of the other on a "white aesthetic" against a "black aesthetic"—and the more or less quiet disregard by both for the complexity of the ena- bling conditions of their utterances. The post-Afrocentric discourse not only quests for different representations but also, simultaneously, queries the *representation of difference.*

A related operative force of the post-Afrocentric formation is therefore its emphasis on historical specificity, which it does in a way that not only reveals the hierarchy between the dominant discourse and the counter- discourse—judging alone from the rhetoric of some of the latter, one would think this hierarchy is no more—but also emphasizes the most frequently related internal differences within each formation. Biodun Je- yifo writes:

> In *this* discourse, the issue is now problematized beyond the parameters of the two previous sets of discourses since analysis characteristically now turns on questions like: *Which* African or European sources and influences do we find operative and combined in any given African theatrical expression? What mo- tivates the interaction and combination of the "foreign" and indigenous," for neo- traditionalism, or a liberating and genuine artistic exploration of the range and diversity of styles, techniques, paradigms and traditions available within both the "foreign" and the "indigenous"? What social and ideological uses and functions mediate, legitimize or problematize the intercultural fusion of the "foreign" and "indigenous"? And what aspects, within the reinvented "in- digenous" forms, appear "foreign" to an indigenous audience and conversely, what absorbed "foreign" elements seem "familiar"?[67]

As an "emerging" practice, the third discourse bears many traces of this form of marginality. Many of its identified features are rarely all present in one work, or are most often muted and needing amplification. And it is not uncommon to find uncritical romances with the Afrocentric dis- course—the main formation with which it shares driving aspirations and subordinate institutional status in relation to the Eurocentric, and whose grounds it *largely occupies* but challenges, extends, and re-visions—or even occasional lapses into assumptions, subtle and refined, characteristic of the Eurocentric—a complex with which it shares ruling standards of dramaturgy, academic performance, and fellowship.

The latter seems to be the case, for instance, with Genevieve Fabre, the distinguished and non-Eurocentric scholar of African-American culture who writes, without any qualification—and as late as 1982—that "[i]n American theatre today hardly a season goes by without one or more black productions appearing on the legitimate stage."[68] The phrase "legitimate stage" goes without even the customary quotation marks, as if it was an uncontestable and uncontested designation without an acrimonious history, even if muted. Even if this were not so, "legitimate stage" still remains a concept that an anti-Eurocentric perspective must view at least with skepticism, or put into historical context. By attempting none of these, a phenomenon in American theater history is flattened and robbed of its due excitement. More important, the subjectivity of the "illegitimate"—since "legitimate" announces little else if not the precariousness of its legitimacy, courtesy of the excluded contenders—is thereby silenced, paradoxically what Fabre's book set out to give voice to, and splendidly did.

The dramatists I examine in detail in the following chapters make strong gestures to this formation and serve well as my illustrations. This is in spite of the irreducible traces of the Afrocentric in them. In other words, they productively straddle both realms. Because of the fact of our imminent engagement with the dramatists, I will restrict instantiating and examining the post-Afrocentric to the outline here.[69] What I will do next is to attempt a delineation of the contours of cultural identity and difference explicit or otherwise in the claims and propositions of the competing discourses, and the implications of their strategies of "othering" for transcultural transactions.

2

Difference, Differently

First, it is necessary to briefly but rigorously sketch the space, muted so far, where the grand drama of subordination and insubordination, colonialist and anticolonialist discourses, is staged. V. Y. Mudimbe proposes a tripartite "colonizing structure" for understanding the European colonial project of organizing and transforming non-European areas into basically European creations: the domination of physical space, the reformation of *natives'* minds, and the integration of local economic histories into the Western perspective. This structure of *complementary* acts, Mudimbe makes clear, "completely embraces the physical, human, and spiritual aspects of the colonizing experience."[1] Although the parts of this structure imply one another and depend on one another for effectiveness, the more immediate and operational terrain of the discourses on black drama belongs to the "reformation of minds," "reformation" here extended as a *complex* of antagonistic projects of reformation and counterreformation.[2] It is in the realm of the reformation of minds that history is processed into nature, and contingency into inevitability; where the subjective *I* is simultaneously real and illusory, and acting is also and at the same time the illusion of acting. It is *simultaneously* the *process* and *space* of securing discursive reproduction and stability. It is thus the realm of the formation of subjectivity and the subject, the latter both as self-knowledge and as subjection to the dictates of "someone else." It is also, therefore, the realm of the contest and refusal of subjectivity and subjection.[3] What underscores the importance of this site *and* prize of social struggles is that it is "where the identity of individuals and groups is at stake, and where order in its broadest meaning is taking form. This is the realm in which culture and power are most closely intertwined."[4]

I thus conceive the immediate thrust of the counterhegemonic discourses on black drama—the Afrocentric and the post-Afrocentric—as a refusal of subjection, of subjectivity imposed by the hegemonic Eurocentric discourse, a refusal to be Europe's civilizational and silent Other. Irrespective of the appropriateness or otherwise, or even the success or failure, of its specific strategies, the Afrocentric's quest for "authentically black" drama is a renunciation in part of what is perceived as an imposed identity, a crippling intellectual dependence on, or, in Mudimbe's description, an undue "epistemological filiation" to, the West.[5]

The Expressive and the Performative

I identify in the three discursive complexes—Eurocentric, Afrocentric, and post-Afrocentric—*tendencies* toward two more or less explicit propositions of cultural identity and difference. These I label the *expressive* and the *performative*. They are intricate structures capable of multiple, even apparently divergent manifestations. It would therefore be difficult simply to abstract their distinctive features out of context. The cost would be to hypostatize their identities and rob them of the fruitful ambiguities characteristic of their status as social actions or, preferably, *performances*. After all, the discourses that call them into being, embody them, and deploy them are never static but in a state of perpetual flux: contestation, confrontation, consolidation, and transformation. The extrapolations that follow concern only the most obvious features; a more detailed exposition follows after the determination of which discursive practice(s) belong(s) to which tendency.

The expressive conception of cultural identity proposes culture—the entire order of the constitutive social processes and practices, spiritual and material, by which a people produce and reproduce themselves[6]—as an essence, transparent, obvious, and unchanging. "Society" itself is taken as given, preconstituted. Culture is a totality, whole, complete, and finished. This self-sufficiency screens out other cultures with an impenetrable rigor. The Other, in this context, remains fixed as an atavistic category of the Same. Or at best a grammar of parallelism is erected as the principle of recognition of difference, rather than the messy *real* of rancorous interference and overlapping. Identity is inviolable and, as James Clifford says, a "boundary to be maintained [rather than a] nexus of relations and transactions actively engaging a subject."[7] Or when heterogeneity is empowered, it is recovered as strands within the norm of the Same or Identity. The expressive identity's mode of representation is axiomatic, transparent, or mimetic; it is a "radical realism," in Said's words, which holds the signified as independent of the means of signification— the very erasure of transformational *work*, and thus of history.[8]

The performative, on the other hand, stresses the historicity of culture, that is, its "made-ness" in space and time.[9] Rather than a given, seamless totality, culture is conceived as an intricate and open process of practices and discriminations through which a people define their "way of life" as distinct. "Society" as a unitary entity is discarded for mutually impinging social networks of differing scales relating to different types of power—political, military, ideological, or economic.[10] Identity in the performative conception is a *process* marked by endless negotiations. It is never closed or positive but always vulnerable, fragile, a "complex historical process of appropriation, compromise, subversion, masking, invention, and revival."[11] The mode of representation it suggests is problematic and opaque, a mode that emphasizes the process of signification, enmeshed as it is in determinate systems and institutions. Performative identity refuses to be an absolute and fixed otherness.

Let us now with some care locate the discourses on black drama within the elicited "models" of conceiving cultural difference. The Eurocentric discourse, in its unyielding insistence on otherness as a negative, inauthentic category of the Same, suggests the expressive notion of identity. "Drama," for the Eurocentric, is not a matrix of institutionalized cultural and ideological conventions but a universal norm—which is European but nevertheless, or precisely for that reason, universal.[12] There could thus be no "drama" among the raw natives, and "tragedy," as the very expression of high culture (= civilization = Europe), is alien to them. They are just "too prosaic, too utilitarian and too lazy to examine things in depth and to note the results of their investigations,"[13] hence, according to the complaints of Ruth Finnegan and others, the lack of "sustained plot" in what could pass as African drama.

Even when it apparently reverses direction, this time conceiving the Other as the more authentic category of the Same, the identity the Eurocentric discourse proposes still remains firmly expressive. This is the ruling logic behind Peter Brook's search for theatrical renewal in nonwestern cultures. The theatrical status quo in the West, it is often argued, is unhealthy because of its showy fripperies; the solution lies in learning from the simple and organic Africa, a continent of *Gemeinschaft* still ruled by a homogeneous *Wesenwille*, as against the *Gesellschaften* West, the center of high culture and high society with an individualistic, dynamic, and free *Kurwille*. Africa is the leaven for the metallic bread of Europe. The Other remains petrified as exotica.[14] It appears that the unacknowledged legislation of Eurocentric thought is that the Other must never be conceived in the time of the Self. This is another instance of the hegemonic power of the Eurocentric discourse, its "flexible *positional* superiority," as Said writes incisively of Orientalism, "which puts the Westerner in a whole series of possible relationships with the Orient without ever losing him the relative upper hand."[15]

The expressive identity, I suggest, is coercive and dominative. This is why it is interesting to note that in spite of its evident antiracist, anticolonial, counterhegemonic character, a sizable proportion of the Afrocentric discourse remains enmeshed in Eurocentrism and proposes what amounts to no less than a fixed, expressive identity. Take for instance the Afrocentric romanticization of culture whose ideological underpinning I have labeled as cultural nationalism. The paradox here can be fully grasped if we briefly consider the resistant character of Afrocentric cultural nationalism and its historical liberating effects—in fact, these effects alone justify all the critical attention we can pay this formation.

Senghor's famous (or even Alain Locke's less famous) racialization of thought—emotion is African as reason is Greek—may be so much goitered cultural theorizing, but it is nevertheless historically a position that revealed the constructedness of the sovereignty of the Western subject by insisting, against Western reason, on *different* rationalities with differing internal points of reference and, what's more, with equal validity. Hellenic "analytical reason" is no more "normal" than African "intuitive reason." Instead of one world, one norm, and many deviants, Afrocentric cultural nationalism authorizes several worlds with several norms. The universalist claim of Europe is shown to be a repression of Otherness in the name of the Same. "Culture," as the West erects it, is hence subverted to "culture," "Truth" to "truth," "Reason" to "reason," "Drama" to "drama." This is the fundamental ethicopolitical point of departure of the Afrocentric cultural nationalist discourse, an empowerment of a grossly tendentiously misrepresented group to speak for and represent itself, says Said, in "domains defined, politically and intellectually, as normally excluding them, usurping their signifying and representing functions, overriding their historical reality." This point of departure is, in Foucault's terms, a subversive recodification of power relations which has the capacity to detach the power of truth from the forms of hegemony in which it operates.[16]

Let me quickly cite two factors for insisting on Afrocentric cultural nationalism as proposing a disabling, expressive identity: its *relativism* and its *culturalism*.

When the cultural nationalist discourse demystifies the Western norm as simply *a* norm, it empowers a plurality of spaces and identities, each with its own validity. "African literature," in Chinweizu, Jemie, and Madubuike's authoritative declaration, "is an autonomous entity separate and apart from all other literature. It has its own traditions, models and norms."[17] And they mean African literature in European languages! Or consider Stephen Henderson's "saturation" theory of black poetry, which posits a unique black difference between Black Experience the reader and Black Experience the text, provable only through black "personal experience," penetrable only to those possessing the necessary stated qualification: Black Experience.[18]

Here then is a central relativist tenet that distinguishes Afrocentric cultural nationalism, and the point where its initial oppositional stance begins to lose steam. Plural spaces, plural traditions, yes, and good. But confronted with the question of any possible, even inevitable relationship between these entities, it can only perambulate. The plural identities empowered, it turns out, are little more than microidentities, perhaps with the possibility of "growth" to a single identity in the horizon. They are in any case "mininorms," organic and self-sufficient, closed to one another. "The unconditional affirmation of African culture," Fanon laments, "has succeeded the unconditional affirmation of European culture"; "the great black mirage" has succeeded "the great white error."[19] The gown of unnegotiable insularity, or rags of it gathered from Eurocentrism, is dusted and donned. Extreme relativism is enthroned: "to everyone *his* truth" becomes the rallying cry, not the mutual abrasion of truths. The problematic of the representation of otherness is translated into the problem of other representations, *competing* rationalities into merely different rationalities. A happy insularity is proposed in a world already too agonistically intermeshed: a most unstrategic strategy especially for a discourse in a position of subordination. Even when a sort of meeting, a "synthesis," is proposed, as Senghor is wont to do, it is a culturalist synthesis that blissfully ignores the inequality of the spaces occupied by the different components.[20] As Fanon argues, cultural relativism is enabling only if "the colonial status," in all its ramifications, "is irreversibly excluded."[21] I find very relevant here Satya P. Mohanty's far-ranging questions and incisive conclusions:

> But the issue of competing rationalities raises a nagging question: how do we negotiate between my history and yours? How would it be possible for us to recover our commonality, not the ambiguous imperial-humanist myth of our shared human attributes, which are supposed to distinguish us all from animals, but, more significantly, the imbrication of our various pasts and presents, the ineluctable relationships of shared and contested meanings, values, materials resources? It is necessary to assert our dense particularities, our lived and imagined differences; but could we afford to leave untheorized the question of how our differences are intertwined and, indeed, hierarchically organized? Could we, in other words, afford to have *entirely* different histories, to see ourselves as living—and having lived—in entirely heterogeneous and discrete spaces? . . . To believe that you have your space and I mine; to believe, further, that there can be no responsible way in which I can adjudicate between your space—cultural and historical—and mine by developing a set of general criteria that would have interpretive validity in both contexts (because there can be no interpretation that is not simultaneously an evaluation) —to believe both these things is also to assert that *all spaces are equivalent*: that they have equal value, that since the lowest common principle of evaluation is all that I can invoke, I cannot— and consequently need not—think about how your space impinges on mine, or how my history is defined together with yours.[22]

Afrocentric cultural nationalism soon discovers that it is actually aided in its aggressive relativism by Eurocentrism. Graham-White's self-appointed task is, after all, to deliver African drama from its racist denigrators.[23] Peter Brook's quest would be impossible without the *humbling* realization that other theatrical traditions exist outside Europe, a humility

coerced in part by vociferous non-European cultural nationalism. Difference, previously defined as deviance, is now authorized and legitimized:
victory for the cultural nationalists, or so it seems. Blacks not only have
theatrical-dramatic traditions, but these are even more authentic than
those of the West. They are the limit of the West, what the West is not:
an affective ankylosis that recuperates difference and freezes identity. The
other is not understood but reified.[24] The relativism of the cultural nationalists is thus recuperable because it is not incompatible with the structure of unequal social relations. Following Hountondji, I have called the
ideology of this relativism, which fits snugly with cultural imperialism,
satisfying both the dominant and the dominated, *culturalism*.[25]

The major boon of culturalism is the manifest differences in the cultures of different peoples; the culturalist practice abstracts these differences, schematizing and mummifying them as the authentic leverage of
contrast among and between cultures. This contrast—"imaginary opposition" in Hountondji's terms—is then given precedence over inter- or
intracultural *real* political and economic conflicts. Culture is reified in its
outward forms, it is denied any historical depth or internal pluralism. The
favorite geopolitical form worshiped by the culturalist is either the *nation*
or the *continent*, entities understood in ahistorical terms as existent and
given, not as social constructions.[26] Here, what are evidently group values
in confrontational competition with other group values are passed off as
values homogeneously shared throughout the entity, irrespective of class,
gender, and other distinctions. African culture, European culture: different entities, different cultures. Ossified this way, the problematic of cultural difference escapes the issue of the historical abrasion of cultures, of
the hierarchy inherent in every proposition of cultural difference, and of
colonial and neocolonial political and economic domination.

Many manifestations of the post-Afrocentric, on the other hand, evince
suggestions of a performative cultural identity. Michael Etherton insists
on a conception of African drama as a "process" beyond the sterile "academic" debates of its "ritualistic" or "festive" character. This "process" is contextually both responsive and catalytic. The continent itself is
to be considered, as Jeyifo puts it, as composed of diverse and heterogeneous social formations and national social-political realities, even as
we insist on the "great affinities of ideological and cultural expressions
which derive from the common historical situation . . . as previously co-
lonially subjugated societies, and in the common aspirations . . . to win
genuine independence from imperialist domination and to resume the
course of self-directed development."[27] The notion of black cultural
identity as a living complex of multiple determinations runs through
some of the recent works of Alexis DeVeaux, Femi Osofisan, Erna Brodber, Amiri Baraka, Wilson Harris, and other names I identified with the
post-Afrocentric. Following their suggestive propositions and leads and
extending their insights, I will briefly give a resistant and anti-imperialist
performative cultural identity a concrete specification: as *articulation*. I

need to make clear a point implicit in the discussion so far. What is at stake in all this is not simply how to think a named cultural form, but also—and perhaps more important—how to think "culture," the "cultural," and cultural translation.

Cultural Identity as Articulation

[C]ultural traditions are always a complex heritage, contradictory and heterogenous, an open set of options, some of which will be actualized by any given generation, which by adopting one choice sacrifices all the others . . . [C]ultural traditions can remain alive only if they are exploited anew, under one of their aspects at the expense of all the others . . . the choice of this privileged aspect is itself a matter for struggle today, for an endlessly restless debate of society.

Paulin Hountondji[28]

Culture as a social practice: this is the ruling idea of culture conceived in performative terms, a conception so well expressed in the preceding epigraph. This conception dispenses with society as a sutured totality of its partial processes. Social relations have no essence, transhistorical or axiomatic, but are always pragmatic, arbitrary, contextual—in short, historical. If society has an "essence," then it is its permanent openness, what Laclau and Mouffe call "negative essence." This openness constitutes the grounds of the antagonistic transactions involved in the "choice" stated by Hountondji. The agonistic process of arriving at this "choice" from the diverse and contradictory "open set of options" I call *articulation*.

Articulation is defined by Stuart Hall as a

complex structure: a structure in which things are related as much through their differences as through their similarities. This requires that the mechanisms which connect dissimilar features must be shown—since no "necessary correspondence" or expressive homology can be assumed as given. It also means— since the combination is a structure (an articulated combination) and not a random association—that there will be structured relations between its parts, i.e. relations of dominance and subordination.[29]

The identity of the parts or elements in the "complex structure" is always modified as a result of the articulatory practice. The parts dominant in the articulated structure constitute what is commonly regarded as a people's distinct "way of life" at a given time. This distinctiveness has a historical character, and it is constantly being refashioned and reconstituted, for it is the site, and also the stake, of most often bitter social struggles. Culture here is perceived as a complicated strategic articulation of diverse and mutually contradictory elements or parts. In fact, the authority and necessity of articulation derive from the fact of cultures as composites of structures, and even its constitutive articulated parts or features are never immutable. In other words, neither the articulated identity—the more or less coherent artificial system of differences taken to distinguish one people from another—nor its constitutive elements possess any natural, sacrosanct character. The emergent theoretical status of articulation is thus as "a discursive practice which does not have a plane of constitution prior to, or outside, the dispersion of the articulated elements."[30] Cultural identity could hence not be closed and positive but necessarily atlerable: a conception of otherness in flux. The performative is the principle of a transgressive and transitional truth.[31]

In spite of this pervasive privileging of dispersion and contingence, the performative model subjects itself to its very own logic by performing its own limits, that is, by admitting "necessity," or indispensable elements. It does this, however, only situationally. It holds as essentialist illusion, even impossibility, absolute expressivity or absolute performativity and therefore eschews both. Both erase the very notion of identity by their erasure of the categories of relation and imbrication with other identities. Between the logic of pure difference and that of pure identity, of absolute contingency and of absolute necessity, there is only ersatz fulfillment. The logic of articulation is alien to these originary and totalitarian quests. Hence true to its character, the performative model accepts honorary expressiveness, or *partial fixations*. This expressive or fixed point is no more than an

> [a]ffirmation of a "ground" which lives only by negating its fundamental character; of an order which exists only as a partial limiting of disorder; of a "meaning" which is constructed only as excess and paradox in the face of meaninglessness—in other words, the field of the [social] as the space for a game which is never "zero-sum," because the rules and the players are never explicit."[32]

This expressiveness, because it is *within* the performative, loses its divine, ahistorical character and becomes an identifiable historically expedient rallying point, or as Laclau and Mouffe would have it, a "nodal point,"[32] or "privileged aspect" according to Hountondji. Since the nodal point is historical and within a general regime of the contingent, it stands little risk of petrifying into an absolute. "The choice of this privileged aspect," Hountondji bears repeating, is "a matter for struggle today, for *an endlessly restless debate whose ever uncertain outcome spells the destiny of society*" (emphasis added). The defining constituent of the nodal point articulates or gives the contingent elements a focus, while the contingent elements constantly challenge and scrutinize the credentials of the defining constituent to the continued occupancy of the privileged, that is, nodal point.[33]

It is important to emphasize that a performative identity is not inherently and automatically insurgent or anti-imperialist, though effective forms of these struggles are hardly conceivable without it. The performative notion enables a conception of society and culture in which more productively resistant, insurgent identities could be thought and fashioned. This it does by subverting expressivity in its different manifestations: either as singular rationality proposed by the Eurocentric discourse or as unnegotiable autonomy put forward by the extreme relativism of Afrocentric cultural nationalism. Identity as "articulation" is enabling, but this is hardly all. Articulation is not simply a complex structure but a *structured* complex structure, that is, a structure of elements in relations of dominance and subordination. It is not only the choice of what aspect of a cultural tradition will be privileged that is always a matter of struggle as Hountondji has written; even more contentious is the character that aspect would take. Witness—as perhaps an unmatchable example—the travails of voodoo in Haiti from independence to the Duvaliers. Performative identity not only needs specific articulation as insurgent and anti-imperialist, but also demands vigilance against domestication.

The Afrocentric discourse is certainly right in identifying the nodal point or identity appropriate to it as African and anti-imperialist. Its problems and limitations lie in pursuing this subaltern position through self-subverting expressive means. The performative identity is proposed here not as a ready solution but as a more useful way to negotiate the minefield of identity and difference. Take, for instance, two of the most intractable problems facing the counterhegemonic discourses (both Afrocentric and post Afrocentric) on black drama in articulating an anti- Eurocentric dramatic subjectivity: genre and language.

Genre

From the Eurocentric denigration of black performance forms or the insistence on European drama in Africa (or none at all) and from the Afrocentric relegation of intercultural influences and affinities, two conceptions of genre, as an attempt at organizing and systematizing conventions into distinct modes of dramatic and theatrical practice,[34] emerge: (1) regulative and prescriptive and (2) descriptive and functional.

Either in the unreflexive propositions or in the erection of an interpreted Aristotle as the norm running from the British Drama League through Finnegan to Graham-White, what is suggested is a conception of genre that is universalist in assumptions and neoclassicist in formal rigorism and unexamined self-assurance. What better accomplices could conservatism find? To the wind is thrown one of the most basic features of genre—and therefore its implications for genre theorizing—the close relationships among genre, writer, and audience, all living in historical time.[35]

Wellek and Warren's statement, "Every 'culture' has its genres,"[36] would certainly receive great applause from the Afrocentric relativists. What their intervention suggests is a descriptive, functional (i.e., culturally bound), and therefore relativist notion of genre.[37] A question this relativist conception is yet to address is the possibility of comparisons, linkages and continuities of genre across cultures—some due, in our particular case, to the colonial experience.

Performative cultural identity suggests investigating and historicizing the kinds and character of influences, relationships, continuities, and discontinuities. Wole Soyinka, in an apparent reference to the claims of the lack of "tragedy" in Africa, argues that "*[t]ragedy* . . . whether we translate it in Yoruba or Tre or Ewe, I think we'll find a correlative somewhere in which we're all talking about the same thing," for

> ultimately there is a certain passage of the human being, a certain development or underdevelopment of the human character, a certain result in the processes of certain events which affects the human being which has that definition of tragedy in no matter what culture. And it is to that kind of linguistic bag, that symbolic bag, which audiences in theater must attune themselves, whether it is Japanese tragedy or Chinese tragedy.[38]

This position, with its implicit acceptance of the name and concept "tragedy" and a recognition of the violent history of the dominance of the language that specifies it, closely approximates Raymond Williams's suggestion of a distinction, in considering genre over time and place, between "nominal continuity" and "substantial continuity," and his preference for the former:

> "Tragedy" for example, has been written, if intermittently and unevenly, in what can appear to be a clear line between fifth-century B.C. Athens and the present day. A relevant factor of this continuity is that authors and others described successive works as "tragedies". But to assume that this is a simple case of the continuity of a "genre" is unhelpful. It leads either to abstract categorization of a supposed single essence, reducing or overriding the extraordinary variations which the name "tragedy" holds together; or to definitions of "true tragedy", "mixed tragedy", "false tragedy", and so on, which cancel the continuity. This way of defining genre is a familiar case of giving category priority over substance.[39]

The "nominal" is patient and humble before the unfamiliar. It is anti-authoritarian and against the colonialist practice of making judgmental classifications even before the alien phenomenon and its complex matrix of determinations have been properly investigated. It is also alert to connections and affiliations over and across space and time.

Language

A major component of Baraka's early call for a "post-white, or post-American form," or the "home" to which Ronald Milner admonishes black theater to go, is as much about genre as about linguistic indigenization, even if little specifically theorized.[40] The difficulty here is the apparently unchallengeable cultural hegemony represented by English. The solidification of the imperial process is virtually impossible without the colonial languages as instruments of pedagogy. Conquest or pacification means the subjection of indigenous populations—or fractions that thereby rule—in the language of the colonizer, a language which, in its partisan intrusion into the indigenous space as the privileged means of knowing, dictates what is or can be known and thought. The great problematic, then, is the intricate connection between language and culture. English Studies, for instance, as the pedagogical arm of the imperial process, is distinguished by the circulating specularity it erects among English language, English literature, British values, Christianity, and civilization. The colonialist discourse of "civilizing mission" is constituted by little else.[41] The imposition of colonial languages is the imposition of colonial culture. English, in our own case, remains the language of law and authority, of social mobility,[42] in short, the "authorized language," in Pierre Bourdieu's words,[43] against either the indigenous languages in Africa,[44] or "Black English" in the United States,[45] or Patwah or Creole or "Nation Language" in the Caribbean.[46]

This points to the dilemma of the counterhegemonic discourses: the paradox of articulating an anti-imperialist identity in the language of the imperialists. Very few English-speaking black writers have not had cause at one time or another to ruminate on this bind.[47] It would seem that the solution suggested by Ashcroft, Griffiths, and Tiffin, that English be turned into english, be altered in radical, new ways,[48] find its greatest applicability in the Caribbean and African-American contexts (though the authors did not discuss the institutional conditions of possibility of this project). This is unlike Africa, where it is not just a case of English against english(es), though it is partly that too in the emerging English-Pidgin question. The choice for the black, whether in Africa, Caribbean, or United States, seems to be at least a *forced* dual socialization or unrelieved marginality and poverty.[49] This is one of the effects of domination that constantly fuels Afrocentrism's basically binary politics.

From the perspective of performative identity, it would be far more rewarding to emphasize the infrastructural conditions of possibility for detaching the power of truth from the hegemony of English rather than any uncritical rejection. Black English may sell at the box office, but it is not a language of social mobility. So with Creole or the African languages. Without ignoring the passionate political investments in the debates, and with due regard for the justifications of the various positions expressed—mainly, the defense of colonial languages as a practical necessity and the proposition of indigenous languages as the only true form of an anticolonial cultural identity—one could nevertheless go "beyond" them to show the complexity of the case the contending positions are wont to ignore. Mudimbe does this by considering African *gnosis*, and the question of the epistemological linkage between Africa and the West, a linkage affirmed in the use of European languages but also not necessarily or automatically escaped simply with the use of African languages or Creole or Black English:

Gnosis is by definition a kind of secret knowledge. The changes of motives, the succession of theses about foundation, and the differences of scale in interpretations that I have tried to bring to light about African *gnosis* witness to the vigour of a knowledge which is sometimes African by virtue of its authors and promoters, but which extends to a Western epistemological territory. The task accomplished so far is certainly impressive. On the other hand, one wonders whether the discourses of African *gnosis* do not obscure a fundamental reality, their own *chose du texte*, the primordial African discourse in its variety and multiplicity. Is it not inverted, modified by anthropological categories used by specialists of dominant discourses? Does the question of how to relate in a more faithful way to *la chose du texte* necessarily imply another epistemological shift? Is it possible to consider this shift outside of the very epistemological field which makes my question both possible and thinkable.[50]

What lies beyond these questions is no simple answer but the promise of a more sober look at history and a re-visioning of the terrains of alien language and local cultural identity.

In general terms, the dramatists examined in the next chapters propose the performative identity. In many instances, however, I find their performative propositions severely abbreviated, interspersed at many junctures with more or less furtive appropriations of norms characteristic of Afrocentric cultural nationalism and its expressive conception of identity. I think it will be too idealistic to expect otherwise, given not only the historically emancipatory effects of Afrocentrism but also the continuing fact of aggressive imperialist cultural domination which often forces the unwary rebel to articulate extreme, ultimately self-defeating positions.

Let me make this peculiar situation clearer. If I borrow Michel Pecheux's tripartite schematic outline of a dominated subject's relationship to the dominating discourse—(1) the "good subject" who "consents" to domination, (2) the rebellious "bad subject" who "counteridentifies" with the discourse of domination, and (3) the subject who "disidentifies" with the existing structures of domination and gestures at their "transformation-displacement" or "overthrow-rearrangement"[51]—I will locate the dramatists at the *interface* between counteridentification and disidentification. They are certainly not Eurocentrism's good subjects; they are simultaneously its bad subjects (because in spite of their rebellion, they still have to work in a world dominated by Eurocentric institutional structures and inevitably bear traces of some of its underlying assumptions) and its disidentified subjects (because they gesture strikingly at a non-Eurocentric order, no matter how much the gestures are circumscribed by their lack of institutional power). The work of these dramatists bears eloquent testimony to the complexity, ambiguity, and yes, productivity, of this space.

II

Inventing Cultural Identities

3

Wole Soyinka:
"Race Retrieval" and Cultural
Self-Apprehension

In their time the great wars came and went, the little wars came
and went; the white slavers came and went, they took away the
heart of our race, they bore away the mind and muscle of our race.
The city fell and was rebuilt; the city fell and our people trudged
through mountain and forest to found a new home but . . . [o]ur
world was never wrenched from its true course.

There is only one home to the life of a river mussel; there is only
one home to the life of a tortoise; there is only one shell to the
soul of a man: there is only one world to the spirit of our race. If
that world leaves its course and smashes on boulders of the great
void, whose world will give us shelter?

Wole Soyinka[1]

No, I have not invoked the Praise-Singer in Soyinka's *Death and the
King's Horesman* in the epigraph only for his arresting lyricism and characteristic rhetorical elan. Noteworthy in it as well is what appears to be
a distinctive feature of Soyinka's articulatory practice in fashioning the
specificity of a collective, cultural self: a complex subtlety. The Praise-
Singer evokes in stirring, even nostalgic terms a solid, self-assured autodynamic organic community, a community that holds tightly to the
essence of itself and whose authentic values survive the ravages of
temporality. This is navel-gazing, the aesthetics of the pristine and the
naive—the aesthetics of *expressive identity*. Only, of course, this reading
is inaccurate. Not even the untethered rhapsody of the Praise-Singer
could hide the dispersed complications located at the heart of his formulations. His "organic" community is baked in the kiln of disorders
and disruptions, the great and little wars; the "authentic" values have the
unbleachable smear of experience, or reconstruction and relocation and

refashioning; and the community's "essence" is shot through with rays from the torch of history. This "complex subtlety" suffuses Soyinka's cultural theory and practice, marked by a combative refusal of subjection to imposed or debilitating norms, local or alien, and the simultaneous exploration of an indigenous African dramatic subjectivity.

Race retrieval is Soyinka's term for the composite project, a project designed to apprehend and register the presence of a culture "whose reference points are taken from within the culture itself."[2] Although this has been the focal point of Soyinka's career since he started in the late 1950s, his now famous formal (re-)statement of position came decades later, in the preface to an important collection of essays, *Myth, Literature and the African World*, published in 1976. "There has . . . developed in recent years," Soyinka writes, "a political reason for this [in the essays] increased obsession with the particular theme." An aspect of the politics involves the presentation of the essays that form the book. They were delivered when Soyinka held an appointment as Fellow of Churchill College, Cambridge. He no doubt believed himself to be discussing literature, but Cambridge thought otherwise. So rather than in the Department of English, the presentation took place entirely in the Department of Social Anthropology—that is, the department responsible for collecting, documenting and theorizing the deviant, exotic cultures that populate the periphery of the Universal = Western Norm. "Casual probing after it was all over," Soyinka says, "indicated that the Department of English (or perhaps some key individual) did not believe in any such mythical beast as 'African Literature.'"[3]

At a related but larger, global level is what Soyinka identifies as the then recent birth and widespread circulation of an insidious colonialist discourse which hides its denial of the existence of an African world under the guise of sophistication. Add to this the discourse's appropriation of Soyinka's well-known stance against Negritude's narcissistic cult of the African world as part of its own project of repudiating the actuality of that world, and the dramatist's "increasing sense of alarm and even betrayal" can be understood:

> [W]e black Africans have been blandly invited to submit ourselves to a second epoch of colonisation—this time by a universal-humanoid abstraction defined and conducted by individuals whose theories and prescriptions are derived from the apprehension of *their* world and *their* history, *their* social neuroses and *their* value systems."[4]

This sounds forbidding but the paradox we are faced with in Soyinka is that the difference being defended is rarely absolutist.

Here then lies the political rationale for the task of *insubjection* (refusal of subjection) and racial self-retrieval,

> the simultaneous act of eliciting from history, mythology and literature, for the benefit of both genuine aliens and alienated Africans, a continuing process of

self-apprehension whose temporary dislocation appears to have persuaded many of its non-existence or irrelevance (= retrogression, reactionarism, racism, etc.) in contemporary world reality."[5]

The rehabilitation of a ruptured continuum of self-apprehension does not mean a call for some mystical, unsoiled pristinism but a "reinstatement of values authentic to [the] society, modified only by the demands of a contemporary world."[6] The *nodal point* that Soyinka passionately elaborates and aggressively defends is the "African world,"[7] though the quest is not for a closed, unnegotiable particularity—difference, after all, is relational and problematic. Soyinka's warning needs no gloss in its intimations of performative identity:

> Nothing in these essays suggests a detailed uniqueness of the African world. Man exists, however, in a comprehensive world of myth, history and mores; in such a total context, the African world, like any other "world" is unique. It possesses, however, in common with other cultures, the virtues of complementarity. To ignore this simple route to a common humanity and pursue the alternative route of negation is, for whatever motives, an attempt to perpetuate the external subjugation of the black continent.[8]

Assimilative Wisdom and Period Dialectics

> I remember my shock as a student of literature and drama when I read that drama originated in Greece. What is this? I couldn't quite deal with it. What are they talking about? I never heard my grandfather talk about Greeks invading Yorubaland. I couldn't understand. I've lived from childhood with drama. I read at the time that tragedy evolved as a result of the rites of Dionysus. Now we all went through this damn thing, so I think the presence [sic] of eradication had better begin. . . . [9]

To the dominant pattern of basing classical (what people generally mean when they say "traditional") African theatrical difference from Europe on such orthodoxies as "communal creativity" against "creative individualism," or unrestrained as opposed to secretive audience participation, Soyinka casts an unhidden disdain. The difference that matters is neither these nor even a simple matter of form or style. And most important, this crucial difference goes beyond the realm of drama alone: it is located in the very operative worldviews of the different cultures. The "Western cast of mind," Soyinka argues, is characterized by a signal "compartmentalising habit of thought" which erects divisive barriers between aspects that are evidently integral to the total, comprehensive experience of culture. Soyinka extravagantly instantiates this spastic "occidental creative rhythm":

> You must picture a steam-engine which shunts itself between rather closely-spaced suburban stations. At the first station it picks up a ballast of allegory, puffs into the next emitting a smokescreen on the eternal landscape of nature truths. At the next it loads up with a different species of logs which we shall

call naturalist timber, puffs into a half-way stop where it fills up with the synthetic fuel of surrealism, from which point yet another holistic world-view is glimpsed and asserted through psychedelic smoke. A new consignment of absurdist coke lures it into the next station from which it departs giving off no smoke at all, and no fire, until it derails briefly along constructivist tracks and is towed back to the starting- point by a neo-classic engine.[10]

The African worldview, on the other hand, is characteristically thorough and catholic: a "relative comprehensiveness of vision" in which parts are apprehended in all their fullness, that is, in their dynamic relationships with themselves, in their constitutive identities as parts and whole. For this worldview, history is not a threat that disperses understanding into unyieldingly "separatist myths (or 'truths')."[11] On the contrary, new experiences, in either harmonious or contradictory relationship to the stock, are absorbed, dealt with, and allocated their proper berths within a vision that resolutely refuses to conceive life and death, evil and good, heaven and earth, past and present, inside and outside, and so on, as irreconcilable absolutes. And this is not simply because *both* sets in opposition are properly within the experiential vista of humanity but largely because they both constitute the very principle of *cosmic adjustment* on which the existence and survival of society are based. The difference being underscored is between a worldview whose creative rhythm is governed by "assimilative wisdom" and another that has surrendered to "period dialectics."[12]

Thus what we find in "The Fourth Stage"—Soyinka's elaboration of a theory of tragic art rooted in an African sensibility, perhaps his finest musing on the philosophy of culture, and unarguably his central document in the task of racial and cultural self-retrieval—is a persuasive concretization of the insistence and conviction broadcast throughout his work: that the sources and roots of African literary creativity, even cultural criticism and sensibility, are to be found in the peculiarities of traditions and cognitive modes characteristic of a continuously changing and lived African world; the elicitation, implicit or explicit, of aesthetic, theoretical, and critical criteria from African sources, epistemologies, and cosmologies; and the general move away from European thought-systems except as illuminating analogies to concepts and principles locally derived. I have borrowed an additional important observation from Biodun Jeyifo: that the essay "ranges beyond this 'return-to-the-source' rubric to an affirmation of the revolutionary impulse in culture and art over the contending and perennial tendency toward inertia and complacency."[13] This essay is considered in detail not only because it is central, in general terms, to Soyinka's artistic practice but also because of the especially close bearing it has to one of the dramatist's plays, *Death and the King's Horseman*, which I will discuss at length later in the chapter.

Soyinka rifles through the swarming haven of heroines and heroes, deities, and legends that constitutes the Yoruba metaphysical landscape to elicit a theory of tragedy from the features, myths, and ritual dramas of two major gods: Ogun and Obatala. Beyond these two figures, the roots of Yoruba tragedy lie deep in the very origin of the pantheon. Once upon a time there was only one being, the Original One, the Essence, assisted by a slave named Atunda (literally, re-creation). Atunda soon turned rebellious and one day rolled a mighty boulder on the first ancestor as he hoed his farm on a slope, shattering the Essence irretrievably into a thousand and one fragments. The Yoruba pantheon originated in this act of revolution. Some fragments became deities, each known by the character of the piece from the First One that constituted its being. The mortal shards, on the other hand, peopled the world of humanity. In no time the entities were separated by an unbridgeable gulf, which signaled the onset of a perpetual sense of incompletion on either side. It was, however, the gods who first contemplated conquering the abyss and fraternizing with humanity, their significant Other. But contemplation of this remedy is of a slightly different order from execution, and so one by one the deities despairingly confessed defeat before the fearful chasm. Until Ogun took over.[14]

Ogun's constitution prepared him well for the great task. He was the one in whom the creative essence fragment from the First One took residence. He is thus the god of creativity and, inevitably, its obverse, destruction; of iron and metallic lore and artistry. His also are the delicate and grave arts of oath-taking, hunting, and war; and praise-chants never forget him as the one in whom orphans and the homeless unfailingly find succor. Ogun gathered his implements, pushed the other gods aside, and, in a manic mobilization of raw, elemental will, plunged into the annihilating bottomless rent *and* succeeded in carving a path from the realm of divinity to that of humanity, heaven to earth.[15]

Two elements of this drama of Ogun are crucial to Soyinka's construction of tragic art: the terrifying void and Ogun's active will. The former is described variously as "incomparable immensity," "natural home of unseen deities," "chthonic realm," "resting-place for the departed," "abyss of transition," "infernal gulf," "storehouse for creative and destructive essence," "seething cauldron of the dark world will and psyche," "psychic abyss of recreative energies," and so on. Only the centrality of this realm in Soyinka's paradigm exculpates the surfeit of significations. In Soyinka's idiosyncratic reading of the Yoruba metaphysical geography, it is the "fourth stage," located between *and* around the other three realms of the *dead*, the *living*, and the *unborn*, corresponding to the time sequences of the past, the present, and the future.[16]

Although for the Yoruba these realms are intimately linked and are in no chronological order or relationship, there is nevertheless a consciousness of otherness, the "primordial disquiet of the Yoruba psyche [which] may be expressed as the existence in collective memory of a primal severance in transitional ether." For the well-being of the community, this gulf "must be constantly diminished by the sacrifices, the rituals, the ceremonies of appeasement to those cosmic powers which lie guardian to the gulf." Here, the Ogun drama becomes the paradigmatic tragedy: his tragic dare (the exercise of Will) is of primal, cosmic proportions, a dare suffused with the possibilities of dissolution and of reassemblage of the self, and which—with unwavering determination—*privileges communal health*. The dare is "an act undertaken on behalf of the community, and the welfare of [the] protagonist is inseparable from that of the total community." The latter particularly explains why "[t]ragic feeling in Yoruba drama stems from sympathetic knowledge of the protagonist's foray into [the] psychic abyss of the re-creative energies."[17]

Following or in the process of Ogun's prodigious foray is a sense of *resolution* characteristic of Obatala, the god of creation and the principle of the serene arts. Not for this god the tragic challenge, and his distance from the willful, venturesome Ogun is evident in the virtues that characterize his drama: "social and individual accommodation: patience, suffering, peaceableness, all the imperatives of harmony in the universe, the essence of quietude and forbearance; in short, the aesthetics of the saint."[18] Obatala's task is mainly formal and plastic—*creation* (his job) comes only after the spark of *creativity* (Ogun's act) is ignited. Obatala is the "aesthetic serenity" that comes after the hubristic, world-changing act.

Soyinka's *African* nodal point is not conceived as exclusivist, so in the elaboration of his tragic schema, he gives full play to his indebtedness to the German philosopher Friedrich Nietzsche and to the common observation of the close resemblance of the Yoruba and Greek pantheons. Thus the dramatist announces early in "The Fourth Stage" that "[o]ur course to the heart of the Yoruba Mysteries leads by its own ironic truths through the light of Nietzsche (*The Birth of Tragedy*) and the Phrygian deity."[19] The essences of the veritable pair Dionysos and Apollo appear to recall those of Ogun and Obatala. The thyrsus of Dionysos parallels the *opa Ogun*; while the Ogun sacrificial dog, slaughtered and torn limb from limb in the mock struggle for its possession by the head priest and his acolytes, recalls the dismemberment of Zagreus, son of Zeus. And "[m]ost significant of all is the brotherhood of the palm and the ivy," telling us of both gods' affinity for wine.[20]

There are, of course, the inevitable significant differences between the two pantheons. While deities in both frequently commit serious transgressions against humanity, "the morality of reparation," unfailingly exacted from, and more or less willingly submitted to, by the Yoruba deities, "appears totally alien to the ethical concepts of the ancient Greeks." The Yoruba insistence on the moral character of their deities constantly forces into focus the dialectic of communal continuity, of restitutions and disharmonies. Hence "the ethical basis of Greek tragedy, not as it began in the ritual *tragodia* but as it developed through the pessimistic line of Aeschylus to Shakespeare's 'As flies to wanton boys, are we to the gods; / They kill us for their sport' " is totally alien to the Yoruba world.[21] Dionysos may resemble Ogun but they are far from equivalent. As the god of ecstasy and creative daring, Ogun may be Dionysos, but Ogun's willfulness is not an end in itself—his creativity is the prelude to creation, hence he is also Apollo. The manic will which he unleashed *on behalf of the community* tells us that Ogun is, in addition, something else: Prometheus. Thus Soyinka's claim that Ogun is "best understood in Hellenic values as a totality of the Dionysian, Apollonian and Promethean virtues."[22]

History as a Mythopoeic Resource

Death and the King's Horseman best embodies the multiplex dimensions of Soyinka's construct of an African poetics. This is so not only in its character as a ritual tragedy—Soyinka's privileged form in "The Fourth Stage"—but also in its concern with the historic issue of the African encounter with Europe. Described by the dramatist as an attempt to "'epochalise' History for its mythopoeic resourcefulness,"[23] the play is based on events which occurred in 1946 in the venerable Yoruba city of Oyo, Nigeria. Part of the final funeral ceremonies for the late king demands the ritual suicide of the commander of his stables, Elesin. This is the tradition, but the Oyo of 1946 is not the Oyo of old. Ultimate political authority has changed residence. Simon Pilkings, the white colonial district officer, motivated by an unreflective, egoistic quest to stamp out "barbaric customs," intervenes and arrests Elesin before the sacrificial act. When Olunde, Elesin's eldest son, returns from his studies in Britain to bury his father, as the rites demand, he is faced with an abomination: his father has not performed the one important duty he has all along been living for. To keep familial honor indoors and affirm the continuity of his people's way of life, Olunde calmly assumes the father's duty. Stung by this tragic reversal, Elesin swiftly strangles himself, while the people lament the passing of a world, the tumbling of their world "in the void of strangers."[24]

Soyinka announces in the "Author's Note" his departures from historical accounts of the events. The changes, he says, are in "matters of detail, sequence, and . . . characterization." He also set the action back "two or three years to while the war [World War II] was still on, for minor reasons of dramaturgy."[25] Other changes of detail, unstated by Soyinka but apparently also crucial "for reasons of dramaturgy" as pressed into the service of a poetics of othering, include Olunde's sojourn in Britain and his suicide; Elesin's wedding on the night of transition, and his subsequent suicide; and the visit of H. R. H. the Prince.[26]

Considered in the light of Soyinka's theory of tragic art, the play yields its peculiarly rich insights and ambiguities. All the tragic ingredients are there: a protagonist who embodies the will and aspirations of the collective, and a tragic issue of cosmic proportions for the community. The altruism of the Promethean ego is not open to doubt, constituted and nurtured as it were by the undiluted goal of communal conservation. The latter requires a *willed* disintegration, which is precisely for that reason not disintegration but a successful crossing and bridging of the chthonic realm, once again renewing the bonds between the ancestors, the living, and the unborn—past, present, and future. Elesin is Soyinka's candidate for the Ogun figure.

To say that Elesin faces his task heroically is not just an understatement but a fundamental error. He knows no other duty; he was born to this hereditary task, and he has gratefully accepted it, lived it, and lived for it, with all its glittering prerequisites:

> In all my life
> As Horseman of the King, the juiciest
> Fruit on every tree was mine. I saw
> I touched, I wooed, rarely was the answer No.

It is in the spirit of this natural acceptance that he lets us know at the outset that

> My rein is loosened
> I am master of my Fate. When the hour comes
> Watch me dance along the narrowing path
> Glazed by the soles of my great precursors.
> My soul is eager. I shall not turn
> aside.[27]

Yet no close reader of his actions and Ogun's in "The Fourth Stage" will fail to discover that there is something amiss. Only a few hours before confronting the "cosmic lair"—during which, according to the drama of Ogun he is aspiring to perform, he would need the most concentrated, gargantuan will—he appears before us not in contemplative mobilization of deep psychic energies but as a man of "enormous vitality [who] speaks, dances and sings with [an] *infectious enjoyment of life* . . ."[28]

A classy, consummate sybarite, Elesin heads for the market among the women, so he can live his fantasy of "a chicken with a hundred mothers," "a monarch whose palace is built with tenderness and beauty." He whistles over "the smell of their flesh, their sweat, the smell of indigo on their cloth." This is "the last air," he announces, "I wish to breathe as I go to meet my great forebears." His eloquence, this time, drowns that of the professional Praise-Singer, who warns that the "hands of women . . . weaken the unwary."[29] What amounts to Elesin's answer is another pleasant surprise: he begins to tell the story of the "Not-I bird," an elaborate, extremely infectious narrative of those who ran away when death, the agent of transition, came calling. Of course, he lets us know that he is not like them. "All is well" with him, he says, for he has "ejected / Fear from home and farm." In fact, he argues that though he loves life, his sense of duty is very much intact:

> When friendship summons
> Is when true comrade goes.
> I go to keep my friend and master company

and that moderation is not a concept alien to him:

> Who says the mouth does not believe in
> "No, I have chewed all that before?" I say I have
> The world is not a constant honey-pot.[26]

Among the market women, Elesin invents an imagined slight which literally sends the women scampering for his appeasement, not daring to offend the one who will soon bear their wishes across to the world beyond. Then, seeing a beautiful young girl among the women, he begins to entertain the idea that even on a night like this he could wander and dilly-dally, and that his rootedness would bring him back to base:

> Coiled
> To the navel of the world is that
> Endless cord that links us all
> To the great origin. If I lose my way
> The trailing cord will bring me to the roots."[31]

Elesin insists on having the girl, requesting that the women honor him with "a bed of honour to lie upon" so that in the coming journey, he could "travel light." Of course, he denies it is for "a moment's pleasure," waxing philosophical about how the "sap of the plantain never dries" but shows the "young shoot swelling / Even as the parent stalk begins to wither." The girl in question is already betrothed to the son of Iyaloja, head of the market-women, but Elesin flatly rejects this as an excuse. Iyaloja finally accedes to Elesin's demand, but not without grave warnings regarding its possible repercussions on the performance of the task at hand. "Eating the awusa nut," she says, "is not so difficult as drinking water afterwards." Elesin swiftly dismisses these doubts on his ability.[32]

Elesin may not be afraid of death, but he has contaminated his own will to a degree he is either unaware of or unwilling to believe. When Iyaloja, in her usual robust, unnerving subtlety, juxtaposes Elesin's present desire with the imminent task,

> Now we must go prepare your bridal chamber.
> Then these same hands will lay your shrouds

the stage direction tells us that Elesin is practically "exasperated," retorting to Iyaloja, "Must you be so blunt?" That is, he wants the coming reality to be thickly robed in soothing metaphors, but the question is, won't these unduly encumber the will when the decisive moment calls? Elesin is at best an unwilling defector whose rhetorical reiterations of his readiness are meant to whip him back on course.[33]

After a brief honeymoon and his exhibition, with a revealing satisfaction, of the "no mere virgin stain," Elesin commences the passage procedures in earnest. What Soyinka makes of the procedure is worth more than mere mention. In what is perhaps one of the most powerful evocations in contemporary African drama of a classical African ritualistic sense of space, all resources are mobilized in aid of the protagonist-actor: the "intensive language of transition," also known as music, the propelling, invocatory laments and exhortations, a massing of communal spiritual energies as a cushioning pool for the protagonist, the dismantling of artificial actor–audience barriers yet with precise collectively recognizable distinctions, and so on. Elesin finally embarks on his destiny.

It is important to emphasize at this juncture the crucial weight Soyinka attaches to music as an indispensable vehicle of the ritual transition. In the "Author's Note," he warns producers against reducing the play to a simple conflict of cultures, and he recommends that they instead face the "far more difficult and risky task of eliciting the play's *threnodic* essence" (emphasis added). In fact, the dramatist argues, the play "can be fully realised only through an evocation of music from the abyss of transition." The underlying assumption here is a mutually propelling relationship between poetry and music in tragic art. But what Soyinka discovers in *The Birth of Tragedy*, from which his theory derives great inspiration, is Nietzsche's antagonistic separation of music and language.[34]

"The cosmic symbolism of music," Nietzsche argues, "resists any adequate treatment by language, for the simple reason that music, in referring to primordial contradiction and pain, symbolizes a sphere which is both earlier than appearance [the realm of "figurative discourse"] and beyond it." Hence language will always perform poorly whenever it attempts to represent music: "[L]anguage, the organ and symbol of appearance, can never succeed in bringing the innermost core of music to the surface. Whenever it engages in the imitation of music, language remains in purely superficial contact with it, and no amount of poetic eloquence will carry us a step closer to the essential secret of that art."[35]

Soyinka takes particular care to distance himself from the Nietzschean conception, for the "nature of Yoruba music is intensively the nature of its language and poetry, highly charged, symbolic, myth-embryonic." For the Yoruba, language does not threaten the consummate ubiquity of music; on the contrary, it is its "cohesive dimension and clarification," which explains why language "reverts in religious rites to its pristine existence, eschewing the sterile limits of particularisation." Soyinka explains this transformative process in detail:

> Language in Yoruba tragic music therefore undergoes transformation through myth into a secret (masonic) correspondence with the symbolism of tragedy, a symbolic medium of spiritual emotions within the heart of the choric union. It transcends particularisation (of meaning) to tap the tragic source whence spring the familiar weird disruptive melodies. This masonic union of sign and melody, the true tragic music, unearths cosmic uncertainties which pervade human existence, reveals the magnitude and power of creation, but above all creates a harrowing sense of omni-directional vastness where the creative Intelligence

resides and prompts the soul to futile exploration. The senses do not at such moments interpret myth in their particular concretions: we are left only with the emotional and spiritual values, the essential experience of cosmic reality.[36]

Only this conception explains why, for instance, Soyinka goes to great lengths to make the poetic, sonorous-lacerating chants of the Praise-Singer and the pervasive intensive drumming (hear Pilkings, the white colonial district officer, to his wife, Jane: ". . . I am getting rattled. Probably the effect of those bloody drums. Do you hear how they go on and on?"[37]) *mutually* underscore one another in a powerful, affective evocation of a ritualistic theatrical space. The following description is of the moment building up to the decisive core of the ritual:

> His [Elesin's] dance is one of solemn, regal motions, each gesture of the body is made with a solemn finality. The women join him, their steps a somewhat more fluid version of his.
> ELESIN dances on, completely in a trance. The dirge wells up louder and stronger.
> ELESIN's dance does not lose its elasticity but his gestures become, if possible, even more weighty.[38]

Soyinka in *Myth* outlines the contours of this ritualistic theatrical space:

> Any individual within the "audience" knows better than to add his voice *arbitrarily* even to the most seductive passages of an invocatory song, or to contribute a refrain to the familiar sequence of liturgical exchanges among the protagonists. The moment for choric participation is well-defined, but this does not imply that until such a moment, participation ceases. The so-called audience is itself an integral part of that arena of conflict; it contributes spiritual strength to the protagonist through its choric reality which must first be conjured up and established, defining and investing the arena through offerings and incantations. The drama would be non-existent except within and against this symbolic representation of earth and cosmos, except within this communal compact whose choric essence supplies the collective energy for the challenger of . . . chthonic realms.[39]

It is this culturally symbolically charged space that District Officer Pilkings violates to arrest Elesin before he can take the decisive plunge.

A consideration of the events leading to Elesin's arrest illuminates Soyinka's assertion in the "Author's Note" that the "Colonial Factor is an incident, a catalytic incident merely." Elesin's actions all along contradict every Ogunnian principle. *Action* is what defines Ogun, and the Ogun figure is the cosmic-scale actor. Elesin knows this, of course, but what he does is to substitute representation, through his rhetorical flamboyance, for action. Yet we all know that death is the unrepresentable, to represent death is to cheat it, tame it, come to terms with it.[40] In confrontation with the chasm, Ogun arms himself with iron ore and unshakeable will; Elesin hangs on to the thin, fragile rope of words, weaving it endlessly in myriad forms, and even makes it the agent for catalyzing his will. Words and iron are, of course, both implements of creativity, and representations are also actions. Yet, perhaps as Elesin himself would say as a Yoruba elder and therefore, as implied by the culture, a repository of wisdom, why give them different names if they are the same? Elesin does not make this difference, between *action* and *promise* of action as action.

Perhaps Elesin misperceives the double-edged nature of action in traditional tragic ritual, in which, according to Soyinka, "[a]cting is . . . a contradiction of the tragic spirit, [but] also its natural complement"; in which "[w]ithout acting, and yet in spite of it [the tragic victim] is forever lost in the maul of tragic tyranny." Not for the Yoruba is this a blind alley; at such moments, the Yoruba chooses action, for it is what defines and gives the tragic act its redemptive character:

> To act, the Promethean instinct of rebellion, channels anguish into a creative purpose which releases man from a totally destructive despair, releasing from within him the most energetic, deeply combative inventions which, without usurping the territory of the infernal gulf, bridges it with visionary hopes.[41]

Elesin not only did not act but also has an uncanny way of putting the cart before the horse. This is not just overenthusiasm, though we would do his honor a great service to hold on to this reading. Elesin has neither performed Ogun's "redemptive action" nor experienced the god's "ritual anguish," yet he represents himself as a "symbol of the alliance of disparities,"[42] of death and life, age and youth; the link between the withering plantain stalk and its new, fresh young shoot—in short, the "twilight hour of the plantain."[43] Perhaps this is what Richard M. Ready means when he says that "Elesin mistakes creation for creativity, supplants accomplishing the fact with the accomplished fact."[44] This is an illusion.[45] Creation, an achievement he is already claiming for himself as the "alliance of disparities," belongs in the office of Obatala, which comes *after* the Ogunnian plunge (creativity). Elesin has not taken this plunge. It is not surprising then that what Elesin claims as creation is mere representation, an "illusion" which belongs to Nietzsche's Apollo, not the Obatalan *essence*:

> Women, let my going be *likened* to
> The twilight hour of the plantain. (Emphasis added)

I think Ready is right not to spare Elesin: "That Elesin would claim for himself the Obatalan achievement of pure essence when in fact he has not even entered the Ogunnian torture is the greatest of illusions."[46]

Elesin is, as we know, given to exaggerations, but he seems unaware that he is not immune from interpellation by his own representations, especially when couched in seductive lyricism as is his wont. On beholding for the second time the beauty of the young girl whom he later would marry, Elesin starts to wonder if he is still in this world or has joined the ancestors—a virtually blasphemous thought: "[C]ould it be my will / Has outleapt the conscious act and I have come / Among the great departed?"[47] If hyperbole has any limits, this is certainly one. Soyinka tells us that even Ogun of the gargantuan will had to synchronize this will with an equally gargantuan *conscious act* before he could subdue the infernal gulf. Is chthonic chaos so easy to conquer that one can actually do it without knowing one has done it? In this formulation by Elesin, Ogun's tragic dare is no more than a picnic, preferably amid beautiful market-women.

Elesin is not the Ogun tragic figure. This point stays in spite of his later suicide when he sees the body of Olunde. His death at this point is too late; he displays heroic will and action (in swiftly strangling himself) but these serve egoistic purposes only (shame on being replaced by his son); and his suicide is not only in a mockery of the ritualistic space (a cell where Pilkings locks him to save him from himself) but it is also not communally redemptive. It is, in short, wasteful. Not about Elesin's suicide could we say: "In the symbolic disintegration of the protagonist ego is reflected the destiny of being."[48] But we could say this of Olunde's suicide, though it too is past the appointed hour. But Olunde's death is meant to right a wrong, and Ogun himself is the god of restorative justice:

> IYALOJA *(moves forward and removes the covering)*:   Your courier Elesin, cast your eyes on the favoured companion of the King.
> *(Rolled up in the mat, his head and feet showing at either end is the body of OLUNDE.)*
> There lies the honour of your household and our race. Because he could not bear to let honour fly out of doors, he stopped it with his life. The son has proved the father Elesin, and there is nothing left in your mouth to gnash but infant gums.[49]

Such a replacement, accompanied by appropriate rites, is well within the "accommodative wisdom" of the Yoruba mind. It is Olunde's death that evokes tragic feeling, winning, as Soyinka writes of Ogun's act, the people's sympathetic knowledge of the protagonist's foray into the psychic abyss of the recreative energies.

Soyinka says in the prefatory "Author's Note" that "the confrontation in the play is largely metaphysical." We add that it is also largely ethical. Pilkings is the typical administrator on Her Majesty's service in one of the colonial possessions. He once expresses a dismissive remark about the project of empire, but of course he says this in a grumbling low tone that even the Resident, his superior whom he is addressing directly, did not hear. Otherwise, he goes about his duty—managing the colonized population for the benefit of empire—with a frame of mind that would be surprising if it was not easily predictable. His attitude to the "native" society is decidedly parochial and positivist; a dripping condescension completes the package:

> JANE: Aren't they all rather close, Simon?
> PILKINGS: These natives here? Good gracious. They'll open their mouths

and yap with you about their family secrets before you can stop them. Only the other day . . .

JANE: But Simon, do they really give anything away? I mean, anything that really counts? This affair for instance, we didn't know they still practised that custom did we?

PILKINGS: Ye–e–es, I suppose you're right there. Sly, devious bastards.

. . .

JANE: Simon, you really must watch your language. Bastard isn't just a simple swear-word in these parts, you know.

. . .

PILKINGS: I thought the extended family system took care of all that. Elastic family, no bastards.[50]

Points of contrast with the colonized are hinged on little more than sets of differences elevated to fetishes: "barbaric custom[s]" versus "civilized traditions." Pilkings may once slyly sneer at the project of empire but he is in no doubt at all—and he publicly expresses it—of the ethical superiority of the Europeans over the Africans, and of the justification, in this regard, of the "c(olonizing)ivilizing mission."

The ethical confrontation is crucial to Soyinka's construct of what he considers significant differences in the (colonizing) European and (colonized) African worldviews, and he is very meticulous in presenting his case. In Pilkings's *expressive* axiological scheme, values are either "normal," "rational"—otherwise known as European—or "abnormal," "irrational"—thus non-European. "The District Officer and his world," writes Soyinka, "*provoked* the argument of the drama . . . the motivating factor for his action, his interference is squarely and hermetically posed within the simple confrontation of 'civilised' values versus the 'barbaric.' "[51] Within a conception of ethics governed by such arrogant and simplistic hermeticism, difference appears as little more than deviance, deserving more of repression, violation, and extermination than understanding: the politics of expressive identity.[52] Hence for the Europeans, revered ancestral masks of the Africans are no more than exotic costumes with which to grace the occasion of the Prince's visit. The truth of the moment belongs to Olunde, who shoulders the burden of debunking the claims and assumptions of ethical superiority by the colonialists. He denies he is shocked by the attitudes of the whites to the colonized culture: "You forget that I have now spent four years among your people. I discovered that you have no respect for what you do not understand."[53] It is significant that Olunde does not reciprocate with a similar parochial vision. His last sentence here is a defense not only of the colonized culture but also of misunderstood redeeming instances in the colonizer's culture. Take the case of the self-sacrificing white captain, who, because it was the only way possible, blew himself up with his ship, which had become dangerous to the other ships in the harbor and to the coastal population. Jane, after relating this story to Olunde, apologizes for welcoming him with such "morbid" news. She is thoroughly flabbergasted when Olunde, in a deep, *performative* act of understanding, coolly replies: "I don't find it morbid at all. I find it rather inspiring. It is an affirmative commentary on life." But the shallow, aggressive positivism of the colonialists won't be defeated that easily. It would cling desperately to props of cliche and dubious logic such as, from Jane: "Life should never be thrown away deliberately," and "The whole thing was probably exaggerated anyway." [54]

In the *white* captain Soyinka locates a true Ogunnian figure who, in a combination of communal responsibility, tragic dare, and Promethean will, plunged into the primeval gulf. If the colonizers could not find reference points within their own culture to properly appreciate the captain's positive, heroic act, what chance have such manifestations in the colonized culture, where they are not likely to be articulated in the "scientific" discursive idiom of "poisonous gases" and "explosions" and "shipping" but in the "primitive" accents of incantations and drumming? There is little or no difference between the willingly accepted self-sacrificing roles of the captain and Elesin. Their suicides are motivated by similar altruistic ends, yet while the captain may not be properly understood, he was not prevented from his self-imposed sacrifice. Elesin, on the other hand, is not only misunderstood but also prevented from the execution of his duties.

It is of significant interest that Pilkings attempts to divest himself of colonial authority by suggesting that his ultimate justification for arresting Elesin comes from the native culture itself:

> I have lived among you long enough to learn a saying or two. One came to mind tonight when I stepped into the market and saw what was going on. You were surrounded by those who egged you on with song and praises. I thought, are these not the same people who say: the elder grimly approaches heaven and you ask him to bear your greetings yonder; do you really think he makes the journey willingly? After that, I did not hesitate.[55]

From this, we can see that Pilkings does indeed try to understand his natives. But through no fault of his, the native culture remains fixed in a mire of ethical confusion. Pilkings deludes himself. The confusion is less in the native culture than in the unyielding binary mode of apprehension with which Pilkings attempts to understand it. His closed, superstitious notion of ethics cannot imagine a culture whose sayings, proverbs, or aphorisms present themselves not as whole and eternally valid but as half-truths: *always* situational and contingent. Unfortunately he is dealing with such a culture. Pilkings's stiff empiricist rationality simply cannot fathom that his "authoritative" saying—the proverb which he says authorizes his action— has been deconstructed several times in the text by other sayings that warn against abandonment of responsibility. The culture which says "the elder grimly approaches . . ." is also the culture which states

> "What elder takes his tongue to his plate,
> Licks its clean of every crumb . . . will encounter

> Silence when he calls on children to fulfill
> The smallest errand!"[56]

Faced with such taut aporia, the colonialist binary logic simply resorts to condemnations:

> JANE [to Olunde]:   You talk! You people with your long-winded, roundabout way of making conversation.[57]
>
> . . .
>
> PILKINGS [to Elesin]:   I wish to ask you to search the quiet of your heart and tell me—do you not find great contradictions in the wisdom of your own race?[58]

Pilkings may indeed have learned "a saying or two" of the local culture, but a saying or two do not a culture make and, if we remember the poet correctly, a little learning is a dangerous thing. . . . The appropriate response here comes from Olunde, talking to Jane of his experiences in Britain: "I saw nothing, finally, that gave you the right to pass judgement on other peoples and their ways. Nothing at all."[59] Olunde's suicide in affirmation of the indigenous culture is the concrete expression of this sanction and a deflation of the colonialists' pretensions to ethical superiority; remember that Pilkings's aim in smuggling Olunde to Britain for medical studies is to "civilize" him and save him from his "primitive" culture.

The Cultural, the Political

A failed suicide, Elesin in great emotional turmoil tries one excuse after another. At times he verges on a submission to the whites' claims of ethical superiority. He actually entertains the thought that his failure signifies the gods' surrender of initiative to the colonizers. But as he himself clearly recognizes, he has committed a great sacrilege, "the awful treachery of relief . . . the unspeakable blasphemy of seeing the hand of the gods in this alien rupture of [our] world."[60] As if this recognition is not painful enough, Olunde's death unequivocally pronounces Elesin guilty on all counts. The colonial presence does not absolve one of responsibility, whatever that responsibility demands. After all, the play again and again insists on the indigenous society as vital, alive, and autodynamic, constantly changing and accommodating new and alien experiences but never losing its moorings. This is the basis for Soyinka's much-discussed statement in the "Author's Note": "The Colonial Factor is an incident, a catalytic incident merely."

For its *strategic* function, Soyinka's statement can hardly be faulted. It is a fitting riposte to the centuries of representation of the African world as stagnant and outside of history before the European incursion. To the extent that the African society represented in the play is like any other—living, changing, and coping with influences—the Colonial Factor is indeed a catalytic incident. We remember, of course, Soyinka's iteration of the "accommodative wisdom" of the Yoruba worldview, a worldview which constructs a linkage between Sango and his thunder and lightning and the handiwork of Benjamin Franklin, between Ogun and space rocket and silicon chips. Besides, the colonial intervention is not the first time the culture's tradition of ritual suicide would receive a critique—historical accounts record several challenges to the tradition from *within* the culture itself.[61] And the play takes great care to indicate Elesin's *personal* weaknesses. In other words, it is not impossible to imagine the same drama without the catalytic factor of colonialism. But then, that would be *an(O)ther* drama and the differential trace between the two would be the Colonial Factor. This is where, in spite of Soyinka's *culturalist* denial, the Colonial Factor comes fully to the foreground.

Amid Soyinka's overinvestment in the representation of *cultural* differences, the theme of *political* domination intrudes repeatedly, covering the gamut of the African encounter with Europe, from slavery to colonialism. After Elesin's arrest, he was locked in the "cellar in the disused annexe of the Residency" "where," in days gone by, "the slaves were stored before being taken down to the coast. . . ." His society irreversibly suffers the imposed strangulating space: "Even the honour of my people you have taken already; it is tied together with those papers of treachery which make you masters in this land."[62] Evidently what we have is more than a confrontation of two "cultures," two "ways of life." It is for this reason that Olunde cuts such a pitiable figure when he argues passionately, in typical cultural nationalist style, that nothing gives the Europeans the right to pass judgment on the culture of others. He is wrong: their political and military power over disparate spaces gave the Europeans that right, not supposed claims of *cultural* superiority. In fact, the seriousness with which Olunde discursively engages colonial hypocrisy—the main target of his culturalist anger—shows his naïveté in believing that colonialism can be usefully engaged in dialogue by the colonized. The white aide-de-camp is right on target here: "These natives put a suit on and they get high opinions of themselves."[63]

If the substance of the drama goes beyond a simple encounter between cultures, then perhaps Olunde's suicide needs a reassessment. His death unequivocally affirms the indigenous culture, but then, as Fanon would say against culturalism, you will not make colonialism blush simply by displaying before it little-known cultural treasures.[64] Olunde's death denies superiority to the morality of the c(olonizing)ivilizing enterprise, but this enterprise was never based on moral superiority. The discourse of barbaric natives/primitive cultures does not precede the enterprise; it is an *after-fact* of conquest. Are we to hold then that Olunde's death is unnecessary? This question is not as simple as it appears.

Soyinka constructs Olunde's suicide (and also Elesin's task) as the redemption of a collective. If we agree that the culture represented is a living, dynamic culture as the "Author's Note" implies and as the play celebrates, then we must also accept that, like other cultures, it is not

univocal. This gives us an opening to question the author's orchestration
of the ritual suicide as communally redemptive. The text itself shows
fissures in the community in the characters of Joseph and Amusa, who
care less for the tradition, but these are presented by Soyinka as evidently
alienated by their surrender to *alien* religions, Christianity and Islam respectively. Otherwise, the whole community—women and men, high and
low—is unanimous in support of the tradition. The interesting point
here, by an ironic turn, is that we are dealing with a tradition whose
origins can be historically dated, whose fortunes can be plotted over the
ages as it had been manipulated by (different factions of) the Yoruba
aristocracy that invented it for its own perpetuation, and whose application had at no time failed to engender great acrimony and rebellion by
many of those at the receiving end, especially palace servants and wives.[65]
Soyinka in the play occludes this fact in the relationship between Elesin
and the aristocracy and the rest of the community.

This leads us to an important aspect of Soyinka's philosophy of culture
and proposition of African cultural identity. The aspect hinges on questions of "internal" heterogeneity and cultural pluralism. Against Sen-
ghorian Negritude's propositions of a conflict-free monolithic Africa,[66]
Soyinka advances a healthily heterogeneous, dynamic, and contradiction-
ridden African world as vital and self-propelling as any other world.[67] His
play *A Dance of the Forests*, produced in 1960 for the Nigerian Independence celebrations, best expresses this vision and is justly famous for its
exorcism of what the author characterizes as the "boring romanticism of
the negro."[68] To add grandeur to the celebration of their "majestic"
history, the gathered tribes appeal to their ancestors to send illustrious
representatives as guests to grace the occasion. But the ancestors would
not be party to such a narcissistic quest and parochial self-apprehension.
They send instead, in a deconstruction of the so-called grandiose history,
clear, accusing pictures the tribes would rather keep, and had indeed
meticulously kept, out of focus. The play, Soyinka confesses, deliberately
"takes a jaundiced view of the much-vaunted glorious past of Africa."[69]

Even later, when Soyinka had to modify his critique of Negritude by
proposing an African essence, he still insists that this is a *dynamic*, not an
unchanging essence.[70] His opponents of the materialist persuasion—
whose debate with Soyinka I will pay some attention to—go beyond the
assertion of the heterogeneity of the African world to insist on stratification
even within a particular culture, a stratification most often along the lines
of the dominant and the subordinate, with all its suggestive implications.
Though Soyinka is also a proponent of heterogeneity as we have seen, he
has consistently challenged this "extension" of it. To be sure—and this is
the paradox of it—Soyinka remains one of the greatest scourges of class
privilege and class oppression in Africa. His interventions in the Nigerian
political terrain, from electoral politics to the civil war and beyond, show a
clear recognition of the existence of class hierarchy. Running through his
corpus are homages to revolutionary will and resistance to tyranny such as

Ogun Abibiman, A Shuttle in the Crypt, Season of Anomy, and *Mandela's Earth,* interspersed with severe sanctions against tyrannical agents, as we have in *Madmen and Specialists, The Man Died, Kongi's Harvest, Opera Wonyosi, A Play of Giants,* and *From Zia with Love.* He has more than once voiced his preference for socialism,[71] and when he joined a political party in Nigeria, his choice was the most left-leaning. Yet Soyinka's insistence, in many theoretical and critical essays, is that a class approach to African culture is self-defeating and subversive of any claim to unique cultural definitions.[72] It is as if "class" is an alien concept which degrades the "original" constitution of the indigenous. Yet in Africa "class" is no more alien than "tragedy" as social and heuristic category. Soyinka here gestures toward the norms of expressive identity.

For Soyinka, the motive cause of history is not class or group but the lone individual hero who acts for and catalyzes the community: the Ogun, the Atunda. Predictably, Soyinka has paid little attention to other intracultural differences, such as gender, which until recently is far less visible than class in modern African literary discourse. Yet we cannot claim that gender difference is irrelevant to a conception of an anti-imperialist cultural identity. Nationalist discourse aggressively appropriates difference as a weapon against foreign domination but arrests the play of difference when it is time for internal analysis. Significantly, no female deity features in Soyinka's elaboration of his tragic paradigm. The dramas of the female gods are perhaps not the stuff of which "tragedy" is fashioned and fundamental insights into Yoruba philosophy of existence derived. The Ogun principle itself is the male principle par excellence, and no one can miss the sumptuous celebration of *virility* that constitutes the symbolic fabric of his passion—the gargantuan will, the penetration of chthonic chaos, the phallic *opa ogun,* and so on. Iyaloja and the market-women unproblematically egg Elesin on to a duty which is undoubtedly of supreme communal significance—for so it has been *constructed* and believed by many for ages—but which is *also* a main pillar of a patriarchal feudalism. "Maidens, Mistresses and Matrons" is how a feminist critic, Carole Boyce Davies, sees many of the women in Soyinka's works.[73] And Florence Stratton raises an apt query of Soyinka's social vision: "Where is Atunda's sister?"[74]

This inadequate attention to culture as a hierarchical structure is central to the terms of a significant debate in the 1970s between Soyinka and African Marxist critics. The encounter was a product of the 1970s unusual explosion of radical consciousness on the African continent, a consciousness at once impatient with the local bourgeoisie and its ideologists and vociferous against Western political, economic, and cultural imperialism. What was at stake was no less than the appropriate contours of a relevant modern African cultural identity. Strands of this multisided encounter[75] that are of immediate relevance here examined the turn to African classical materials by the contemporary artist for inspiration, *and* the proper—that is, with contemporary mass aspiration in view—theoretical and dramaturgic mode of appropriation of such materials. This led to an interrogation of Soyinka's "African world," which was found to be too myth-informed, "ahistorical," and "essentialist"; and his resolute refusal at a class appreciation of African cultures was seen as an inadequate grasp of the problematic of difference in the construction of cultural identity. In short, the charges suggested that Soyinka constructs an expressive rather than a performative cultural identity. The two Marxist critics of Soyinka who best articulated these issues are Femi Osofisan and Biodun Jeyifo.

Soyinka's special predilection, as "The Fourth Stage" shows, is for the ritual form. For him, ritual is not only a cultural anchor but also a creative ideal for the representation of experience and phenomena that resist simplistic rationalism or socioeconomic calculation. Ritual "is a metaphor for the perennial," he wrote, "and the perennial is not located in any one such and such event. Birth is a perennial event, so is death. So are courage, cowardice, fear, motion, rain, drought, storm . . . Ritual is the irreducible formal agent for event-disparate and time-separated actions of human beings in human society."[76] In addition, ritual has a revolutionary imperative to it, located as it is at "that point where the cementing communal roots of theatre are made one with the liberating direction of the present." No one will deny, concluded Soyinka, that this "universal idiom" is "a language of the masses."[77] Femi Osofisan, himself a poet, distinguished dramatist, and mythopoeist, challenged Soyinka's claim by asserting that ritual is *not* inherently revolutionary. He cited as evidence some of Soyinka's own dramas such as *Madmen and Specialists* and *Death and the King's Horseman*, which he argued work as powerful theatrical rituals but express little more than "idealist illusion," "spiritual homeostasis," reconciliation with the status quo, and "fatalism, that antidote to human progress."[78] Soyinka did not deny that these are possible directions for ritual but, citing copiously from "The Fourth Stage," disagreed that they are exemplary of his own work. Besides this, he cautioned that to describe the entirety of ritual in such narrow and predetermined ways is to give short-shrift to the necessarily complex transactions between the stage and the audience.[77]

Osofisan, of course, was far from saying that ritual is incompatible with revolutionary ethos. His point was that the animist worldview inherent in traditional ritual was irrelevant to the needs of the moment:

> The truth is that this moment in history, the world -view which made for animist metaphysics has all but disintegrated in the acceleration, caused by colonialism, of man's economic separation from Nature. However one may regret it, myth and history are no longer complementary, and to insist otherwise is to voice a plea for reaction. For it is obvious now that in order to adequately come to terms with the rapacious, dehumanized white men of Europe and America, the ancient modes of life must dissolve and yield place to an empiric mastery of life, and of the means of production. There seems no other alternative in a

world dominated by the West's capitalist predatoriness. . . . [B]ecause the animist world accommodates and sublimates disaster within the matrix of ritual, the Red Indian world collapsed, and so did ours, perhaps with slower speed.[80]

What is to be done is to unsparingly dialectically mediate ritual if it is to serve a revolutionary purpose. Osofisan then cited another set of plays in which he suggested that Soyinka actually did this: *The Road* and *The Strong Breed*.

Soyinka responded that Osofisan's claims fly in the face of historical facts. The animist worldview is not inherently reactionary or antiprogress. Superstition, which for Soyinka includes " 'animism', 'bhuddism', 'roman catholicism', 'islam', 'protestantism', etc. etc.," has never prevented the rise of any society to technological heights. Otherwise, why is it that an "unfair proportion" of the world's scientific geniuses belong to one of the most "unliberalised religions—the Judaic[?]" For Soyinka, ours and the American Indian worlds collapsed not because of animist metaphysics but because of lack of superior military technology at the moment of contact—what makes empires if not guns?[81] Osofisan is hence guilty of a superficial grasp of his history. And Soyinka did not mince words about this, especially because he perceived an "alien" framework—Marxism—as the guiding light of the superficiality: ". . . in the haste to identify with progressive minds outside their own immediate polity, our intellectuals tend to construct a false or adumbrated reality of their own social milieu. The more 'historical' their claims the less factually history-conscious their analysis."[82]

There is a sense in which Osofisan's now enormous work can be seen as one long, continuing dialogue with Soyinka. The latter's influence on the former is substantial, and this is easily seen both in their similarities and differences.[83] Osofisan's own adopted deity is Orunmila, the god of divination. Here we have a major critique of Soyinka from within the source-tradition. In Osofisan's opinion, Ogun may be all those features elicited from him by Soyinka, but Ogun is also something else: the individualist par excellence, the god who braved the void and chaos alone to singlehandedly cut a path through which other gods descend to earth. This individualism may once have been relevant, but given the complexity and multidimensionality of Africa's problems today, success is better ensured, in Osofisan's opinion, with a vision that privileges collective participation. The days of the "Promethean protagonists," he insisted, are over. Orunmila as the god of divination, the mediator between ill and sound health, the one who incarnates "the tension between the existing and the visionary, between the past, the present and the future," for Osofisan, enables the collectivist perspective.[84] To Osofisan's charge of individualism, Soyinka answered yes, but he has always emphasized the communal agency role of the individual protagonist-ego. Fidel Castro is after all an individual, yet no one can deny, in the plunge through the marshes and subsequent successful revolution against Batista, the communal agency role of his will.[85] Osofisan would probably insist on his point against overprivileging the lone individual ego. After all, Castro was not the only one who braved the odds. This last argument will not, of course, resolve with any finality what is at issue here: the old, undying individual–collective dialectic.

The recurring themes in Jeyifo's criticism were the ahistoricism of Soyinka's constructs and the absence of a class perspective in the universe of his cultural theorizing. Jeyifo read Soyinka's formulation of tragedy and tragic consciousness as "unexceptionable" only if we leave unquestioned its "symbolic, idealistic" character, and the fact that it is achieved "within an entirely *hypostasized* reality." Ogun's passion exists in "pure mythology" and is therefore a "fabulous lie." In the choice of a tragic archetype, Soyinka privileges Ogun, who exists in pure essence, over another possible candidate, Sango, because he was a deified human being and so supposedly tainted by the specks of mundanity and of history. Jeyifo read in this choice a partisanship which is ideologically exceptionable:

> [T]he reification which gives victory to Ogun's timeless ahistoricism belongs in that realm of thought in which imagined beings and relationships have absolute, autonomous existence. Hence it is easy victory, illusory, undialectical: thought, in a bewitched, becalmed, vaporous zone of absolute self-subsistence, frees itself from its moorings in the sea of real life processes.[86]

For Jeyifo here, realism is apparently the only radical mode. The hermetic ritual space constructed by Soyinka, he argued, amounted to "literary idealization," whose aim is "the rout of objective representation and the rout of critical realism and in this case, of true revolutionary potential."[87]

The wide sweep of Jeyifo's "categorical distortions," in Soyinka's view, betrayed a consciousness immersed in narrow, unreflective scientism frightened by the *"irrational* dynamics of great art." It thus failed to recognize the materiality of metaphysics, the historicity of essence:

> When radical criticism claims that idealism reinforces a static, historical, irremediable world-view, I recognize immediately that we have a problem of language. Music, whose nature lends itself to largely idealist striving, is not static; on the contrary, the interiority of its language provokes a constant dialectic with the world of reality, which is action, development, motion.[88]

To those who think they can have the world completely within their grasp, Soyinka sounded a warning tinged with derision; it is also a combative defense of mythopoesis: "Historical 'data' is permanently, irretrievably and, irrevocably, incomplete. (Dedicated materialists of the ideological paradise—take note!) Which is why the creative (or re-creative) imagination has any function in the world."[89]

To the ubiquitous charge of the absence of a class perspective in his works, Soyinka's response was to return the charges of ahistoricism and failure to historicize—the Marxists' wholesale importation of European concepts with questionable indigenous applicability:

We must take into account but reject the burden of bourgeois development of other societies, reject the framework of their bourgeois values and conceptualizations yet, in the process, ensure that concepts which are termed bourgeois in the societies of their origination also correspond to the values of bourgeois development of our own societies. . . . The existence of classes, however, is a universal reality: What remains permanently contestable is the universality of concepts and values attaching to each group.[90]

In this way, Soyinka accepted "class" merely grammatically as a tool of differentiation, but not technically in the Marxist sense as a location in a historically determined system of social production.

Beyond the *obvious* specific positions of the two main sides of the encounter, what is of crucial relevance to my project is how to identify and comprehend the difference(s) between them in regard to a recurring problematic throughout the exchanges: the African intellectuals' undue epistemological dependence on the West. I discussed this in Chapter 2, relating it to the status of European languages as the African intellectuals' preeminent tools of cognition. It appears that Soyinka, in his turn to Yoruba metaphysics, recognizes and makes Western epistemological domination an issue, while his Marxist critics, except perhaps Osofisan, appear to be little concerned with the bind, too self-assured in the "manifest persuasiveness"[91] of historical and dialectical materialism. This undue self-assurance somewhat suggests a closure of history—a denial or disregard of other ways and means of knowing—and thus of an expressive identity.

The profound shift in African Marxist criticism of Soyinka since the early and mid-1980s affirms the credibility of my preceding analysis. The shift is also, as in the earlier criticism, spearheaded by Biodun Jeyifo. Apparently an instance of the contemporary general interrogation of predominant epistemologies, but with its own distinctive accents, what distinguishes the new criticism is an openness that is alert to the complexities of artistic representation of difference and its politics. Paradox, contradiction, aporia, and so on, are no longer irrationalities to be explained and transcended or forced into conformity by dialectical materialism, but are seen as yielding useful indispensable insights of their own.

Thus Jeyifo, who earlier pronounced Soyinka's mythologizing as "illusory" and the "rout of true revolutionary potential," can now propose that "[i]f the gods of mythology and traditional religious ritual and their attributes yield central ideas of traditional African thought, what Soyinka has done is to return to these ideas in order to re-vitalise them for contemporary society." Consider also his spirited efforts to now show how Soyinka makes "his rationalisation of African traditions consistent with the will to liberation and revolution in contemporary Africa."[92] Or his discovery of a "most intriguing" Soyinkan practice in which the dramatist's "rarefied" mythic constructs actually evince a convergence with history in a manner as potent as it is culturally rooted.[93] Even where significant disagreements still remain, such as the precise character of a liberating postcolonial epistemology, it is a sign of the changed circumstances that Jeyifo's proposition is now an open-ended comment: that the debate "is not foreclosed and remains open."[94]

Lessons from this productive if acrimonious encounter will serve well as my conclusion. Apart from the heady radical ferment of the time, Soyinka's extremely abstruse formulations did not always help matters. And here, perhaps, is one of the immediate gains of the encounter, that Soyinka's clarifications and reformulations of his positions *after* the criticisms are now indispensable toward more sensitive appreciations of his project. An instance of the yield of this sensitivity is the discovery of a complex subtlety I argue as located in Soyinka's proposition of an African cultural identity. Another facet of this discovery is that even within this complex subtlety, issues such as Soyinka's tendency to overinvest in the *cultural* in matters relating to the historical Africa–Europe encounter; his anxiety—as a localized example of the stated tendency—that *Death and the King's Horseman* would be read in terms more *political* (as a case of clash of cultures due to colonialism) than *cultural* (as a case of an exploration of an eventful disjunction in a people's way of life); and his inadequate attention to intracultural differences *and* stratifications such as class and gender as necessary perspectives of analysis, all remain and constitute expressive spots in his vast canvas of performative articulation.

4

LeRoi Jones/Amiri Baraka:
The Motion of History

The Violence of Naming

We cannot begin to properly comprehend Amiri Baraka's proposition of an African-American cultural difference without cutting through the tangle of critical mass surrounding his artistic production and examining his relationship with the critical establishment. One of the tales about Baraka's many engagements with the American academy concerns a well-respected English department of a well-respected university. When a member of the search committee for an open visiting professorship suggested Amiri Baraka's name, the chair*man* instantly fainted. When he regained consciousness at the college health center an hour and a half later, to the worried looks of faculty and friends, the first thing he said was, "Che without a jungle—over my dead body!" and promptly again faded into momentary oblivion.[1] It is difficult to say precisely what this utterance means, not in the least because it is one of those fuzzy irruptions characteristic of the twilight zone between consciousness and unconsciousness. Although it is clearly a case of excess coding, my suggestion is that if placed within the larger discourse of Baraka criticism, the code may not be that resistant to our *curiosity*.[2]

Let us attempt then some extrapolations from the utterance's multiple significations. Che without a jungle, or the veteran guerrilla without forests for camouflage, cuts a pitiable figure indeed, much like a fish out of water, Castro without Cuba, or Reagan without the USA. Baraka (Che, the guerrilla-political activist) in an English department (which is neither a jungle nor a political field) is, without debate, truly incongruous. Baraka should be *out* there, where politics is played, not *in* an English department, where literature is studied and scholarship is pursued. Baraka is writing not literature but political pamphlets.[3] Variations of this position dominate Baraka criticism today.

Lloyd W. Brown, in his synthetic account of the life and works of Baraka, describes the playwright as an "unsubtle ideologue" who is yet to resolve the tension in himself and his works "between a passion for literal political statement and an interest in art as an imaginatively conceived, expressive, and committed design." Hence Baraka's theater is more a theater of "ideological positions" than of "character and situation," a theater that offers "hackneyed and literal statements in lieu of artistic forms that are both imaginative and sociopolitically significant."[4] This closely echoes Werner Sollors, who sees in Baraka's Marxist works "only occasional flashes of poetry," which are even then "often overshadowed by hammering political slogans." *The Motion of History*, for instance, lacks literature's characteristic "literary logic of progression and resolution." In Baraka, Sollors concludes, "politics wins out over aesthetics."[5] The leading Caribbean dramatist, Derek Walcott, in a review of *Dutchman and The Slave* in 1965, labeled Baraka's theater as "The Theatre of Abuse,"[6] an assessment mimicked in exactly the same way about twenty years later by Greg Tate in his description of Baraka's later output as "diatribe disguised as literature."[7]

If these judgments appear absolute, I say that it is only apparent, for none of the critics denies or would deny that Baraka had indeed once written works that qualify as "literature." Baraka is simply the grand apostate who missed some steps and soiled his apparel. Thus Baraka's "prenationalist" works, such as *Preface to A Twenty Volume Suicide Note*, *Dutchman*, *The Dead Lecturer*, and *The System of Dante's Hell*, are regarded as "literature," while very few since his nationalism are so honored.[8]

My interest in these pronouncements as part of a larger enterprise of the critical production of the Amiri Baraka text is not so much in their being encomiums or condemnations or both as in the issues they allow us to raise about their own conditions of possibility. And the issues, I propose, hold some promise for a different appreciation of Baraka and his suggestion of an African-American cultural difference. The issues ask not so much what makes a "good" or "bad" literature as *what is* "literature"; they debate not so much what is a theater of "ideological positions" or of "character" as what is (accepted as) "theater." These questions implicate many hidden and potent instruments and mechanisms of subjection (and subjectivity) such as institutions, genre, and value (the last two themselves as institutions).

The canons of the "dominant liberal aesthetic faith" outlined by Anne McClintock, writing on the relations between black South African poetry and the white critical establishment, appear to me to approximate closely the constituents of the resource pool from which the ruling body of Baraka criticism draws sustenance: "individual creativity, immanent and 'universal' literary values, unity of vision, wholeness of experience, complexity of form, refined moral discrimination untainted by political platitude, irony, taste, cultivated sensibility, and the formal completion of the work of art."[9] Baraka's practice unequivocally challenges many of these nostrums, and he has mostly been condemned for it. According to the "faith," literature is not a social institution and an ideological form as W. L. Hogue has usefully argued,[10] but it is a repository of aesthetic value which critics are to transparently reveal and display for our culture and edification. However, since a literary text has no value or meaning except that which is attributed by criticism, a self-feeding circularity results: "normative criticism establishes a 'universal' model, albeit ideological, that corrects literary texts. The worth and value of literary texts are determined by how closely they approximate the model."[11] In this process, history is held in abeyance, after all, what *value* as a term appears to do cunningly well is describe phenomena "that display their spiritual status while hiding whatever material processes have created and sustained them."[12] What is worshiped is the transcendental, the immanent, and the immutable: the expressive identity.

To reflect critically on these issues is to conclude that "the ways we judge and experience literature, as well as the ways we organize, articulate, and disseminate our judgment and experience, result from institutional mediations that seek to obliterate their own traces."[13] And the effects of the mediations can be really hard to break. What we are faced with in Baraka's practice is *not* his dogmatism, literalism, penchant for politics and propaganda, and so on, but, as Foucault says, our glaringly "inadequate means for thinking about everything that is happening."[14] What we have in Baraka is Fanon's irreverent, unassimilable Negro who is needed, demanded, and quested for if only "he" would allow himself to be made palatable, but the unyielding Negro "knocks down the system and breaks the treaties"[15]—the treaties we have established between literature and nonliterature, art and politics, "literary writer" and "political pamphleteer," genre and history, value and its material and historical determinants, and the scholar and the activist or the intellectual and the politician. In Baraka's artistic practice, identity is a process, in motion, perpetually becoming. I think the challenge of reading Baraka's *performative* articulatory practice is the challenge Raymond Williams implicitly formulates when he identifies "the true crisis in cultural theory" today as the conflict "between [the] view of the work of art as object and the alternative view of art as a practice."[16]

The Protean Essence

I know I've always tried to be a revolutionary. That's been consistent. From the time I could open my mouth in terms of talking about art I've wanted to talk about change and revolution. I think the methods and ways I've seen have changed as my own understanding has deepened.

Amiri Baraka[17]

I suggest that the vision governing Baraka's work is that of art as a *practice*. It is a practice deeply embroiled in what Cornel West calls "the brutal side of American capital," the "reality *that one cannot not know*. The ragged edges of the Real, of Necessity. . . ."[18] Against the brutal side and its hegemonic literary and ideological practices, Baraka has fashioned an artistic practice that is defined at every point by its provisional, *strategic*, and tactical character. This is at the service of a difference that has relentlessly moved away to the left of accepted and authorized differences, an *oppositional* difference with a polemic, protean essence.

Baraka in the epigraph to this section explains the paradoxical, performative identity of "protean essence." There is a sense in which his artistic career, from the bohemian days of the late 1950s to the current "Marxism–Leninism–Mao Tse-Tung Thought" and feminism, can be seen as one grand narrative of *consistency* to some declared objectives. But there is also, simultaneously, an equally valid sense in which the same career is conceivable in terms of radical ruptures, discontinuities, and *changes*. Baraka has ever been consistent but it is a consistency that subverts itself by being a changing consistency. I think this is the site in which Amiri Baraka's practice suggests we situate African-American cultural identity. He once described this problematic space in a cryptic phrase "The Changing Same."[19]

From Barbara Ann Teer, founder and director of the National Black Theatre I have borrowed the word-concept *decrudin* to characterize Baraka's construction of an African-American cultural identity. Teer, well-known as an activist and innovator of acting styles immersed in African and African-American popular performance forms, outlines the standards evolved by her group:

Our art standard requires that all theatrical presentations be they dramatic plays, musical, rituals, revivals, etc., must:
1) *Raise the level of consciousness* through liberating the spirits and strengthening the minds of its people.
2) *Be political*, i.e., must deal in a positive manner with the existing conditions of oppression.
3) In some way *educate*, i.e., "educate to bring out that which is already within." Give Knowledge and truth.
4) *Clarify issues*, i.e., enlighten the participants as to why so many negative conditions and images exist in their community in order to eliminate the negative condition and strengthen the positive condition.
5) Lastly, it must *entertain*.[20]

The strategic goal of these standards is a "decrudin" or "decrudification" of the consciousness of the African-American target audience diagnosed as hamstrung by an oppressive and dehumanizing reality. Decrudin is thus a process of refusing subjection and reforming subjectivity, a *conscientizing* (consciousness-raising) pedagogy that is at once critical and visionary. It is a prodigious ritual for the exorcism of the accreted dead weight of centuries of forced residence at the peripheries of society. The periphery, decrudin teaches in a gesture to destroy the low self-esteem it sees as pervasive among African-Americans, may be represented negatively and as unimportant in the discursive transactions of society, but it is actually an indispensable condition of possibility of the center.[21] The result—positive self-appreciation and reformed subjectivity—is proposed as guarantor of the capacity to deal in a "positive manner" with the "existing conditions of oppression." In other words, only a decruded African-American consciousness can subversively read its situation of subjugation *and* fashion the most appropriate strategies for ending that condition. This is why, to Teer and her group, participants in the decrudin process (rehearsals and performances) are called not actors or artists or performers but "liberators."

Baraka thus is the liberator in an elaborate decrudin process in which many famous milestones can be identified: the American avant-garde, black cultural nationalism, and Marxism. W. J. Harris has written suggestively on how the method Baraka employs in the decrudin process closely "emulates a transformation process typical of jazz revision."[22] Baraka's techniques include inversion, mutilation, repetition, parody, rejection, extremism, signifying, and complex fusion, all utilized in relation to the dominant literary structures. Harris thus labels the decrudin art the "*jazz aesthetic*, a procedure that uses jazz variations as paradigms for the conversion of white poetic and social ideas into black ones,"[23] or more appropriately, to cite Kimberly W. Benston, for "self-consciously shaping his material, changing the forms available to him, and ultimately fashioning new ones."[24] In Baraka's artistic practice, decrudin is the articulatory practice of performative identity.

> Let my poems be a graph of me.
> "Balboa, The Entertainer," LeRoi Jones
>
> . . . I am a man
> who is loud
> on the birth
> of his ways. Publicly redefining
> each change in my soul . . .
> "The Liar," LeRoi Jones[25]

In his own scheme of values, Baraka started out as a victim of what he did not choose and could not erase: his lower-middle-class birth and upbringing. In the elaborate spectrum of metaphorical colors he invents to map his transformations—"Brown," "Yellow," "White," and "Black," in the order of progress—this background into which he was thrown was already a diseased condition.[26] Labeled "brown," its location a few rungs on the social ladder above the "black" masses measures the scale of its subjection to the dominant white American norms. The hope of the brown, of course, is for a deeper inroad into the "mainstream," but the obstacle to any smooth sail is the "yellow," the black–middle class proper, whose condescension for the brown is shown in its stolid refusal to make any distinction between the brown and the black. The yellow is only some steps or so away from the ultimate objective, "white," and would just not tolerate any distractions from below. Catalyzed by mutual insecurities in relation to the absolute ends of the spectrum (black–white), the brown and the yellow are constantly at each other's throats.

Baraka takes great pains to show that for the brown, especially in his own case, the black reality was inescapable, "no matter the brown inside game plan your mama hammered out with piano lessons, drum lessons, art lessons, singing and dancing in the summer school. . . ."[27] But Baraka did fulfill one of the brown's main aspirations: make the brown condition a temporary liability, a passageway *up*.[28] His brief stint as a student at Howard University in Washington, D.C., convinces him of the middle class's self-devaluation and surrender of African-American cultural identity. Although Howard is generally regarded as "the capstone of Negro education," it is for Baraka the very embodiment of, and prime maternity home for, yellowness. "The Howard thing," Baraka writes with disgust, "let me understand the Negro sickness . . . They teach you how to pretend to be white."[29]

But Baraka did not reverse directions. It was as if he was destined to (b)reach the *top*, so that his subsequent valorization of the *bottom* will come out in very sharp relief. His Howard stay was followed by service in the United States Air Force from 1954 to 1957. Here too Baraka found another or a related "sickness": ". . . the Air Force made me understand the white sickness. It shocked me into realizing what was happening to me and others. By oppressing Negroes, the whites have become oppressors, twisted in the sense of doing bad things to people and justifying them finally, convincing themselves they are right, as people have always convinced themselves."[30] But Baraka also found what appeared to be a weapon against the entrenched culture of conviction, domination, and silence: poetry, and the revelation that he could be a poet. It is not that poetry or a poet is immune from the "sickness." In fact, as Baraka discovered, poetry in the dominant practice is a potent carrier of the sickness, convincing, sanctioning, and justifying domination and social hierarchy. Considering what it entails for *him* to be a poet in this circumstance brought tears to his eyes:

> I had been reading one of the carefully put together exercises *The New Yorker* publishes constantly as high poetic art, and gradually I could feel my eyes fill up with tears, and my cheeks were wet and I was crying, quietly softly but like it was the end of the world. I had been moved by the writer's words, but in

another, very personal way. A way that should have taught me more than it did. Perhaps it would have saved me many more painful scenes and conflicts. But I was crying because I realized that I could never write like that writer. Not that I had any real desire to, but I knew even if I had had the desire I could not do it. I realized that there was something in me so out, so unconnected with what this writer was and what that magazine was that what was in me that wanted to come out as poetry would never come out like that and be my poetry. The verse spoke of lawns and trees and dew and birds and some subtlety of feeling amidst the jingling rhymes that spoke of a world almost completely alien to me.[31]

Luckily Baraka found a small, marginal rebellious part of the white world to which the establishment aesthetic was also odious: the American avant-garde. After a dishonorable discharge from the Air Force (in those days, who would believe that a black male U.S. Air Force sergeant with stacks of a magazine called *Partisan Review* is concerned only with the poetry pages![32]), Baraka settled in New York's Greenwich Village, the haven of the post–World War II avant-garde, the Bohemia of the Beat Generation.[33] The Beat world provided Baraka with an intellectual tradition and a literary practice with which to articulate his pent-up enmity against the bourgeoisie, both white and black—but the latter especially—and the hegemony of philistinism and conventionalism they have so assiduously cultivated.

Central to the cultural politics of bohemianism is a virulent *inversion* of bourgeois hegemonic norms. Thus against the conformism, order, hierarchy, and privilege so vital to "civilized society," bohemians valorize the outcast and the excluded, "such peoples and races, social classes, castes, strata and groups . . . which are suppressed and persecuted . . . or simply discriminated against socially."[34] Bohemianism offers "an artistic cult of youth, beauty, truth and flourishing life against the bourgeois desert of hypocrisy, vanity, and fraudulence."[35] Baraka acknowledged the influence of Allen Ginsberg's *Howl* (1956), which, unlike the alien *New Yorker* poems that celebrated upper-class aristocratic morality and made him cry, talked about "the 'nigger streets' and junkies and all kinds of things that I could see and I could identify with, then I said, yeah, that's closer to what I want to do."[36]

Soon to be dubbed "King of the East Village"[37] and already married to a middle-class Jewish woman "as protection against Bohemia,"[38] Baraka's graduation into the "white" world could not have been easier. He had chosen, though, a rebellious fringe of that world. As a black in bohemia, Baraka had only moved from one margin to another. But there is a world of difference between the margin of white America and the margin of multiracial America. Baraka at this time confused the two, imagining his bohemian revolt to be also a black (from his color code) revolt against bourgeois values. His aesthetic propositions were a-racial, lacking any specificity in regard to the African-American condition. Every dissenter against bourgeois norms, from whatever race, class, or group, was welcome. An empowering African-American identity was no more than a nonbourgeois American identity. When a reviewer attacked bohemians and charged that bohemia is for the black "a means of entry into the world of whites," Baraka replied that "Harlem is today the veritable capitol city of the Black Bourgeoisie. The Negro Bohemian's flight from Harlem is not a flight from the world of color but the flight of any would-be Bohemian from . . . 'the provinciality, philistinism and moral hypocrisy of American life.' "[39] In other words, there is no difference between Harlem and white America. Baraka here unsubtly neutralizes the question of race and difference. Harlem life is American life, and vice versa, a poor attention to difference which makes Baraka's postulations constitutive of expressive identity. He also turns a question of an antagonistic group struggle into that of an individual rebellion against the group.

The occlusion of African-American difference and emphasis on individual revolt mark Baraka's aesthetic theory and practice of this period:

> MY POETRY is whatever I think I am . . . I CAN BE   ANYTHING I CAN. . . . I *must* be completely free to   do just what I want, in the poem. "All is permitted"   . . . There cannot be anything I must *fit* the poem   into. Everything must be made to fit into the poem.   There must not be any preconceived notion or *design*   for what the poem *ought* to be.[40]

Baraka's introduction to *The Moderns* and his inclusion in the appendix of especially Jack Kerouac's "Essentials of Spontaneous Prose" are eloquent statements of a theory of art[41] as "extremely privatistic" as it is "elitist."[42] This is the aesthetic and ideological vision behind such early works as *Preface to a Twenty Volume Suicide Note* and *The Dead Lecturer*, both poetry collections, and the fiction, *The System of Dante's Hell*. They are distinguished by an unwavering commitment to the deformation of English and aesthetic experimentation, expressed in such features as unusual or "disorderly" graphic formations, an irreverent mesh of diverse orthographic styles such as abbreviations ("sd" for "said"; "yr" for "your," etc), capitalizations, and italicizations.

But Baraka's consuming passion for decrudin and antibourgeois revolt soon found these techniques inadequate. The page may be filled with cobwebs and fowl scratches presented as poetry, the poem itself may be all remote allusions and orthographic irregularities and severe abbreviations,[43] but it is still dead, lifeless, and—Baraka's bitterest disappointment—lacking in "action." "[U]nconsciously at first, but then very openly, dramatic dialogue began to appear" in Baraka's poetry:

> I can see now that the dramatic form began to interest me because I wanted some kind of action literature, where one has to put characters upon a stage and make them living metaphors. Drama proliferates during periods of social upsurge, because it makes real live people the fuel of ideas. It is also a much more popular form than poetry. . . .[44]

But the early dramatic pieces such as "The Eight Ditch (Is Drama," *The Baptism*, and *The Toilet* are, like the poetry, largely unconcerned with representing African-American difference, though the use of black urban streetwise speech patterns in *The Toilet* is striking.

The Baptism best represents Baraka at this stage. All the characters are nameless—"Boy," "Minister," "Homosexual," "Old Woman," "Messenger," and "Women"—and very little in their characterization provides any clue to their identities in relation to the myriad permutations of multiracial America. The play pits the agents of love, life, and natural unpretentious morality—the bohemian intellectual, Homosexual, and the Christ figure, Boy, who goes into fits of masturbation at every prayer time—against the hypocritical managers of crippling Christian asceticism and sanctimoniousness—the Minister and his congregation. The former, of course, prevail in the end. The Homosexual's bohemian solution to the cult of the soul over the flesh propagated throughout the play by the Minister is a Dionysiac affirmation of life and unpoliced morality:

> MINISTER: Son, there are no temptations for the wise man. The sins of the flesh, are not the sins of the leopards. Cast down your lies and fall on me praying.
>
> HOMOSEXUAL: *(ballet steps. Takes colored confetti from his pocket and tosses it over the assembly. Sings.)*: The pride of life is life. And flesh must take its move. I am the sinister lover of love. The mysterious villain of thought. I love my mind, my asshole too. I love things. As they are issued from you know who. God. God. God. God. Go-od. The great insouciant dilettante. My lovers, priests, immolated queers, how many other worlds are there, less happy, less sorrowful than ours? God. God. God. God. Go-od. The thug of creation. Our holy dilettante.[45]

In the context of Baraka's later militant nationalism, Taylor Mead, who is listed as having played Homosexual in the 1964 Writer's Stage Theatre production, remembered with nostalgia and regret that

> no mention was made in the play of turgid unfathomable racial irreconcilabilities. No mention was made [i]f you are black or white, and I like to think we all worked together so well that more was said for racial equality than all the right-wing black utterances of Jones and his buddies since.[46]

What Mead appreciated most in the early Baraka—*colorlessness*—is precisely what shows up the inadequacies of the dramatist's conception of African-American difference and his naive bohemian cultural politics. Baraka was never "black"; he started out as "brown," then moved to "yellow" and "white," always setting camp at the left-of-center or periphery of these formations. But bohemianism, very high in the valorization of the margin, is very low—and nearly blind—in the recognition of hierarchies within the margin. "Bohemia, for many of its white affiliates a place of refuge from a secure middle-class background," writes Werner Sollors, "offered some of its Black members exactly what many whites were apparently trying to escape: a job with a modest income."[47]

Evident in *The Baptism* is this: to the "sicknesses" of brown, yellow, and white, all of which for Baraka equals the *bourgeoisification* of values, he recommends as solution (white) bohemianism, which for him equals the *debourgeoisification* of values. These are the two monolithic forces in combat; they have nothing to do with race, gender, class, or other differences—even homosexuality is little more than a catachrestic ploy to foil the "provinciality" and "philistinism" of American life. And besides, only *values* are in conflict. This is an aesthetics of the expressive that overlooks the multiple determinants of any identity.

The year that punctured Baraka's colorless bubble was 1960. Not only were civil rights agitations gathering steam at home but there was also a young defiant revolution a mere stone's throw away. Baraka was invited to visit Cuba during the July 26 celebrations and his experience there, he recorded, "was a turning point in my life."[48] He met Castro and other leaders of the revolution and was particularly impressed not only by their evident courage, determination, and sense of purpose, but by their *youth*. Baraka, of course, was no stranger to the manifold significations of youthfulness; the bohemians, after all, made a cult of the vivacity of youth against the stiffness and languor of old age. In bohemian protest, however, an enervating cynicism often replaces what should also have been involved, "actual change." But the Cuban youth? "Seeing youth not just turning on and dropping out, not just hiply cynical or cynically hip, but using their strength and energy to *change* the real world—that was too much."[49]

During the trip, Baraka was taken to task about his political sympathies by a Mexican delegate. The bohemian artist lived true to his calling: "I'm a poet . . . what can I do? I write, that's all, I'm not even interested in politics.'" Baraka reports with laconic plainness that he was promptly dubbed a "cowardly bourgeois individualist." Another delegate sealed the damnation: "You want to cultivate your soul? In that ugliness you live in, you want to cultivate your soul? Well, we've got millions of starving people to feed, and that moves me enough to make poems out of."[50] Here is Baraka on the profound effects of that trip on him: "I carried so much back with me that I was never the same again."[51] Bohemianism for him henceforth became

> this so called rebellion against what is most crass and ugly in our society, but without the slightest thought of, say, any kind of direction or purpose. Certainly, without any knowledge of what could be put up as alternatives. To fight against one kind of dullness with an even more subtle dullness is, I suppose, the highwater mark of social degeneracy. Worse than mere lying.[52]

Roland Barthes could have been talking about Baraka when he wrote in a short and justly famous critique of the avant-garde published in 1964: "to tell the truth, the *avant-garde* is threatened by only one force, which is not the bourgeoisie: political consciousness."[53] Baraka's essays collected in *Home*, arranged chronologically from 1960 to 1965, starting with the account of his Cuban trip, "Cuba Libre," document in interesting ways the dramatist's gradual attention to the specificity of the

African-American condition in the United States as well as its links with the condition of African and Third World countries generally.

A 1961 "Letter to Jules Feiffer" vigorously defended the use of the term "Afro-American" against right-wing caricatures of it as a passing fad, while also not forgetting "[t]he new countries of Asia, Africa, and Latin America" that need freedom not from Communism as American propaganda says, but from "exploitation at the hands of this 'bastion of freedom.'"[54] Baraka wrote in 1958 that Harlem was no different from philistinic and hypocritical America and that Bohemia was the only safe haven of radical and uninhibited mental growth. In the 1962 historical study, "City of Harlem," he made a complete turnaround. Harlem became the abode of Americans "whose singularity . . . is that they are black and can never honestly enter into the lunatic asylum of white America":

> Harlem for this reason is a community of nonconformists, since any black American, simply by virtue of his blackness, is weird, a nonconformist in this society. A community of nonconformists, not an artists' colony—though blind "ministers" still wander sometimes along 137th Street, whispering along the strings of their guitars—but a colony of old-line Americans, who can hold out, even if it is a great deal of the time in misery and ignorance, but still hold out, against the hypocrisy and sterility of big-time America, and still try to make their own lives, simply because of their color, but by now, not so so simply, because that color now does serve to identify people in America whose feelings about it are not broadcast every day on television.[55]

Baraka turned to black literature, a literature he had rarely previously given any attention. Black music had been his first and major artistic influence—and would remain his undying inspiration, manifested most extensively in the poetry and in the speech styles of his characters.[56] All his literary influences had been white, and the black writers he promoted in the various avant-garde journals he edited either were or aspired to be bohemians.

"The Myth of a 'Negro Literature,' " written in 1962, could be taken as Baraka's formal recognition of black literature. Its sumptuous effusion of vitriol is less a denial of the literature than an affirmation of its existence and of the need for a redirection of its focus. What most readily distinguished black literature, Baraka argued, is, "with a few notable exceptions," an "almost agonizing mediocrity." Among the complex of social, economic, and political factors responsible for this is that the black middle-class, the privileged producer of this art, "has always gone out of its way to cultivate *any* mediocrity, as long as that mediocrity was guaranteed to prove to America, and recently to the world at large, that they were not really who they were, i.e., Negroes." The black American art form which is yet exempt from this gangrene, and in which the originality and genius of the African-American can be glimpsed, is music. This is because "the bearers of its tradition maintained their essential identities as Ne-

groes," rather than, like the writers, "imitating the meanest of social intelligences to be found in American culture, i.e., the white middle class." A solution, Baraka suggested, begins from a proper grasp of the peculiar location of the black experience in America, an experience "separate . . . but inseparable from the complete fabric of American life," "completely invisible to white America, but so essentially part of it as to stain its whole being an ominous gray." This terrain, the paradigmatic location of black music, is where the black writer could "propose his own symbols" and "erect his own personal myths" to produce a literature based on "*real* categories of human activity" and "*truthful* accounts of human life": a literature that captures the black experience "in exactly the terms America has proposed for it, in its most ruthless identity."[57]

Dutchman, first produced in 1964, is almost a programmatic embodiment of the dramatist's new conception of African-American difference. The play is sure enough about "real categories of human activity," by which Baraka means that black reality in America is made prominent, but it is not the conventional slice-of-life naturalistic drama. Its apparent realism is undercut by, among other things, its abbreviated but deeply performative language whose substance insistently advertises itself as deliberately elsewhere: in the cultural repertoires of the characters and the audience; its unnerving humor, delicately arrested between a laugh and a foreboding grunt; its ironic turns of logic and events; and a mythic formal circularity, all encased within a powerfully constructed claustrophobic space which is, however, changing, in motion—a moving subway car. Baraka has found a new use for his mastery of Western avant-garde poetics.[58]

Clay, the twenty-year-old apprentice black bourgeois, is simultaneously a creation and victim of white America and an enemy of the black masses. The latter relationship of enmity is not irrevocable if only Clay would commit class suicide and reclaim his despised heritage. With the attractive thirty-year-old white *bohemian* Lula, the black middle-class victim is in good and sympathetic company—or so it seems. Lula, who dominates most of the play, variously lambastes, ridicules, and taunts Clay's middle-class pretensions, in tones ranging from condemnatory to understanding. However, at no time does her discourse abandon its roots in unapologetic eurocentrism. She divides Clay into two: the *individual*, Clay; and the *genus*, black middle class. She knows everything about the latter and very little about the former, which is not surprising since the genus is the realm of sweeping frameworks and frozen identities, while the individual is the field in/of motion. Her conception of Clay is entirely as a genre:

> I told you I didn't know anything about *you* . . .
> you're a well-known type.[59]

For instance, Clay confesses an earlier subjection and denial of difference: "Well, in college I thought I was Baudelaire. But I've slowed down since." Lula latches on to the first statement, which is really for blacks a

socially generic problem—thanks to a Eurocentric education—and completely ignores the volatility and unpredictability located in the second. She responds: "I bet you never once thought you were a black nigger," and rubs this in with a scornful "A black Baudelaire."[60]

Against Lula's homogenizing discourse, Clay constantly insists on specificity, and his insistence regularly decelerates Lula's pace. But Clay is not doing this to be deliberately subversive; he is simply a pitiful product of inexperience. When Lula chides him for wearing "those narrow-shoulder clothes . . . from a tradition you ought to feel oppressed by. A three-button suit. . . . Your grandfather was a slave, he didn't go to Harvard," Clay replies with an amusing literality: "My grandfather was a night watchman."[61] And he completely ignores the double-edged proposition that he ought to feel oppressed by his sartorial proclivities: it could liberate as well as ghettoize. It is apparent that Lula's aim is for the latter, the garish, carnivalesque display of exotic difference:

> And that's how blues was born.
> Yes. Come on, Clay. Let's do the nasty.
> Rub bellies. Rub bellies.[62]

And so from the genus *bourgeoisia*, Lula suggests another monolithic identity for the appropriation of Clay: *minstrelsia*. Clay, however, would not budge, and the tauntings of Lula push him into that zone of "invisible strength" and vision that Baraka identified as peculiarly open to the black for re-visioning the self: the interface between inside and outside, America and black America, and in Lula's caricature, bourgeoisia and minstrelsia. Clay, with his middle-class pretensions, would not dare to enter this terrain on his own, for there is a fearful price for every rebirth. His elaborate poetics of decrudin and identity violently assails the empiricism and positivism of the Eurocentric imagination:

> You don't know anything except what's there for you   to see. An act. Lies.
> Device. Not the pure heart,   the pumping black heart. You don't ever know
> that.

and reveals that black creativity, which includes "this buttoned-up suit"[63] and the music of Bessie Smith and Charlie Parker, is an artistic sublimation to prevent blacks from living their necessary and justified "ruthless identity" proposed by white America itself: the murder of whites. Lula's bohemian politics is completely confounded by this paradoxical theory of conscious subjection as subjectivity, for the bohemian's self-righteous valorization of the victim here becomes probematic: *against* the bohemian (the Self's) assumption, the victim (the Other) in this case is *no* object or fixed identity. Any recognition of this fact by the Self must lead to a revaluation of the identity of the righteous Self, but this is on the condition of equality with the Other, which is absent in the bohemian–victim encounter. In the power game, the Other, weaker, Clay, loses, stabbed to death by Lula.

But Clay is no absolute and helpless victim. Not only is he forced into the zone of "invisible strength" but, once there, and with all the attending insights, he actually tries to retrace his steps and to continue the order of "metaphors" and sublimation and compromise and masquerade:

> Ahhh. shit. But who needs it? I'd rather be a fool. Insane. Safe with my words, and no deaths, and clean, hard thoughts, urging me to new conquest.[64]

His death is Baraka's valediction to an aesthetic revolt divorced from African-American reality. Enter Baraka the ex-"brown," once-"yellow," lately-"white," and newly- "black."

> We want a black poem. And a
> Black World.
> Let the world be a Black Poem
> And Let All Black People Speak This Poem
> Silently
> or LOUD.[65]

Clay's resurrection was immediate. As Walker in *The Slave*, he still has his "words," but also something else irreconcilable with bohemian aesthetics: a revolver. Clay wanted "no deaths," but for Walker, nothing else is good for one's oppressors. Though the white liberal and "loyal opposition," Easley, would argue to the contrary—"Your inept formless poetry. Hah. Poetry? A flashy doggerel for inducing all those unfortunate troops of yours to spill their blood in your behalf"[66]—the poet can also be a revolutionary. After all, the hand that managed the trigger against Moncada barracks is also the hand that crafted the famous, elegant lines:

> Esta tierra
> Este aire
> Esto cielo
> Son los nuestros
> Defenderemos![67]

Baraka certainly did not miss this observation. Walker is the poet–guerrilla commander for whom the subjection of blacks—he calls this "an ugliness that has worked all my life to twist me"[68]—is unachievable outside a political separation from white America. The process may not necessarily be nonviolent, and the struggle would demand new, that is, *black*, songs. Baraka's strategy has changed but decrudin as the goal remains.

Baraka's central theoretical document of this mood is "The Revolutionary Theatre," a document that radically coerces Antonin Artaud and his Theater of Cruelty to take account of blackness. The new theater, the essay begins, "should force change; it should be change." It is a "theatre of Victims" that will "Accuse and Attack" and teach "the victims to look at the strength in their minds and their bodies." White people of whatever ideological hue will hate this theater. That is just as well, for this theater also "hates them . . . must hate them for hating . . . must teach them their deaths . . . must crack their faces open to the mad cries of the poor." The theater will perform this function through its politics of representation: it will show whites as "abstract and cowardly" and thereby be "a political weapon to help in the[ir] slaughter." The most careful treatment will, however, be reserved for the victims. For this people, the "Revolutionary Theatre" will "take dreams and give them a reality." It will galvanize the people to stand and seize that reality:

> Our theatre will show victims so that their brothers in the audience will be better able to understand that they are the brothers of victims, and that they themselves are victims if they are blood brothers. And what we show must cause the blood to rush, so that pre- revolutionary temperaments will be bathed in this blood, and it will cause their deepest souls to move, and they will find themselves tensed and clenched, even ready to die, at what the soul has been taught. We will scream and cry, murder, run through the streets in agony, if it means some soul will be moved, moved to actual life understanding of what the world is, and what it ought to be. We are preaching virtue and feeling, and a natural sense of the self in the world. All men live in the world, and the world ought to be a place for them to live.[69]

Against the stultifying ascetic rationality of the dominant worldview, this theater proposes the more competent force of "World Spirit," in which language will no longer be the type serving "tired white lives" but one capable of summoning a new world with magical precision, a language "tightened by the poet's backbone." Baraka is groping toward an autochthonous ritual which "must function like an incendiary pencil planted in Curtis Lemay's cap. So that when the final curtain goes down brains are splattered over the seats and the floor. . . ." Against the unrelieved decadence and reaction of the Broadway stage, the new theatre proposes a unity of revolutionary ethics and aesthetics. Thus it will show and stock in its repertory beautiful "horrible coming attractions" of such necessary plays as "*The Crumbling of the West*," and "THE DESTRUCTION OF AMERICA." And when these necessity-plays come to be finally performed, the world will be seeing a transformation: not "victims" any more but "new kinds of heroes—not weak Hamlets debating whether or not they are ready to die for what's on their minds, but men and women (and minds) digging out from under a thousand years of 'high art' and weak-faced dalliance."[70] This *black* aesthetic is a "post white, or post american form."[71]

Baraka abandoned his racially integrated beat life—white wife,[72] friends, and relations—and took off for Harlem, where he set up the Black Arts Repertory Theater/School (BART/S) to put his theories into practice and to disseminate his ideas. Similar institutions shot up in several centers across the country. The process of decrudin reached a decisively different and *popular* phase and seemed unstoppable, even with the closure of BART/S a few months later. Baraka moved to Newark to found a black community and arts center, Spirit House, devoted to the propagation of "black values."[73] Baraka, who started being "black" with *Dutchman*, was now his blackest self. As a cultural nationalist, what were thought of as "authentic" African values and traditions were exhumed and valorized, out of context. Culture lost its defining suppleness and was reduced to mere modes of dress and haircut and naming. A free reign for cultural nationalism and for expressive identity. For instance, "LeRoi Jones" became "Ameer Barakat," meaning the Blessed Prince (later "Bantuized" or "Swahilized" to Imamu Amiri Baraka), showing Islamic influence mainly through Malcolm X. This is, to be sure, a vital part of the decrudin process, for a religion that has ministered to three centuries of a people's enslavement can hardly be expected to be the honorable one to nurse the articulation of a new, resistant identity. But as Baraka himself discovered later, "[i]t is Chancellor Williams, the historian, who points out, however, that the many new Yusefs and Omars should remember that those Arabic names for black people are as much slave names as Joseph and Homer. One from Anglo-American slavery and the other from Arab slavery."[74]

If it is impossible to define Baraka's "black aesthetic" with any precision, we can at least point to some of the features of the dramatist's works of this period: extreme valorization of blackness and the opposite, a denigration of whiteness; absolute cultural separatism, explicit political nationalist content, celebration of black collectivity and communality, violent, scatological language, urban and rural black expressive forms, and the old compulsive formal experimentation but now in search of "authentically black" techniques.[75] Some of Baraka's well-known black aesthetic plays include *Experimental Death Unit #1* (1965), *A Black Mass* (1965), *Great Goodness of Life: A Coon Show* (1966), and *Madheart* (1966), all published as *Four Black Revolutionary Plays* (1969); and *J-E-L-L-O* (1970), *Junkies Are Full of (Shhh...)* (1971), and *Bloodrites* (1971). These are mostly deliberately didactic and direct agitprop pieces dealing with violent rebellion and racial stereotypes or unapologetic Afrocentric cultural nationalist myth-making.[76]

Slave Ship (1967), perhaps the most discussed of Baraka's plays of this period, has a significantly different orientation. It is thematically the most reflective, a deep introspective exploration of the origins of the present struggles for black self-fashioning, a genealogy of, to paraphrase Chinua Achebe, how, where, and when the rain began to beat us. Thus far more than we could say of the other plays, the audience assumed is largely black, and this assumption is woven into the very fabric of the play. It is not a "play"[77] as such but, more appropriately, a presentational, gigantic ritual, a pageant. It has no defined plot. Dialogue or discursive language is spare and very sparse. The series of scenes or tableaux are juxtaposed with drumming, singing, dancing, laughing, screaming, wailing, miming, and various theatrical devices: sounds of the sea, chains, and whips, smells, dramatic light shifts, and so on—atmosphere ceases to be a mere backdrop for the action but a character in its own right:

> Whole theater in darkness. . . . Occasional sound, like groaning, squeaking, rocking. Sea smells. Burn incense . . . make a significant, almost stifling smell come up. Pee. Shit. Death. Life processes . . . Eating. Those smells and cries, the slash and tear of the lash, in a total atmosfeeling, African drums like the worship of some Orisha. Obatala. Mbwanga rattles of the priests. . . . Rocking of the slave ship . . . sounds . . . of people, dropped down in the darkness, frightened, angry, mashed together in common terror.[78]

This "historical pageant," as the playwright calls it, attempts to show its African-American audience their origin and the direction to be taken in the present. It dramatizes the ordeal of Africans from the time of capture as slaves, through the horrors of the Middle Passage, to slavery in the New World, and finally to liberation.

The contradictions arising from the historical black–white encounter still define the moving force of the action but, unlike the calculatingly crafted rhetorical and confrontational bombast of the earlier plays, *Slave Ship* simply shows the negative effects of the encounter on the victims and proceeds with its more urgent task of celebrating their courage and community, especially as these traits resist total disintegration through alien invasion to betrayal of kin. A critic, Stefan Brecht, also notes this crucial turn in Baraka and contemplates its implication:

> This play is devoted to showing the evil done (& suffered), not the evil doer. On the contrary: it neglects him. It focuses on the good, though on its destruction. . . . This play's principles being profoundly humanitarian, if the course of action it suggests carries the day, the outlook, even for us, i.e., for the survivors among us, is hopeful.[79]

The play's identified task is made poignant by a series of oppositions that seem to be its basic principle of composition: the screams and wails of agony of the slaves versus the satisfied, voluminous laughter of the slavermasters: "We head West! . . . (Long laughter) Black gold in the West. We got our full cargo"[80]; courageous women killing themselves and their children in order to escape the ignominy of slavery versus the white slavemasters looking on and laughing in blissful contentment; the slaves' degrading condition versus their intact humanity and fellow feeling; drums of ancient African warriors versus images of detestable "yassa massa" sellouts; rebellion versus betrayal; and so on.

These oppositions, generously bathed in affective music and evocative oppressive atmosphere, tug insistently on the audience's emotional chord. The brief successive "scenes" are like pages in a history book of a people under an imposed, dehumanizing condition. This condition is not static but evinces a clear, unmistakable—though many times lost and recaptured—progression, from origin to elimination. The protagonist in this movement is the people, as a collective: the characters are not only anon-ymous but nonindividualized, and their effectiveness is shown to be most potent only in that unity. A united African-American community, we remember, is central to nationalist thought. The renegades, the "Toms," who veered away from the group, lose both ways: they are not only treated with contempt and condescension by the oppressors they ally with, but they are also the first to be consumed by their people's wrath. The play is unsparing in their condemnation:

> (. . . *speaking in the pseudo-intelligent patter he uses for the boss. He tries to be, in fact, assumes he is, dignified, trying to hold his shoulders straight, but only succeeds in giving his body an odd slant like a diseased coal chute*)
> PREACHER: Yass, understand . . . the problem. And, personally, I think some agreement can be reached. We will be nonviolenk . . . to the last. . . .
> (*Screams . . . moans . . . drums . . . mournful death-tone. . . . The preacher looks, head turned just slightly, as if embarrassed, trying still to talk to the white man. Then, one of the black men, out of the darkness, comes and sits before the Tom, a wrapped-up bloody corpse of a dead burned baby as if they had just taken the body from a blown-up church, sets the corpse in front of the preacher. Preacher stops. Looks up at "person" he's Tomming before, then, with his foot, tries to push baby's body behind him, grinning, and jeffing, all the time, showing teeth, and being "dignified"*)[81]

Central to the play then is an exploration of the dynamics of collective self-construction inscribed in the African-American experience.

At the beginning, the slaves are Africans held captive and carted away from their land. Their wailings and invocations are replete with references to spaces that had been intimate parts of their lives, that had defined and given them an identity: Shango, Obatala, Ifanami, and so on. With whips, chains, and time, *captives* are broken to submission as slaves, and there is a concomitant loss of a self-directed sense of self: "Now the same voices, as if transported in time to the slave farms, call names, English slave names" and metaphysical spaces like Luke, John, Jesus. But the slaves deny the planters' hegemony any completeness. A subversive "New-sound saxophone" by the slaves begins a new tune, drawing on aboriginal memory to forge a self-reflexive, hybrid identity: "sounds of slave ship, saxophone and drums," and "a new-old dance, Boogalooyo-ruba line. . . ." The resistant character of the new subjectivity is testified to by the fact that what the new music and dance articulate are "sounds of people picking up. Like dead people rising."[82] The play's final call is for the destruction of all enemies, black or white, and the eradication of the existing condition of oppression.

Apart from the advertised targets, whites and black Toms, Baraka's project of cultural nationalism is not without other significant victims. Most important is the black woman. Baraka's essay "Black Woman" is an exposition on the role of the black female in the decrudin process, black-aesthetic, black-cultural-nationalist style. The "deed and the proc-ess of slavery," Baraka theorized, had separated the black man and the black woman and created a front too weak for any sustained resistance. The erasure of the "separateness" is thus a major constituent of decrudin. Though this is first and fundamentally the task of the black male, the black woman, allocated her *proper* province, is indispensable to the project. The proper role of the black woman, according to Baraka, is to be the complement of the black man, for the black value system "knows of no separation but only of the divine complement the black woman is for her man." A complement completes an incomplete, suggesting that black female and male are mutual complements: "we will complement each other . . . ," in a relationship of equals. No one gives the lie to this reading of equality better than Baraka himself: "[W]e do not believe in 'equality' of men and women. We cannot understand what devils and the devilishly influenced mean when they say equality for women. We could never be equals . . . nature has not provided thus." What nature has provided, and what the black woman must do in the nationalist struggle, is to "inspire her man," be his "house" and the "nation," bear and "teach our children," and be "submissive." What Baraka's theory of complementarity authorized, in its profoundly sexist, chauvinistic, and coercive character, is a normative identity—which is unquestionably male—to which all others are merely adjuncts: a negation of identity as the product of a ceaseless articulatory practice. "[W]e are simply different aspects of a single entity," Baraka concluded his elaboration of a repressive, expressive identity.[83]

This vision of gender relations in and for the "new" black nation occurs in its most famous and graphic form in the "revolutionary" play *Madheart*:

BLACK WOMAN: I'm the black. The one who disappeared. The sleepwalker. The one who runs through your dreams with your life and your seed. I am the black woman. The one you need. You know this. Now you must discover a way to get me back, Black Man. You and you alone, must get me. Or you'll never . . . lord . . . be a man. My man. Never know your own life needs. You'll walk around white ladies breathing their stink, and lose your seed, your future to them.

BLACK MAN: I'll get you back.

BLACK WOMAN: *(Laughs)* You need to, baby . . . just know what's good for you . . . you better.

BLACK MAN: *(Looking around at her squarely, he advances.)* I better? . . . (A soft laugh) Yes. Now is where we always are . . . that now . . . *(he wheels and suddenly slaps her crosswise, back and forth across the face.)*

BLACK WOMAN: Wha . . . What . . . oh love . . . please . . . don't hit me. *(He hits her, slaps her again.)*

BLACK MAN: I want you, as a woman. Go down. *(He slaps again.)* Go down, submit, submit . . . to love . . . and to man, now, forever.

BLACK WOMAN: *(Weeping, turning her head from side to side)* Please don't hit me . . . please . . . *(She bends.)* The years are so long, without you, man, I've waited for you . . .

BLACK MAN: And I've waited.

BLACK WOMAN: I've seen you humbled, black man, seen you crawl for dogs
    and devils.
BLACK MAN: And I've seen you raped by savages and beasts, and bear bleach
    shit children of apes.
BLACK WOMAN: You permitted it . . . you could . . . do nothing.
BLACK MAN: But now I can. *(He slaps her, drags her to him, kissing her deeply
    on the lips.)* That shit is ended, woman, you with me, and the world is
    mine.
BLACK WOMAN: I . . . oh love, please stay with me. . . .
BLACK MAN: Submit, for love.
BLACK WOMAN: I submit. *(She goes down, weeping.)* I submit . . . for love
    . . . please love. *(The* MAN *sinks to his knees and embraces her, draws her
    with him up again. They both begin to cry and then laugh, laugh, laugh,
    wildly at everything and themselves.)*
BLACK MAN: You are my woman, now, forever. Black woman.
BLACK WOMAN: I am your woman, and you are the strongest of God. Fill
    me with your seed. *(They embrace. . . .)*[84]

In Baraka's "black value system," equality of the sexes was a white, that
is, devilish, idea that the new black nation can and should do happily
without.

But this was not the only evil threatening black values. Another one,
important in view of Baraka's subsequent move, was Marxism. "Lenin,
Marx, Trotsky," Baraka's blackest self argued, are "just the names of
some more 'great white men,'" no different from Washington, Jefferson,
Nixon, and so on.[85] And "when you speak of capitalism you speak of the
European mind. We do not want to be European. No, not of any persuasion."[86] Baraka did not go uncensured. Various Barakan portraits (in
1969) by *The Black Panther* paper included "bourgeois" or "pork-chop"
nationalist; "Papa Doc," who replaces "white oppression with Black oppression"; "The names are different but the madness being perpetrated
is the same"; and so on.[87] In 1973, a thirty-page pamphlet, *Papa Doc
Baraka: Fascism in Newark* was released by the National Caucus of Labor
Committee detailing similar and even more acerbic political charges
against Baraka. Baraka, of course, replied, "exposing" the caucus's "anti-
black, anti–Third World, Rightist tone," and labeling the caucus "pater-
nalist reactionaries . . . supported by the oppressive elements of the
society." The reply continued later in an essay, "Nationalism, Pan-
Africanism, Ujamaa, Their Future in America," written between late
1973 and early 1974:

> Capitalist vs Proletariat is a secondary contradiction in America. Whether you
> lefties like it or not, any serious analysis will show you that. Black vs White
> influences all other contradictions in America. Rich vs Poor. Educated vs Un-
> educated. Men vs Women. Polluters vs Ecologists. Homosexuals vs Heterosex-
> uals. Old People vs Young People, Jews vs Gentiles, &c., Black vs White is the
> most influential, it influences all the others, defines their terminologies, shapes
> their rhetoric, must be dealt with even after left communists denounce nation-
> alists as reactionaries and talk wildly about the coming hegemony of the pro-

letariat (in spotless university dining rooms) it is still Black vs White, throughout, over and above, undercutting all other talk or movement in America. Capitalist vs Proletariat is a secondary contradiction in America.[88]

By November 1974 Baraka, now singing an entirely different tune, published a lengthy position paper, "Toward Ideological Clarity." Beginning with an approving quotation from Lenin, Baraka traced the history of contemporary "monopoly capitalism" back to its roots in the slave trade. And drawing from such other sources as Du Bois, Cox, Rodney, Cabral, Marx, and Mao, he discovered that imperialism of the West was the real enemy of not only the African-American but the masses of the world. The retainers of this system could be of any color, so a correct attitude must label the previous black–white opposition simplistic and obsolete. Henceforth, any analysis of the diverse aspects of society, economic, political, cultural, and so on, must "utilize the universally applicable scientific method . . . Marxism–Leninism–Mao Tse Tung thought."

From this perspective, "culture" ceased to be an inextricable appendage to skin coloration; it was now "the historical and contemporary unfolding of the life of a people in all its ramifications, associations, and implications, in their most dynamic and fluid character." For Baraka, this was where to situate the myopia of the "so-called cultural nationalists": "their use . . . of the concept of culture as a static concept." The oppression of African-Americans, he argued, is "at base economic," though without forgetting the factor of racism, "an integral part of the capitalist mode of production." National liberation should still be pursued, but the objective should be to liberate "the national productive forces" from imperialist stranglehold. In other words, "[d]ialectically our struggle takes on a nationalistic character if only because it is a struggle against oppression. But there is also a class nature to our struggle, since we understand the economic reasons behind that oppression."[89] Of the lamentable "male chauvinism" of cultural nationalism, Baraka could only wish that

> one day that story will be told from some of those women's mouths how they had to stand up under [its] incredible and bizarre neo-feudalist yoke. . . . How they fought it for every inch. How they improvised and sidestepped and even threw real pots and pans to try to get free of their master the slave.[90]

African-American cultural difference was no longer to be posed in exclusivist, ontological black–white terms; it was now a strategic performative identity articulating the complexities of gender, race, class, and international solidarities. Baraka, as in the previous phase, was still "black," but his blackness now was more open, aerated by history. Baraka again had shifted position, but decrudin is a process whose only enemy is stasis.

Thereafter for Baraka the task of the black revolutionary writer was to "transform his culture to a militant fighting culture," "*an international anti-imperialist culture.*"[91] In the introduction to *Hard Facts*, a volume of poetry published in 1974 after the shift, Baraka reiterated the earlier black cultural nationalist utilitarian notion of art as a "weapon of revolutionary struggle." But the approach was now different. Cultural nationalism remained a "subjective mystification" as long as it continued to holler "White people as the cause of our oppression," rather than point to and confront "the system of monopoly capitalism." In an obvious echo of Mao Tse-Tung's *Talks at the Yenan Forum on Literature and Art*, Baraka outlined the new aesthetics:

> We want to raise the level of the people, but to do that we must start where they are which is on much higher level than the majority of intellectuals and artists. We also want to popularize, to make popular, to make a popular mass art. To take the popular and combine it with the advanced. Not to compromise, but to synthesize. To raise and to popularize.

The new poems must be "odes of strength, attack pieces, bomb, machine gun and rocket poems. Poems describing reality and methods of changing it."[92] A similar statement of the new position introduced his *Motion of History and Other Plays*.

The title play, written between late 1975 and early 1976, attempts to put the new theory into practice. It is a vast, panoramic view of situations of oppression and rebellion in America from the seventeenth century to the present. It draws generously on history and there is an appendix of some of those sources. The play, according to Baraka, was aimed at "telling a part of this nation's history through its recurrent rebellions." The other main task was to expose the "treachery and sham" of the "conscious separation created between black and white workers who are both exploited by the same enemy."[93] As a result, one of the new insights in the play is an emphasis on class division and antagonism *among* whites. They are no longer a homogeneous category counterposed simply as enemies of blacks. The play thus presents a 1676 rebellion as interracial revolt against slavery and servitude and reveals the divisive tactics of the oppressors:

> GRANTHAM: I say import more blacks, more black slaves, and relieve all the whites from debtor's servitude. Then use the whites to enslave the blacks. Use the ex-debtors, vagrants, the lower classes of Englishmen to be the overseers, the guards, the gendarmes for the blacks.[94]

The struggle against oppression must therefore be collective, that is, include white lower classes, who are mere tools bribed with a few privileges. Lenny, the apostle of "Marxism-Leninism–Mao Tse-Tung Thought," later in the play lectures on the need for this collectivity:

> If you are interested in revolution . . . not just word games and posturing, but the absolute transformation of society, the smashing of this bourgeois state and the replacing of it with socialism, you must understand that that will not be done by just black people or by just white workers, or just by the Puerto Ricans or the Mexicans or the Indians or Asiatic peoples in this country alone. it will be done by means of a party, a political party, a revolutionary Marxist-Leninist

party . . . a party leading a union of the whole working class here in the United States, the entire multinational working class, the black brown red yellow white of it, in combination. Guided by the science of revolution![95]

The structure of the play supports this less exclusivist approach to black self-fashioning. If *Slave Ship* undermines conventional play identity by simultaneously being an expansive festival and a compact, evocative ritual, *The Motion of History* keeps the subversive thrust but secularizes and alters it in very different ways.

The *Motion*'s mode of exposition is more decisively *democratic*, drawing largely on the narrative techniques of a mass medium, the cinema. The short, fragmentlike divisions of the drama are more like shots, frames, or sequences of a film than "scenes" in a play. In fact, the drama commences by announcing itself as a film:

> Film of rebellion is playing on screen. Police beating black people savagely. Put all the rebellion films together. One big rebellion film, in all countries the people struggling. Third World struggling against imperialism, colonialism, neo-colonialism, hegemonism. In the west, the workers battling police, the oppressed nationalities, black people prominently, getting smashed and bashed but fighting back.[96]

But the play's relationship with the conventions of the medium it borrows from is not an unproblematic one. Jean-Louis Baudry has shown persuasively how the process of cinematic screening, especially the arrangement of its constituent elements such as projector, darkened hall, and screen, and the effects on the spectator such as corporeal immobility but great visual excitation, strikingly reproduce "the mise-en-scène of Plato's cave (prototypical set for all transcendence and the tropological model of idealism)," thus fulfilling the structural and ideological function of "occultation or of filling the gap, the split, of the subject on the order of the signifier."[97] Baraka's play short-circuits and denies this process any completion. Amid the film of rebellion, two characters stick their heads out of the screen and not only try to see the film being screened (thereby turning the screen-mirror back on itself), but soon begin a conversation— on the film (thus interrupting the screen–audience alliance and its suture effects). A cannibal of genres, the play is not a play or a film or simply one with a measure of the other in it.

It is this radical interrogation of formal identities that appears to govern the aesthetic and ideological vision of the play. The theater's—indispensable—fixation with the performer's corporeal presence ("live!") is juxtaposed and grated against cinema's nature as a performance with absent performers. Timothy Murray reads this agonistic juxtaposition as a blending of "corpor[e]al presence and technological image into one representational filmic body, a membrane depicting . . . 'a confrontation of world views.' "[98] And in the richness of its appropriation of historical data, the play could be accused of a documentary overkill. Yet it avoids, like a plague, the masterful totalizing eye characteristic of the documentary form in dominant practice, and it even parodies stock techniques such as voiceover and what I call the visual address, or "dumb show."[99] A contemporary narrative of the coming-to-consciousness of the two Dudes is woven into and around a narrative of historical occasions of oppression, repression, and rebellion, thereby disordering chronology and temporality. The two Dudes are set up as simultaneously inside—as characters and actors in the drama, and outside—as spectators and commentators on the film of rebellion, of the play, and so on.

The latter technique is particularly deeply implicated in Baraka's professed aim of showing through the play that "the only solution to our problems, i.e., the majority of us in this society, is revolution! And that revolution, socialist revolution, is inevitable."[100] The two Dudes, black and white, mediate, as spectators *in* the play, between the theater audience and the play. Baraka has set up a surrogate audience *within* the play for the theater audience, who thus can psychologically compare its own reactions with that of its surrogate and probably adopt the duo as role models—after all, they are not just spectators, they are also performers, closer to or in the action. "What happens to these characters in the course of the play," argues W. D. E. Andrews, "thus becomes paradigmatic of the transformations called for in the real-life audience."[101] The two Dudes set out as socially passive and uncommitted individuals. The bohemian White Dude sees only the aesthetic of politics, swooning at the "profound choreography" of the smashing and bashing of the oppressed going on in the film, while the pipe-smoking, bourgeois middle-class Black Dude only talks evasively about the "obviousness" of inequality.[102]

But the two Dudes are soon swept along by a reality they "cannot not know." Within the terrain of the social, and even more one marked by crises, identity cannot be fixed. The first roles they found themselves playing are those of the black James Chaney and the white Andrew Goodman, active participants in an interracial freedom struggle. But this struggle which failed stands as a prototype of several struggles with similar composition and fate throughout the play. Yet they do not give up. They learn, organize study groups, and advance in consciousness, until their experience reveals that only solid institutional structures of resistance can effectively combat imperialism. The play ends with the formation of a multinational working class "Marxist-Leninist vanguard party"[103] for this purpose, with the the two Dudes, now *nameworthy* and identified as Lenny and Richie, prominently involved. A decruded subjectivity is not an end in itself but only a beginning, albeit a crucial one.

Many critics are irked by what they regard as the "propaganda," the absolutism, of Baraka's politics in this play. I think Baraka's practice suggests, whether the author wills it or not, precisely this: that people should be irked rather than be comforted by it. Extremism, we know, remained a major component of Baraka's practice all through his various positional shifts. The common negative conception of the extreme and the outrageous has prevented critics from paying any attention, beyond bland dismissals, to its creative potential *in Baraka*: the way in which it very often calls a critical attention to, and boldly risks subverting itself. I suggest we need to envisage extremism-propaganda in more productive, performative ways. If the goal of propaganda is to indoctrinate and induce passive acceptance, Baraka's propaganda is so extreme, so "obviously propaganda," as the cliché goes, that it induces anything but quiescent endorsement. What it regularly meets with is active resistance and interrogation. Here, I think, lies the strategic usefulness of the playwright's propaganda. Rather than approximate our expectations and actuate passive consumption—the paradigmatic form of which we have in television advertising—Baraka's propaganda is so "incompetent" as propaganda that it activates only our meticulous, alert, and discriminating faculties. Take, for instance, the following unsubtle, nonironic speech of a character in a play in late 1970s United States:

> Comrades, we have come together today to do serious work, the most serious work of our epoch, putting together the antirevisionist, Marxist-Leninist vanguard party. The revolutionary party. The new Communist Party, guided by the science of revolution, Marxism–Leninism–Mao Tse-Tung Thought, the best of all possible weapons for liberation of the people from . . . the clutches of the bloody beast imperialism-monopoly-capitalism. . . . To paraphrase Stalin in his book, *The Foundations of Leninism*, such a party must be "an advanced detachment of the working class and armed with revolutionary theory.". . .[104]

The legend that someone thought this was from a Richard Pryor or Eddie Murphy routine is easily believable! But that, precisely, is the problem: our obssessive quest for the familiar, the safe, and the easily categorized. Baraka's "propaganda" undoes, subverts itself, by suggesting critical appropriation. As Bertolt Brecht once said, propaganda that stimulates thinking, in whatever form, is useful to the cause of the oppressed.[105]

A related point is that what appears to be the play's remorseless politics of uniformity occurs at the verbal level only, and it is contradicted forcefully at the level of structure, where the play is a veritable *open* form: its deconstruction of genre boundaries, its temporal flux, fragmentary, collagelike character, and so on. It is significant that toward the play's end, this openness irrupts into the verbal realm:

> RICHIE: Yeh, yeh. But there's some types here we can't agree with thoroughly.
> LENNY: Who agrees thoroughly? We don't agree with you all on everything. And I know you got plenty of them chauvinists lurking in the wings. But let's get it on, so we can get the big push on.[106]

Of course, there is no need to agree "thoroughly." To hold on to the canon of "thorough agreement" in matters such as this is to abandon the strategic and suggest coercion and tyranny, principal supports of expressive identity.

I have argued that Baraka's practice suggests the performative identity. Yet I have shown specific significant moments when only the expressive best defines his art. I will clarify the "contradiction." Let us make a distinction in Baraka's career (so far) between the *parts* (the different positional aesthetic and ideological shifts) and the *whole*. My readings show Baraka, as a Bohemian and as a cultural nationalist, to propose the expressive identity, while the performative is evident in his current Marxism, which is in many instances doctrinaire, though self-subverting in its orthodoxy. However, looking at this career graph or the writer's practice as a whole, what is its animating force is none other than a major component of performative identity: *change*, emphasis on change, change as a privileged category. To privilege change is to acknowledge history and contingency. It is to be, as in Baraka's career, autocritical, sensitive to criticisms, bold enough to accept one's misapprehensions and embark on reeducation and rectifications; it is to be able to move from the effete aestheticism of bohemia to a garrulous, extremist cult of blackness to an openness which is so far the most liberating of all the stops; it is to be unafraid of improvisation, as in jazz revision: acting, stumbling, *learning*, rising, and acting again.[107] *Change* is the nodal point of Baraka's practice; decrudin, a performative articulatory practice, is its African-American specificity.

Elaborating a measurement scale for decrudin, Barbara Ann Teer identifies "Five Cycles of Evolution": The Nigger, The Negro, The Militant, The Nationalist, and The Revolutionary, in order of desirability.[108] In the last, the "spirituality of blackness" has been absorbed, that is, blackness is no longer an encumbrance to thought and action, and consciousness is free of parochialisms usually associated with the preceding stages. We can grant that Baraka is at present in this cycle. But the cycles are not fixed or immobile, and even revolutionary consciousness must continuously examine and reexamine itself as it confronts concrete practice. Baraka himself acknowledges as much:

> [I]n comparing and measuring, in summing up, all the roads I've traveled have been the preparation, *hopefully, this present period [Marxist] is more preparation.*[109]

5

Derek Walcott: Islands of History at a Rendezvous with a Muse

Now, the sibyl I honour, mother of memory,
Bears in her black hand a white frangipani,
with berries of blood,
She gibbers with the cries
Of the Guinean odyssey

Derek Walcott, "Origins"

I met History once, but he ain't recognize me,
a parchment Creole, with warts,
like an old sea-bottle, crawling like a crab
through the holes of shadow cast by the net
of a grille balcony; cream linen, cream hat.
I confront him and shout, "Sir, is Shabine!
They say I'se your grandson. You remember Grandma,
your black cook, at all?" The bitch hawk and spat.
A spit like that worth any number of words.
But that's all them bastards have left us: words.

Derek Walcott, "The Schooner Flight"[1]

A popular lore has it that while Old World griots, African, European, or Asian, preface panegyrics for their lineages and cities with "from times immemorial," their New World counterparts are doomed to the very inferior task of factual calculations and concatenation of dates. For the Old World, "origin" is a bottomless abyss that traverses grandiose monuments and/or monumental ruins, appropriating their multiple significations: agedness, stability, authenticity. Old World scions are supposed to "walk tall" and assured, given the "solidity" of their tradition; "from times immemorial" is the ultimate hymn to this taproot without end.

The worst thing that could happen to a tradition, in this kind of historiography, is for it to be datable, to be mere verifiable history.

Writing on the region that from 1492 "rapidly became the dramatic proscenium of the European invasion and domination of the Americas," F. W. Knight and C. A. Palmer argue that "the modern Caribbean states represent a unique and challenging experience in the history of mankind."[2] Part of the experience they challenge is the Old World fable of mythical origins. The islands are not just the creations of *known* history, but this history is also their very constitution. The inhabitants were virtually *unknown*, practically *did not exist*, before the "European intrusion," which "abruptly interrupted the original pattern of their historical development . . . severely altered their physical environment . . . diversified their diet, complicated their epidemiological systems, produced new biological strains, and linked them inextricably to the wider world beyond the Atlantic Ocean."[3] The combined experiences of slavery and colonialism have conspired to produce a classic situation of imperial dominance in which a majority of the population, oppressors and oppressed alike, are, in the legal parlance of today's nation-states, "aliens," originally from far-flung locations in Europe, Africa, and Asia. They stayed, endured, but were never to be free from the enervating afflictions of a known history, a history of dates. Edward Brathwaite, the distinguished Barbadian poet, testifies to the perpetual stress of adjustment to such a terrain by offsprings of both planter and slave, when he writes: "The most significant feature of West Indian life and imagination since Emancipation has been its sense of rootlessness, of not belonging to the landscape."[4]

All the West Indies has to show for decolonization today is a maze of multicolored flags and the composite of intellectual, social, cultural, and economic conditions that political scientists mean when they say "Third World."[5] Perhaps no anglophone Caribbean writer best captures the complexities of this historical present than its greatest poet and dramatist, the St. Lucia-born Derek Walcott.

"History is the nightmare," Walcott prefaces a seminal essay with this statement from James Joyce, "from which I am trying to awake."[6] Beyond the immediate ambience of the essay, Walcott here states a preoccupation apart from which he has virtually been unable to do anything else: history and the West Indian writer; what *is* this history and what *should* it be? But first, a fundamental question: does the West Indies have a history?

> Where are your monuments, your battles, martyrs?
> Where is your tribal memory? Sirs,
> in that grey vault. The sea. The sea
> has locked them up. The sea is History.[7]

The sea is the unappeasable customs officer who at the primal moment coldly seized the histories of all arrivees, cargo or captain. Either the New World is going to do without the unnecessary encumbrance called history, or a new history would have to be created. Yet, if one cares to look, the iniquities of the postcolonial present stare unblinkingly, throwing shards of light across negatives of time, illuminating Empire and absentee landlords and canefields and "Bones ground by windmills / into marl and cornmeal." But, Walcott insists, "that was just lamentations, / it was not History."[8] These islands, it seems, are irretrievably "history-orphaned."[9]

However, it is Walcott himself who reveals that the sea was not impartial in the execution of its immigration duties. Some peoples' histories were actually allowed in, to circulate and dominate other peoples'. The favored histories were those of captain rather than of cargo. "I remember as a child," Walcott says, "singing *Brittania Rules the Waves*. I sang it just as fervently as a million other black children. Including the line 'Britons never, never shall be slaves.' Amazing, isn't it, that we didn't feel any contradiction there!"[10] He also remembers he "saw history through the sea-washed eyes / of our choleric, ginger-haired headmaster" who told narratives that were little more than "Nostalgia! Hymns of battles not our own."[11] When Michel Foucault, the eminent theorist of subjection and subjectivity, was listing the retainers of the disciplinary mechanisms so central to the "normal" functioning of today's carceral world, he did not forget to include the "teacher-judge."[12] Walcott's experience substantiates his point.

"Hallucination though it was," Walcott comments on the subjection, "we saw ourselves as Britons, not blacks. We saw ourselves, you might say, as parts of something bigger, more universal than mere race—the ideal Britain—the England of Shakespeare."[13] It would astonish if this did not lead to entrenched self-devaluation and rejection. Thus when the young Walcott scanned West Indian history and read about the Haitian revolutionaries Dessalines and Christophe—"our only noble ruins," he later calls them—he could pardon all their excesses but not the inspiring "size, mania, the fire of great heretics" they, in their circumstances, had: "Here were slaves who by divine right could never be kings, because by claiming kingship they abrogated the law of God. Despite my race, I could not believe that He would choose such people as his engines." Hence they deserve all the punishment God and the slavemaster could muster, for their blasphemous presumption that slavery was not their unalterable destiny. "He," Walcott writes of his past, hallucinating self,

> believed then that the moral of tragedy could only be Christian, that their fate was the debt exacted by the sin of pride, that they were punished by a white God as masters punished servants for presumption. He saw history as hierarchy and to him these heroes, despite their meteoric passages, were damned to the old darkness because they had challenged an ordered universe.[14]

But subjection is never total or a one-way process; it also *enables*—in fact, this is its condition of effectiveness. What Walcott did in the circumstance was to appropriate with productive greed the history that was everywhere made available to him. He fell "madly in love with English,"[15] he says, and the possibility of possibilities precluded any apologies:

> like Christofer he bears
> in speech mnemonic as a missionary's
> the Word to Savages,
> its shape an earthen, water-bearing vessel's
> whose sprinkling alters us
> into good Fridays who recite His praise,
> parroting our master's
> style and voice, we make his language ours,
> coverted cannibals
> we learn with him to eat the flesh of
> Christ.[16]

Subjection insists on conformity through acts of "free will," but it trusts too much by hiring no sentinel against free will's interrogation of its own premises. By the time the hallucination began to clear, revealing that "this was not the way the world went, that the acolyte would have to defrock himself of that servitude,"[17] the Word had been given and irretrievably taken or, rather, seized.

The painful process of learning and understanding difference—defrocking oneself of "that servitude"—needed a self-protective weapon to survive. Paradoxically, this weapon turned out to be the Word acquired in servitude. Henceforth, the Word would perform the twin functions of asserting and interrogating difference. This would be the ammunition for registering West Indian subjectivity. Thus an urgent task immediately presented itself to the muse: the fact that "no one had yet written of this landscape / that it was possible"[18]:

> So the self-inflicted role of martyr came naturally, the melodramatic belief that one was message-bearer for the millennium, that the inflamed ego was enacting their will. In that simple schizophrenic boyhood one could lead two lives: the interior life of poetry, the outward life of action and dialect. Yet the writers of my generation were natural assimilators. We knew the literature of Empires, Greek, Roman, British, through their essential classics; and both the patois of the street and the language of the classroom hid the elation of discovery. If there was nothing, there was everything to be made. With this prodigious ambition one began.[19]

But the *process* of negotiating difference is discovered to be the least of easy tasks, more so when one's only tool—which is appropriated from the "enemy" one is freeing oneself from—is taken for granted. "[M]y first poems and plays," Walcott confesses, "expressed [the] yearning to be adopted, as the bastard longs for his father's household." Such a yearning is often accompanied by displeasures but Walcott could only get wiser:

I saw myself legitimately prolonging the mighty line of Marlowe, of Milton, but my sense of inheritance was stronger because it came from estrangement. I would learn that every tribe hoards its culture as fiercely as its prejudices, that English literature, even in the theatre, was hallowed ground and trespass, that colonial literatures could grow to resemble it closely, but could never be considered its legitimate heir. There was folk poetry, colonial poetry, Commonwealth verse, etc., and their function, as far as their mother country was concerned, was filial and tributary.[20]

In spite of the frustrations, Walcott persevered, graduating from a yearning for adoption to an assured independence. The rest, to borrow the cliché, is history.

History as Culture: The Romance of Adam

In the articulation of a Caribbean cultural identity, Walcott privileges a particular understanding of history: history as myth. Three of Walcott's critical essays are central in this regard: "What the Twilight Says," "The Caribbean: Culture or Mimicry," and "The Muse of History." The critical thrust in these essays is also evident in the autobiographical volume of poems *Another Life* (1973), the epic poem *Omeros,* and the plays *The Last Carnival* (1986, produced 1982) and *Remembrance* (1980, produced 1977).[21]

Walcott distinguishes two ideas of history: "history as time" and "its original concept as myth." In its characteristic chronological rigorism and accumulation of details, the former is history that arraigns and judges in absolute terms. Its consciousness assumes an unnegotiable polarity between Prospero and Caliban, hence whatever it has to say of the past is channeled parochially through the memory of hero or of victim, reeling off absurd, will-crippling images of discoveries and conquests and pacifications and revenge. The "rational madness of history seen as sequential time," Walcott contends, could do little else but "contemplate only the shipwreck." History as myth shuns this groveling submission to the paralyzing grip of historic time. Here, "history is fiction, subject to a fitful muse, memory." This fitful guardian of the past admits breaks, bridges, continuities, and amnesia: imagination is its only god. Rather than contemplate the shipwreck, it offers elation at the "elemental privilege of naming the new world." Rather than debilitating nostalgic quests, its "vision of man in the New World is Adamic . . . a world without monuments and ruins."[22] "We make too much of that long groan that underlines the past"—Walcott returns again in 1992 to his choice critique in his Nobel acceptance speech.[23]

From Walcott's outline above, it is clear that he intends history as time to approximate, in my terms, the expressive identity, and his own privileged history as myth to gesture toward the performative. What I discover, however, is a more complex scenario. There is a great disjunction between Walcott's *critical formulations* of history as myth and the *dramatic form* into which he translates this vision. While the former decisively registers the expressive identity, evident in the latter is a significantly enabling performative articulation. To unravel this enigma, we must begin with a proper situation of the writer's idea of history in the context of its elaboration.

Walcott conceives his vision of history as deeply embattled by the proponents of the idea of history as time. Given the highly polemical tone of Walcott's formulations, it is amazing that he does *not* specifically identify his opponents but simply takes the liberty of representing their claims. Thus Walcott points to a trend in West Indian literature which he argues is sponsored by the unimaginative idea of history as time:

> In the New World servitude to the muse of history has produced a literature of recrimination and despair, a literature of revenge written by the descendants of slaves or a literature of remorse written by the descendants of masters. Because this literature serves historical truth, it yellows into polemic or evaporates into pathos. The truly tough aesthetic of the New World neither explains nor forgives history. It refuses to recognize it as a creative or culpable force. This shame and awe of history possess poets of the Third World who think of language as enslavement and who, in a rage for identity, respect only incoherence or nostalgia.[24]

If we place Walcott's denunciation into its general social context, it is really not difficult to identify concretely his target. "The Muse of History," from which the preceding passage is quoted, and the other two essays were written between the late 1960s and 1974, the height of the Black Power phenomenon in the Caribbean.[25]

The literary tradition that Walcott has made an intimate part of himself, the center from where he feels and seeks other sources for inspiration, is the Western tradition. It was precisely this tradition that poets influenced by Black Power made a target of attack in their quest for a "black aesthetic." In the words of Edward Brathwaite, a leading poet and proponent of a black Caribbean aesthetic, the search is for "a possible alternative to the European cultural tradition which has been imposed upon us and which we have more or less accepted and absorbed, for obvious historical reasons, as the only way of going about our business."[26] I cite below Gordon Rohlehr, a perceptive watcher of the Caribbean cultural scene, on the features of the aesthetic—as manifested in Brathwaite's work—that prompts so much denunciation from Walcott:

> Brathwaite's trilogy treated all the themes that Walcott had criticised as inhibiting influences on the West Indian sensibility, namely, the themes of exile, journey, the quest for identity, Africa, history, race and return. The instantaneous reception which Brathwaite's poetry received, especially since it appeared at the height of the Black Power movement, angered Walcott even more, since it seemed that the same wave of politics and history which had caused his work

to be neglected (a number of theses were being written on Walcott at the time) had catapulted an inferior writer to the forefront. Walcott's bitterness against "History" and "Politics" and "Race" and "Africa" increased, as did his need to negate Brathwaite's achievement, which he viewed as the mediocre embodiment of all these themes.[27]

According to Walcott's paradigm, this is the identity of the poets enslaved to "historical truth," the defenders of the idea of history as time.

To the challenge of the Black Power poets against the hegemonic tradition, Walcott argues that "those who break a tradition first hold it in awe" and that "by openly fighting tradition, we perpetuate it." For him, "revolutionary literature is filial impulse," and "maturity is the assimilation of the features of every ancestor." Of course, says Walcott, those who derive their inspiration from history as time cannot see this; they see instead the " 'classic style' as stasis . . . rejecting it as the language of the master," a self-devaluation which results "when the poet . . . limits his memory to the suffering of the victim." For the attempt of some of the poets to integrate concepts from African languages, cultural traditions and cosmological systems, and West Indian Creole, Walcott has only scorn, insisting that Calibanism is a greater virtue:

> Their admirable wish to honor the degraded ancestor limits their language to phonetic pain, the groan of suffering, the curse of revenge. The tone of the past becomes an unbearable burden, for they must abuse the master or hero in his own language, and this implies self-deceit. Their view of Caliban is of the enraged pupil. They cannot separate the rage of Caliban from the beauty of his speech when the speeches of Caliban are equal in their elemental power to those of his tutor. The language of the torturer mastered by the victim. This is viewed as servitude, not as victory. [28]

The result, observes Walcott, is that the poets hypocritically cannibalize dialect and glorify experimentation but the product is little more than the "degeneration of technique" hiding itself in originality: "Bad verse written by blacks is better than good verse written by whites, because, say the revolutionaries, the same standards do not apply. This is seen as pride, as the opposite of inferiority." For them, the efficacy of poetry lies in its subject, so they see "all form as hypocrisy," hence "[t]heir poetry becomes a kind of musical accompaniment to certain theses. . . ."[29] The venom is unmistakable.

Subtending Walcott's critique is an interesting view of identity and difference. In the earlier essay, "What the Twilight Says," Walcott argues that "[o]nce the New World black had tried to prove that he was as good as his master, when he should have proven not his equality but his difference." By the time of "The Muse of History," when Black Power had turned inward from proving its difference, from its grand distinctions Them and Us to also include the disparate "thems"—toms, traitors, and so on—within a formerly held homogeneous Us,[30] Walcott executes an about-face: "Blacks are different, and the pathos is that most blacks have been led to believe this, and into the tragedy of proclaiming their difference."[31] This undue equivocation before the demands of difference, hardly a feature of performative articulation, defines Walcott's critical elaboration of history as myth, and it is a main theoretical pillar of his concept of Adam/ic poetics.

Walcott proposes that the common experience of the New World, for scions of both slave and master, is colonialism and that the great minds of this world have always refused to be incapacitated by its history. "Their philosophy, based on a contempt for historic time, is revolutionary, for what they repeat to the New World is its simultaneity with the Old." They revere and assimilate every tradition, but "their veneration subtilizes an arrogance which is tougher than violent rejection." They are the models of the "truly tough aesthetic" which neither explains nor forgives history. In Saint-John Perse, Borges, Whitman, Cesaire, and Neruda, Walcott sees the clear outlines of this aesthetic. In all of them, he sees excitement eloquent at mastering a strange environment and naming the world anew, rather than the anthropological exhumation of dead customs—the preoccupation of the other unmentionable kind of poet:

> It is this awe of the numinous, this elemental privilege of naming the new world which annihilates history in our great poets, an elation common to all of them, whether they are aligned by heritage to Crusoe and Prospero or to Friday and Caliban. They reject ethnic ancestry for faith in elemental man.[32]

Comparing the poetry of Perse and Cesaire, Walcott concludes:

> Perse and Cesaire, men of diametrically challenging backgrounds, racial opposites to use the language of politics, one patrician and conservative, the other proletarian and revolutionary, classic and romantic, Prospero and Caliban, all such opposites balance easily, but they balance on the axis of a shared sensibility, and this sensibility, with or deprived of the presence of a visible tradition, is the sensibility of walking to a New World. Perse sees in this New World vestiges of the old, of order and of hierarchy, Cesaire sees in it evidence of past humiliations and the need for a new order, but the deeper truth is that both poets perceive this New World through mystery. . . . If we think of one as poor and the other as privileged when we read their addresses to the New World, if we must see one as black and one as white, we are not only dividing this sensibility by the process of the sociologist, but we are denying the range of either poet, the power of compassion and the power of fury.

It is significant that Walcott finds it necessary to check himself at this point. "One is not making out a case for assimilation and for the common simplicity of all men," he says, "we are interested in their differences, openly, but what astonishes us in both poets is their elation, their staggering elation in possibility."[33] Both poets see possibility, but as Walcott himself shows, the possibility they see is diametrically opposed. This is of little interest to Walcott, who thereby thinks he is being less parochial

than his detractors who bow to sociology. In exchange for exclusive sociology, Walcott hands out exclusive mythopoeia.

Here then is the fabric of Walcott's Adam, the "original instinct" at-
tainable only by the "annihilation of what is known."[34] For the Caribbean, "history is irrelevant, not because it is not being created, or because
it was sordid; but because it has never mattered, what has mattered is the
loss of history, the amnesia of the races, what has become necessary is
imagination, imagination as necessity, as invention."[35] The slave's assimilation of Christianity, a religion of the Old World, is not a sign of defeat;
no, "[t]he slave converted himself, he changed weapons, spiritual
weapons, and as he adapted his master's religion, he also adapted his
language, and it is here that what we can look at as our poetic tradition
begins. Now began the new naming of things."[36]

We arrive at a problematic juncture. Walcott attacks historical truth
and proposes amnesia and Adamic vision, yet he repeatedly insists that
this Adam is not a saint dropped from heaven but holds a borrowed
language and is neither innocent nor naive; the golden apples of his "second Eden have the tartness of experience . . . are shot with acid." What
Walcott refuses to accept is that the constitutive fabric of this "acid" or
"tartness" is little else if not the historical truth he rails so much about.
Because the acceptance is not made, it is quite easy for Walcott to often
erase historical specificity and revert to a reified Adam so that, for instance, in reading the British Ted Hughes and the Guyanese Denis Williams or Wilson Harris, or even Samuel Beckett, the important thing he
sees in them, irrespective of context, is universal alienation, "the displaced, searching psyche of modern man, the reversion of twentieth-
century man whether in Africa or Yorkshire to his pre-Adamic beginning, to pre-history." Or, for another instance, this soppy Methodist
moralism:

> . . . I felt history to be the burden of others. I was not excited by continuation
> of its process but by discovery, by the plain burden of work, for there was too
> much to do here. Yet the older and more assured I grew, the stronger my
> isolation as a poet, the more I needed to become omnivorous about the art
> and literature of Europe to understand my own world. I write "my own world"
> because I had no doubt that it was mine, that it was given to me, by God, not
> by history, with my gift.[37]

Many of Walcott's named Adamic poets are, interestingly, those catalyzed
by a passionate, radical obsession with historical truth. And my own insistence is that even the Walcott corpus is unthinkable outside the historical truth of the Caribbean area.

One important related question is how Walcott *translates* his idea of
history as myth and its derivative Adamic vision to a choice of *form* for
the construction of a Caribbean poetics and cultural identity. In view of
the historical status of the Caribbean as a confluence of disparate cultural

traditions, the question is best approached through a consideration of Walcott's attitude to appropriating theatrical forms from the different traditions.

Part of Walcott's disagreement with those he calls the poets of history as time is their insistence that the Western tradition in the Caribbean be displaced in favor of the African, the tradition of the majority. His own view of history as myth, he suggests in his elaborations, is more open and enabling, encompassing Crusoe and Friday, free to borrow from any direction, refusing ultimately, after the usual pitfalls of apprenticeship, to be parochially compartmentalized. Walcott's early plays labored heavily in attempted domestication of the Western tradition, his long-accepted and central model. Of *Henri Christophe*, the playwright, with the benefit of hindsight, mocks its "Jacobean style" and its "cynical aristocratic flourish."[38] Synge provided the model for *The Sea at Dauphin* (first produced in 1954); classical Greek tragedy served the same purpose for *Ione* (1957). Since *Ti-Jean and His Brothers* (1958), which Walcott describes as the "first real experience I had of writing a stylized West Indian play," Walcott has moved from mere domestication to an assured synthesis and originality for which many of his later plays are justly well-known. Synthesis is a process of continuous experimentation, something Walcott could well afford since his formation of the Trinidad Theatre Workshop in 1959. The crucial new elements in the synthesis are the Nō and the Kabuki, *Japanese* forms first learned in the late 1950s from Brecht's appropriation of them. And then "I began to go to the texts themselves. . . . I used to look very carefully at the woodcuts of Hokusai and Hiroshige. There was then a very strong popular interest in Japanese cinema—in Kurosawa, and films such as *Ugetsu, Gate of Hell, Rashomon*, etc." The immediate homage to this influence was the play *Malcochon or, The Six in the Rain* (1959), derived from *Rashomon*.[39]

Walcott needs the Japanese theater for what he calls its classic discipline, to act as a chastening antidote to West Indian theater, too oriented to the *carnival*: "Our sin . . . is the sin of exuberance, of self-indulgence, and I wanted to impose a theatre that observed certain rules. The use of choruses required precise measure; the use of narration required precise mime."[40] Walcott calls attention to the "adverse" effects of carnival's untetherable mutability and mobility. "The essential law of Carnival is movement," and this is hardly the kind of terrain in which enduring classics are fashioned. Hence the artist "works in isolation from the crude, popular forms."[41] The playwright would subsequently declare carnival to be of dubious value to the stage: "The truth is that West Indian theatre will continue to be literary, humanistic in its concept just as much as the West Indian novel is."[42] If carnival is to be useful at all, the strong folk content would have to be tamed, by Japanese and English, specifically Elizabethan, traditions. The dance patterns, for instance, would need to be more compressed, to move "from popular language into metaphor";

and the music must be subtler, and do more "underlining" than "accompanying" movement. "The West Indies has not yet produced an original composer," Walcott laments, "because the folk element in [its] music is so strong."[43] It is important that Walcott here did not elaborate on what an "original" composition is, for it is only a question of taste to hold Kitchener or Mighty Sparrow inferior to Beethoven, a taste predicated on produced, disseminated, and consolidated modes of music appreciation. It does not come to one naturally and the process of learning is not innocent. Walcott's "classics" are eternal and heaven-made.

These are good grounds for being suspicious of Walcott's history as myth and its vaunted openness. In fact, his kind of reading of carnival could not but sound elitist and Eurocentric to its committed defenders.[44] An interesting point here is that aspects of carnival have been indispensable to Walcott's dramaturgy since *Drums and Colours* (1958),[45] which gives full play to the expansiveness of carnival, and *Ti-Jean*. And he has also defended the carnival, sometimes forcefully. In "The Caribbean: Culture or Mimicry?," for instance, he stresses the uncompromising inventiveness of carnival, even celebrating its protean character as liberating.[46] On his scornful remarks about carnival, he insists that he is not attacking carnival but the Caribbean states and their intellectuals, who make a business of vulgarizing it. No, the "enemy was not the people or the people's crude aesthetic which he [he means himself] refined and orchestrated," but the fraudulent self-proclaimed protectors of the people:

> Every state sees its image in those forms which have the mass appeal of sport, seasonal and amateurish. Stamped on that image is the old colonial grimace of the laughing nigger, steelbandsman, carnival masker, calypsonian and limbo dancer. These popular artists are trapped in the State's concept of the folk form, for they preserve the colonial demeanour and threaten nothing. The folk arts have become the symbol of a carefree, accommodating culture, an adjunct to tourism, since the State is impatient with anything which it cannot trade.[47]

Walcott's West Indian play would thus be a composite of treated but still earthy Creole, dance and music, sometimes the unapologetic coarseness of carnival forms, the "lyricism and savagery of Lorca," the "rawness and crudity of Elizabethan or Greek staging," and the physicality and volubility of a movie theater—"A theatre that has the excitement of a boxing ring," as he says Brecht once put it. The profound, expressive subtlety of Asian art completes the collage.[48] And Walcott sees this eclecticism authorized and enabled by history as myth and Adamic vision as particularly West Indian, waxing rhapsodic about the "fusion of formalism with exuberance, a delight in both the precision and power of language . . . this combination of classic discipline inherited through the language, with a strength of physical expression that comes from folk music."[49] Walcott has a name for this performative aesthetics, "mulatto," and himself as a practitioner, the "mulatto of style."[50]

Toward Inflammatory Dreams (for the New World Black)

Dream on Monkey Mountain, first produced in 1967,[51] is a particularly illuminating instance of Walcott's mulatto aesthetics. The play is a poignant dramatization of the refusal of debilitating definitions of the self and the concomitant self-reappreciation by the dominated in the Caribbean. The central character, Makak, begins as the exemplary victim of a hegemonic racist Eurocentric discourse, living fully his constitution—his subjection—as "black, ugly, poor [and so] worse than nothing,"[52] and then gradually negotiating his way toward self-definition through a wide-sweeping seriocomic interrogation of the dominant discourse of "race" and its conception of the relationship between the visible, corporeal body and the discourses that map and territorialize it. While the discourse of "black is ugly–white is beautiful" that the text signifies upon overprivileges the corporeal in the attribution of cultural definitions (for example, black = ugly = lack of culture), its own suggestion is that the relation between corporeal and discursive bodies is one of *mutual* determination, influence, and interaction.

Makak—black, charcoal burner, psychologically subdued, and topmost on the scale of poverty and ugliness—dreams one night of a white moon goddess who cleanses him of his inferiority complex by narrating to him his royal ancestry in precolonial Africa. His attempts to make his friends believe him leads him through a tavern brawl into jail. He escapes after a mock trial and succeeds this time in selling the rebellious but naive dream to the masses. He travels to Africa of the mind where he is king and ruler of immense power and wealth. However, he soon notices contradictions in the dream and he decides to give up the charade of an Edenic Africa. He "returns" awake to his poor but now psychologically liberated West Indian self.

The main excuse for dragging Makak into the vortex of visibility, the prison, is that he is "[d]runk and disorderly." But this is not exactly the case. He is taken as drunk and disorderly because he has commenced the discursive (re)constitution of his corporeality *differently*. He had a dream that he is "the direct descendant of African Kings, a healer of leprosy and the Saviour of his race." He claims that God spoke to him directly—"in the form of a woman"—and that at a point in the dream, he felt he was "God self, walking through cloud." This is how Corporal Lestrade, the agent of normality and the representative preserver of the law and the order of "Her Majesty's Government," records the offense in his book of charges: "You claimed that with the camera of your eye you had taken a photograph of God and all that you could see was blackness." The didascalia tells us that "[t]he judges rise in horror": horror at the potential disruptive effect of this dream on the ruling "order" and the discourse that constitutes it. Only Lestrade is able to go beyond the gestural to verbalize the "horror":

Blackness, my lords. What did the prisoner imply? That God was neither white nor black but nothing? That God was not white but black, that he had lost his faith? Or . . . or . . . what . . .[53]

Notice already the effects of the counterdiscourse: manic insecurity and uncertainty evinced by the string of rhetorical questions, the ellipses, and the general implicit hankering for the restoration of a destabilized meaning. It surprises none then that Makak's dream is officially described as "vile, ambitious, and obscene." But what exactly is the order being destabilized? What are its contours? An answer will be none other than a narration of how a Eurocentric hegemonic order constitutes Makak as a spoken subject, forces him to occupy a spoken position in the operations of discourse.[54]

The order operates through a Manichean opposition between "black" and "white." In its expressive rules, white is the solvent of all values and the entrenched symbol of all positive attributes, while black is its irredeemable opposite. *With* the aid of the law, which Lestrade insightfully defines as "a whore" that "will adjust her price," blackness automatically consigns the body to surveillance and subordination. And this law, we are told in unmistakable terms, is the law of the "white man": "I am an instrument of the law . . . I got the white man work to do." In the statutes, to be black is to be "[a]nimals, beasts, savages, cannibals, niggers. . . ." According to Lestrade's theory of evolution, God created the human being as ape; after some time, some "tribes" of this ape straightened their backs and began to walk upright, but one "lingered behind, and that was the nigger."[55]

The major black characters are therefore mapped and territorialized as ugly beasts not only directly but also by association: monkey, mouse, tiger, and mosquito. Makak is not only a monkey as the name says, but he is also a *charcoal* burner, and lives in the "forest," in the jungle, on Monkey *mountain*. He is the Other, the obverse face of civilization. The cell in which he is locked becomes a "stinking zoo" and Lestrade, the guard, wants "a transfer to civilization." In addition, whatever law operates in Africa, his ancestral home, is nothing but "the law of the jungle."[56] In one telling scene, we see not only the process of the "robotization" of Makak but also its immediate effects. Before his mock trial, Lestrade takes him through a grueling drill. As "the CORPORAL, like an animal tamer, cracks out his orders"—sit, stand, kneel, turn, and so on—Makak responds like an automaton. The chorus to all this is "Everything I say this monkey does do / I don't know what to say this monkey won't do." At the end of it all, Makak, the stage direction says, flops down "wearily," a zombie.[57]

The law effectively prevents Makak from contesting this discourse; he is simply the passive, obliging surface on which it is inscribed. When he is brought into the prison, he has totally forgotten his name, and his "race" is "I am tired." His corporeality is mapped physically and pro-

duces in him a supportive—quietistic—consciousness. He adores whiteness, the only thing his reality tells him is worth striving for, and secretly
keeps a white mask in his work bag. He has completely absorbed the
psychological relations of power that map his corporeality. He not only
believes he is ugly and a beast because he is black, but he actually lives
and *voices* this subjection: "Is thirty years now I have look in no mirror,
/ Not a pool of cold water, when I must drink, / I stir my hands first,
to break up my image."[58] His case tends dangerously close to that classic
stage of self-subjection narrated by Foucault:

> The efficiency of power, its constraining force have, in a sense, passed over to
> the other side—to the side of its surface of application. He who is subjected
> to a field of visibility, and who knows it, assumes responsibility for the con-
> straints of power; he makes them play spontaneously upon himself; he inscribes
> in himself the power relation in which he simultaneously plays both roles; he
> becomes the principle of his own subjection. By this very fact, the external
> power may throw off its physical weight; it tends to the non- corporeal; and,
> the more it approaches this limit, the more constant, profound and permanent
> are its effects: it is a perpetual victory that avoids any physical confrontation
> and which is always decided in advance.[59]

Lestrade is correct, after all: "In some places the law does not allow you
to be black, not even black but tinged with black."[60] However, no hegemony is total, and this play powerfully makes the point obvious. The
reality of Makak's revolt indicates there are some areas of experience and
consciousness not yet accessible to regimentation.

Makak's strategy of negotiating the colonialist discourse is an instance
of the Afrocentric counterdiscourse, manifested here by his discursive negation of the negative representations of him. With the dream—in which
the moon goddess–white woman tells him he is neither ugly nor "nothing" but a worthy human being, a descendant of emperors and kings in
great Africa—as catalyst, Makak begins the inversion of the hegemonic
discourse. In the first place, he believes that the woman he sees in his
dream, whom he takes in his arms, is not only the "loveliest" and most
beautiful in the world but also is *white*—Moustique, his assistant, swears
that Makak is mentally unbalanced to have dreamed up such an abomination. The woman not only tells him he is a handsome man with a royal
ancestry—"She say I should not live so any more, here in the forest,
frighten of people because I think I ugly. She say that I come from the
family of lions and kings"—but also, and more important, that he is not
a monkey—"That Makak is not my name." I say the latter is "more
important" because "monkey" is, in the dominant discourse, his implacable badge, the signifier of his subjection, his nothingness and his spoken-
ness.[61]

Expectedly, Makak describes the morning of his dream as "resurrection
morning." Of course, the authorities see this attempt at self-
reconstitution as nothing other than "the rage for whiteness that does

drive niggers mad." In fact, Makak is so gripped with the burgeoning possibilities for self-definition that he emphatically denies he has only dreamed them. Henceforth, he stops at nothing but the superlative: from a "nothing" he becomes a prince, a "God's warrior." Although he co-owns only an overworked ass, he roars, "Saddle my horse!," in preparation for the triumphant journey to Africa. From the zombie who flops down "wearily" in the mock trial scene, Makak now strides with his spear in agile agitation. He barely hesitates before stabbing the corporal in order to escape from prison, *acting* out an earlier proposition: "If we dead . . . is not better to die, fighting like men, than to hide in this forest?" The Afrocentric discourse reverses the gaze of the supervised on the supervisor and makes "orderly" government difficult. The crowning example is the jailbreak. Again, it is Lestrade who brilliantly expresses the implication:

> Attempting to escape. Attempting to escape from the prison of their lives. That's the most dangerous crime. It brings about revolution.[62]

The function of this strategy of resistance is to transform Makak from a nonentity to a king, a political figure. Which exactly happened. His "royal" experience in Africa, however, tells him that his vision of that continent is extremely idealized. He finds the different peoples warring when he had supposed them united, their continent homogeneous, and their cultures univocal.[63]

The tribes, led by the converted Lestrade, now the chief ideologue of Afrocentric culturalism, are more of praise-singers than effective monitors of their leader. Once in control of power, their preoccupation seems to be with revenge, and this they pursue with reckless abandon:

> We have no time for patient reforms. Mindless as the hawk, impetuous as lions, as dried of compassion as the bowels of a jackal. Elsewhere, the swiftness of justice is barbarously slow, but our progress cannot stop to think.[64]

A trial is set up. Makak, in kingly splendor, sits enthroned. History is dragged out from the deepest recesses and accused of having trampled blackness underfoot. Aristotle, Shakespeare, Galileo, Lincoln, Drake, Tarzan, Cecil Rhodes, William Wilberforce, Mandrake the Magician . . . — all are sentenced to the gallows, because they are "indubitably . . . white." The enemies of the present—the Pope, the United States, apartheid South Africa, the Ku Klux Klan, and so on—"fearing revenge," offer apologies and hands of fellowship; the tribes, of course, reject all. Makak, however, begins to interrogate his vision when Moustique alleges that he—Makak—is only a puppet now, surrounded by power-hungry hounds, and that the original dream has been corrupted. But let us not mistake Moustique for a visionary; he deserves his two deaths because he started the corruption: he began selling the dream for profit even before it had barely taken shape.[65]

Makak's suspicion of his vision is an eloquent critique of his Afrocentric counterdiscourse and its proposition of expressive identity as a weapon of resistance. It dawns on him that his dream of a pristine, glorious Africa is extremely idealized and ironically an acceptance still of whiteness as a measure of value. He wants to *exhibit* his black heritage, to counterpose it to whiteness, not necessarily because he believes in it. And remember it was a *white* woman—part of his self-annihilating fantasies—that set him on the wild utopian chase. In other words, Makak's Afrocentric counterdiscourse is operating within, and therefore already circumscribed by, the Manichean terrains of the dominant Eurocentric discourse. It would be crude, however, to belittle his resistance because of this limitation. Such a strategy often proves to be quite subversive and therefore indispensable as a *stage* to more effective forms of resistance.[66]

Ultimately, however, Makak does go beyond an inversion of the hegemonic discourse. He confronts the apparition of the white woman that catalyzes his epic quest for Africa. "Why have you caused me all the pain?" he queries her. As Lestrade appropriately cuts in, the woman's "vision is exhausted." What remains is to get rid of her. Her "theory" of negritude, her message of an innocent Africa, is discovered to be, in the last instance, some poisonous honey: another and more insidious form of enslavement. I will quote Lestrade, addressing Makak, in some detail:

> She . . . was but an image of your longing . . . as fatal as leprosy . . . destroy her; otherwise . . . [y]ou will come out in blotches . . . neither one thing nor the other . . . kill her! . . . She is the mirror of the moon that this ape look into and find himself unbearable. . . . She is . . . mother of civilization, and the confounder of blackness. I too have longed for her. She is the colour of law, religion, paper, art, and if you want peace, if you want to discover the beautiful depth of your blackness, nigger, chop her head! . . . She is the white light that paralysed your mind, that led you into this confusion. It is you who created her, so kill her!

And the result?

> MAKAK: *(Removing his robe)* Now, O God, now I am free. *(He holds the curved sword in both hands and brings it down. The WOMAN is beheaded.)*[67]

Makak rejects the deception by beheading the white goddess. It is significant that he steps *out* of the charade of a splendor-filled imperial Africa, by "[r]emoving his robe," before performing the decisive act. The challenge of resistance is no longer simply to invert the hegemonic discourse, but to radically alter the terrain of production of discourse and the relations of the subordinated to it. With Makak's final act—a rejection of black–white essentializing narratives—the dominant discourse's main supporting pillar, Manichaeism, becomes obsolete. This is the enabling moment of history as myth, the authority to be irreverent to settled relations and traditions and to invent. "Our mistake," writes Walcott of

West Indians, "has been to try to align our real power, a human thing, with the hallucination of *sharing* it, either with Africa or America. Going back to Africa is assuming an inferiority. We must look *inside*. West Indies exists but we must find it." For Walcott, Makak's treatment of the white woman is justified on the grounds that "[g]etting rid of his overwhelming awe of everything white is the first thing a colonial must take."[68]

The foregoing liberating insight raises an important query. All colonials are males—"his"—and it is they that need to get rid of their "overwhelming awe of everything white." The black female colonial, if such an entity exists, remains securely locked in the colony's conventional roles and needs no such liberation. "Sisters of the Revelation," "Market Women," "Wives of Makak," as the designations suggest, serve excellently as atmosphere or setting. Elaine Savory Fido writes perceptively that this is symptomatic of Walcott's "creative world," a world whose "treatment of women is full of cliches, stereotypes and negativity,"[69] a world subtended by the patriarchal colonial construct of Adam. In Walcott's narrative, *only* Adam named the world. Also, racism and Eurocentrism, unfulfillable and recalcitrant desires—in short, everything the black *man* should run away from—are mapped onto the white *woman*, who is then *justifiably* beheaded. This is as it happened in Baraka's *Dutchman*, though Lula does the stabbing. Even *if*, for the oppressed black man, either the white man or the white woman would do as target, we see in the case of Baraka's *Madheart* how the same structure, suffused with violence, is easily reshaped to fit the black woman. Walcott apparently interprets his concept of mulatto too narrowly and conventionally. "Mulatto" is supposedly a deconstructor of rigid identities, but Walcott's mulatto aesthetics is paradoxically unsubtly masculinist.

The dream, or nightmare, serves as a spiritual cleansing for Makak. The signal of his reformed consciousness is that in the end he not only smartly names himself but also rejects the white mask found in his bag. From being a slave to whiteness and then to an imaginary Africa, he is now his real West Indian self, a cultural mulatto, without any illusions: "Lord, I have been washed from shore to shore, as a tree in the ocean. The branches of my fingers, the roots of my feet, could grip nothing, but now, God, they have found ground." Even the elements celebrate this rebirth: the sun appears in all its bright glory as Makak is freed from prison, the symbolic prison of mental enslavement.[70]

Author as Text and Character

It is impossible not to notice in Walcott's several narrations of his experience in developing an aesthetics proper to the Caribbean a struggle similar to Makak's. Just like the latter's, three stages of the journey can be identified: European, African, and West Indian. As a fact of his Western education, Walcott starts out, as he says, a natural assimilator of the "great" tradition of English literature. The literature of the "mother country" provided the challenge and the inspiration to fill the literary desert named Caribbean and to create a viable extension of those "masterpieces" he considers as universal classics. Walcott's earliest play, *Flight and Sanctuary*, written in 1946 when he was sixteen years old, best represents this phase. The play was written entirely in verse, and not typically West Indian in setting, characterization, language, and story line.[71] Finally convinced of his Englishness, the young dramatist knocked at the doors of the Great Tradition but was rudely turned back, by Mr. F. R. Leavis, of course. Walcott had seen himself as "legitimately prolonging the mighty line of Marlowe," but he was told in no uncertain terms that nowhere beyond the Atlantic had Marlowe any legitimate heir.

Walcott retraced his steps and gradually "began" his "African phase," shown in the bitter engagement with those he calls the pastoralists and revivalists, the advocates of history as time. Walcott and Makak never found a comfortable position in this stage. Outside of an escapist dance of self-deception, any unproblematic look to Africa for cultural and spiritual succour was virtually impossible. The dramatist writes: "If one went in search of the African experience, carrying the luggage of a few phrases and a crude map, where would it end? We had no language for the bush and there was a conflicting grammar in the pace of our movement." In dramatic and theatrical terms, this quandary is demonstrated concretely when Walcott directed one of Soyinka's plays with his company, the Trinidad Theatre Workshop:

> When we produced Soyinka's masterpiece *The Road*, one truth, like the murderous headlamps of his mammy-wagons, transfixed us, and this was that our frenzy goes by another name, that it is this naming, ironically enough, which weakens our effort at being African. We tried in the words of his Professor, to "hold the god captive," but for us, Afro-Christians, the naming of the god estranged him. Ogun was an exotic for us, not a force. We could pretend to enter his power but he would never possess us, for our invocations were not prayer but devices . . . only blasphemy was left.[72]

The "dilemma" is movingly expressed, but it is not clear why Walcott, a West Indian, would expect to be able to "hold the god captive" exactly as a Yoruba would. Why quest for the absolute, an unproblematic translation? This dilemma is alien to the many neo-African religions in the New World.

Finally, author and character had to reject the exclusivist African dream. "West Indies exists," the author assured himself, "but we must find it. It's a mosaic, you might say."[73] The mosaic is the vast inlay of diverse cultures. For Walcott, therefore, an authentic cultural identity for the Caribbean cannot be forged outside the parameters of conscious assemblage: a mulatto style to confront West Indian schizophrenia, a "bastard" aesthetics for a "bastard" reality.

It appears that the text too is on a mission similar to that of author and character. The text is intricately structured upon an elaborate system of contrary pulls, hence the *agonistic* tension between such elements as inside and outside theatrical spaces; seriousness and horseplay or buffoonery; animal and human characters; poetry and prose passages; stylistic complexity and popular theme; dream and wakefulness or reality; Creole and Queen's English; the material poverty of the setting and the intellectual richness of the dramatic discourse; history and fable; and local earthy folk forms and extensive, sophisticated and foreign high-brow allusions and borrowings. I will briefly examine those with an especially close bearing on Walcott's poetics.

Coherent Deformation and Its Context

Creole and English. When Walcott penned the famous lines "how choose / Between this Africa and the English tongue I love?" in "A Far Cry from Africa," the dominant response was predictable: here comes the red nigger with an "identity crisis."[74] Walcott admits to a certain anguish on the question of language choice in the Caribbean, but he insists it is partly this "that enriches our literature and our theatre":

> I'm not denying that there was this anguish of choice. It's dramatised by the fact that, here I am, a black man, writing, using a language which is beautiful, to describe a situation which is perpetuated by the people who are the authors of that language.[75]

Unlike many other West Indian writers, Walcott boasts a triple linguistic heritage: French Creole, English Creole, and English. French Creole is the predominant language of St. Lucia but English is the language of government, the result of a legendary drama of thirteen flag changes in which the main actors were the French and the British.[76] And then the Creole of Trinidad, Walcott's second home, is English-based.

One immediate observation on examining the Walcott *dramatic* corpus is that he seems to have found Creole virtually indispensable, though he laments all the time the difficulties in its creative appropriation.[77] For instance, there is the problem of intelligibility across national borders. "Every island in the Caribbean has its own syntactical structure," explains Walcott; "a Trinidadian is not going to understand a Jamaican the first time off." This is apart from the common fact that no English Creole has a standardized orthography. Walcott's solution has been to theatrically dilute Creole forms to arrive at a median, "using syntaxes from various dialects" to articulate a "form that would be comprehensible not only to all the people in the region that speak in that tone of voice, but to people everywhere" with a knowledge of the basic component of the particular Creole (largely English and some French, in Walcott).[78] Thus in *Dream*, we have vast linguistic variations such as the following:

Let us go on, *compere*. These niggers too tired to believe anything again. Remember, is you all self that is your own enemy.

I was a king among shadows. Either the shadows were real, and I was no king, or it is my own kingliness that created the shadows. Either way, I am lonely, lost, an old man again. No more. I wanted to leave this world.

Yes. *Oui*. Hobain. Sur Morne Macaque, *charbonnier*. I does burn and sell coals. And my friend . . . well, he is dead. . . . Sixty-five years I have. And they calling me Makak, for my face, you see? Is as I so ugly.[79]

For the question "Creole or English?" fostered by the political turmoil of the 1960s and 1970s, Walcott, as we have seen, has little regard. "One works within a language," he says, arguing that it is "a futile, stupid and political exercise to insist on 'creating' language":[80]

Pastoralists of the African revival should know that what is needed is not new names for old things, or old names for old things, but the faith of using the old names anew, so that mongrel as I am, something prickles in me when I see the word Ashanti as with the word Warwickshire, both separately intimating my grandfathers' roots, both baptising this neither proud nor ashamed bastard, this hybrid, this West Indian.[81]

This then is the linguistic form the West Indian writer must forge. "The dialect of the tribe" must be purified and in this task, English, the language "learnt by imitation," is indispensable. Creole must be apprenticed to English, but the "feelings" must be local, must "have their roots in [the writer's] own earth."[82] The last statement, ironically, best defines the practice of many of those whom Walcott attacked, for English Creole is barely intelligible outside the parameters of English.

Poor theater and affluent discourse. Except, perhaps, in the "Apotheosis," where an atmosphere of material splendor and opulence is created, *Dream* virtually operates on the barest material theatrical accoutrements. Perhaps little is to be expected from a setting that is a cell, a country road, a forest, a hut, or a village market. And what is more, the stage direction pays only minimal attention to the materiality of the scenes. The "style should be spare, essential as the details of a dream," the playwright insists.[83] Borrowing Grotowski's phrase, this instruction intimates the playwright's agenda for "The Poor Theatre," which he asserts

has never been more applicable to our own situation here in the islands, both as economics and as chord of compassion for theatre artists, playwrights, actors, musicians and craftsmen continue to labour under embittering conditions. Our culture needs preservation and resurgence, our crises need an epiphany, a spiritual definition, and an art that can emerge from our poverty, creating its own elation.[84]

Hence the emphasis in the play is on the actor's body as the chief theatrical resource, its capability to switch roles and create spectacle. The quest is "for a staging that would be easy under some backyard tree as with the devices of the rich theatre. The wealth of this bareness is in the nakedness of spirit, in the pliant and magical metamorphoses of the body."[85] It is upon this material barrenness of the play's setting—"A West Indian Island"—that Walcott erects a dramatic discourse that has all the trappings of affluence: it is poetic, highly textured, and theatrically and intellectually challenging; and its extensive canvas bears marks of disparate philosophical, theological, and artistic systems and traditions from several parts of the world. I will touch upon this extensive reach again.

History and fable. The play as fable is evident not only in its self-advertisement as a dream but also in the assignation of animal names to the characters, the symbolic use of masks, the journey to Africa of the mind, and the corporal's consistent theatrical overkill and rhetorical excess. History, however, retains an equally strong pull, and the most obvious evidence of this is the effusion of "definite references"[86] that threaten to drown the play: Africa, Lion of Judah, Esau, Ashanti, Moses, Sharpeville, Marlowe, Ibo, Pushkin, and so on. Besides, the play can hardly deny that it could stand, symbolically, as a history of the Afro-Caribbean. We know, of course, Walcott's preference for history as fable or myth rather than as time. But the play, unlike the author's critical pronouncements, resolutely refuses to absolutize the distinction. Here, history does not in any way exclude the fabulous, or vice versa; the historical nurtures and authenticates the fabulous while the fabulous competently exorcizes the (onerous burden of the) historical.

Indigenous base and foreign highbrow allusions. Built upon the play's rich local fabric—the characters, songs, dances, humor, and Creole—is an edifice of extensive, intellectually disparate allusions. We have the Strindbergian trait of the "Note on Production"; Brechtian estranging effects such as Lestrade's direct addresses to the audience; the author's indebtedness to the Kabuki theater; and appropriations from Lorca, Büchner, Cervantes, and Christian theology (the last is the most pervasive: Makak as a Christ figure, Tigre and Souris as the two thieves, and so on). This is perhaps a demonstration of Walcott's rejection of what he sees as "stylistic careerism": the wholesale and uncritical adoption of models from any or one of the cultural tributaries that feed the Caribbean. The ideal, he says and *Dream* shows, is to be a "traitor," "the mulatto of style," free to borrow not only from Aeschylus, Shakespeare, Brecht, and Soyinka but also from ancient Japanese and Chinese theaters, contemporary American opera, and West Indian carnival and folktale. "I am a kind of split writer," Walcott confesses: "The mimetic, the narrative, and dance element is strong on one side, and the literary, the classical tradition is strong on the other."[87]

Walcott is certainly an accomplished craftsman who is able to turn challenge into great creative resource. In making sense of the text's creative plunder of disparate, both canonical and noncanonical philosophical systems and artistic traditions, I suggest we identify its organizing principle as *coherent deformation*. There is the extensive parody of the established law by none other than its officer, a parody that subtly but accurately reveals the law's alpine weight on the dominated. Makak is black, poor, and "ugly as sin" but he is the Christ, complete with the healing power and the two thieves (especially in the cell scenes). He is also Moses, coming down from the mountain with good tidings. Or one might look in another direction and see him as Don Quixote, and Moustique as his Sancho Panza, set to exorcise the age-old oppression of their kind.[88] But neither Makak-Moustique nor their goal could be said to be exactly quixotic. And what could this speech by Lestrade signify if not that *that* famous, lofty declaration still remains little more than mere rhetoric for some category of people?

> Your right? Listen, nigger! according to this world you have the inalienable right to life, liberty, and three green figs. No more, maybe less. You can do what you want with your life, you can hardly call this liberty, and as for the pursuit of happiness, you never hear the expression, give a nigger an inch and he'll take a mile?[89]

"Coherent deformation," Allen Weiss explains, "is the process whereby the form, the facticity of the world is shattered by praxis, with the result that a new meaning ensues. The 'coherency' maintains the equivalence between signs; the 'deformation' achieves the differences between signs." Weiss quotes Merleau-Ponty: "It is just this 'coherent deformation' of available significations which arranges them in a new sense and takes not only the hearers but the speaking subject as well through a decisive step."[90] Coherent deformation is subversive in its undermining the stability of signs, the destruction of the established order of meaning and classification, and the suggestion of the possibility of a realignment of forces. It is this coherent deformation, this mulatto style, that is the nodal point of Walcott's dramatic articulatory practice. In conscious and controlled eclecticism, the dramatist's work suggests, lies an enabling Caribbean cultural identity.

It is within this space that the theater of Walcott speaks. Perhaps no intervention is more appropriate for the Caribbean, but only as a means that must constantly interrogate its own blindnesses. For there is a certain Walcottian trust in the canonical and the established that borders on utter reaction and closure of history. This has made many of his critics argue that his so-called mulatto aesthetics is in fact a mask to hide his crippling awe for, and self-immolation at the altar of, the Western tradition. As if to justify this, Walcott's writings are littered, as we have seen, with shallow and scabrous attacks on all propositions of a black aesthetic in which black aesthetic equals revenge aesthetic equals escape aesthetic equals low art equals the killing of art equals politics. What Walcott forgets is that there is no such thing as hybridity qua hybridity, that is, hybridity or mulatto aesthetics that is unanchored to a particular source.[91] The source and sponsor in his own case is, as we have seen, the Western tradition, and this is not necessarily a negative thing, but only with a self-conscious acknowledgment that it is only one tradition in many open to the Caribbean artist: the choice is not natural, self-evident, or automatic but thoroughly ideological.

Closely related to this is Walcott's universalist and aristocratic notion of form and literary greatness, as if greatness inheres in texts outside the entrenched and codified fantasies of those who read them, as if "classics" are eternal and created outside the discourse(s) of history, as if culture is static, as if identity is formed and fixed once and for all time. For him, it is not so much the rage of Caliban that is important as the beauty of his speech—as if one could separate the speech from what it utters, as if rage necessarily corrupts beauty. And what the Caribbean requires of its poets is "highest language," majestic tone and intense diction, rather than "predictable sentiment." Language is the empire, "and great poets its princes."[92] Thus Walcott's mulatto aesthetics depends greatly on his opposition between what I call *history as culture* (his "history as myth") and *history as politics* (his "history as time"). As if these are absolutes, he privileges the former and condemns the latter. It is not surprising then that to the innumerable neocolonial problems of the Caribbean world he writes so well of, his proposition is that "[t]he future of West Indian militancy lies in art."[93] Here lies a core expressive problematic in Walcott's performative practice: his constant recourse to a *culturalist* reading of the great encounter between Europe and Africa, between Euro-America and the Caribbean.

6

Ntozake Shange: The Vengeance of Difference, or The Gender of Black Cultural Identity

> To Terdiman's "no discourse is ever a monologue," we should add, the site of counter discourse is itself contested terrain.
>
> E. Frances White[1]

> Through the multiple voices that enunciate her complex subjectivity, the black woman writer not only speaks familiarly in the dicourse of the other(s), but as Other she is in contestorial dialogue with the hegemonic dominant and subdominant or . . . "ambiguously (non)hegemonic" discourses.
>
> Mae G. Henderson[2]

In the main, I locate the interventions of Wole Soyinka, Amiri Baraka, and Derek Walcott in the discourse of black anti-imperialist cultural identity, both in their dispersed accents and close affinities, at the juncture between the counterhegemonic Afrocentric and post-Afrocentric discourses. This is a terrain, as we have seen, of a promising dynamic—performative—conception of difference in general and cultural identity in particular. In the dramatists' theatrical practices if not always in their theoretical formulations, identity is conceived as open, an articulation, interculturally negotiable, and always in the making: a *process*.

But these dramatists, I suggest, have yet to interrogate deeply their roots in Afrocentric cultural nationalism and its characteristic expressive and fundamentalist propositions of difference. Soyinka remains suspicious of considerations of class (and by implication, other crucial kinds of) differences in the formulation of African cultural identity. Walcott would have Caribbean history as *culture* rather than as *politics*, as if the realm of the social admits of such a choice or distinction. And the force and energy of Baraka's vision and creative practice have always depended on a certain radical absolutism—but absolutism nonetheless—which is impatient with or distrustful of compromises, minute details, or fine intermeshings: bohemian–bourgeois, black–white, and proletariat–bourgeoisie. In his Marxist phase, Baraka is at his most sensitive to the myriad determinations of the social, but in large part only as they are subsumable to the great proletariat-bourgeoisie battle.

The recalcitrant expressiveness in the dramatists' practices can be traced to their appropriation of the very weapon that authorized their projects and the originary weapon of all black anticolonialist discourses: difference and its affirmation against Eurocentrism's definition of it as deviance. The affirmation of difference and its concomitant project of decolonization have proved truly liberating and a worthy cause against the aggressive global character of Western hegemony. It is, however, still the exception rather than the rule that difference is approached with all the complexity and subtlety it merits. Difference is hardly conceived as a double-edged weapon that not only cuts both ways but is also ceaselessly active. Hence the sword of difference is promptly sheathed when the interlocutor is no longer the Euro-American world but "ourselves." This peculiar arrest of difference has been insightfully read by many scholars as a "unanimist illusion"[3] of "deep horizontal comradeship."[4] It is as if the multiplex constitutive differences of the dominated cultures have little or no bearing on the great project of formulating a resistant cultural identity against Western imperialism. But difference is not to be cheaply repressed in the cultures we are dealing with, so "unequally divided along gender and class lines"[5] as they are.

Gender, the most obscured difference, has emerged of late to wreak deserved havoc on the anti-Eurocentric discourse of black cultural identity as constituted by our three dramatists, unequivocally pronouncing it as *masculinist*. I have attempted to capture—in spirit if not in letter—the ideologically sexist character of this occlusion by quoting in full a poem written by the reknowned Malawian male poet Felix Mthali to the distinguished Nigerian female poet and feminist critic 'Molara Ogundipe-Leslie. The title of the poem is "Letter to a Feminist Friend."

> I will not pretend
> to see the light
> in the rhythm of your paragraphs:
> illuminated pages
> need not contain
> any copy-rights
> on history
>
> My world has been raped,
> looted and squeezed
> by Europe and America
> and I have been scattered

over three continents
to please Europe and America

AND NOW
the women of Europe and America
after drinking and carousing
on my sweat
rise up to castigate and
castrate their menfolk
from the cushions of a world
I have built!

Why should they be allowed
to come between us?
You and I were slaves together
Rapes and lynchings—
the lash of the overseer
and the lust of the slave-owner
do your friends "in the movement"
understanding these things?

The wile of the coloniser,
the juggernaut of apartheid
the massacres of Sharpeville and Langa,
"interrogation" unto death
unreal inquests have
your friends seen these?
like the children of Soweto?

No, no, my sister, my love,
first things first!
Too many gangsters
still stalk this continent
too many pirates
too many looters
far too many
still stalk this land—
every inch of it should be sure
yet inch by inch
day by day we see it ceded
to forces beyond our control.

Where then do we sit
where build our tent
while sorting out
the faults between you and me?
Miracles still happen,
I agree,
and privilege and the underdog
can unite to undo privilege
but sister, not every yawning of the privileged
amounts to a sacrifice!

> When Africa
> at home and across the seas
> is truly free
> there will be time for me
> and time for you
> to share the cooking
> and change the nappies—
> till then,
> first things first![6]

It is impossible to miss the poet's meticulous construction of a hierarchy of oppression in which the one from "without," which impinges on both him and his feminist friend, is far more important than the one "within," in which *he* is a beneficiary and his friend a sufferer. And there are even strong gestures of doubt of the existence of any oppression within, between him and his friend, after all, "You and I were slaves together / uprooted and humiliated together" (note the repetition of the homogenizing cue, "together"). But the poet could just not risk not convincing his feminist friend, hence he does not, strategically, end with these gestures of doubts—apparently he himself knows that they are dishonest doubts and thus open to attack. He thus proposes a compromise by assuming the existence of internal oppression but erecting a *hierarchy* of resistance. The oppression from without is to be resisted first before attention is shifted to the one within. So while the poem constructs a resistant subjectivity against Euro-American imperialism now, it insists that "sorting out / the faults between you and me" will come at a later date, only "When Africa / at home and across the seas / is truly free." "The Promethean persona that endured slavery and the slave trade, colonialism, imperialism and neo-colonialism," Ogundipe-Leslie says with irony, "does not have time for women's rights yet."[7] The anticolonialist, anti-imperialist identity being fashioned could not possibly include everyone, especially not the oppressed of the oppressed whose interests are relegated to "later," the victims also of the "imperialism of patriarchy"[8] within, as bell hooks forbiddingly puts it.

The challenge of gender, as E. Frances White proposes in the first of the chapter's epigraphs, is that the site of the counterhegemonic discourses is itself contested terrain. This is part of the problematic suggested by the title of this chapter, "The Gender of Black Cultural Identity." The phrasing directs attention not only to the gendered character of black cultural identity as it is proposed by the dramatists, but also to the gender dimension to be faced in any constitution of such a project.[9] The gender of black cultural identity, as Soyinka, Baraka, and Walcott formulate it, is male, though presented as nongendered: "black" or "African," "African-American," "Caribbean." I will cite three notable challenges to this tradition. The Kamiriithu Community Education and Cultural Centre Theatre Group, before being hounded out of existence by the neocolonial Kenyan government, stressed in its practices the intricate relations between and among gender and class *and* the deadly competing interests of the masses of Kenyan people, the neocolonial national bourgeoisie, and metropolitan capital.[10] Engaged in a similar practice is the Sistren Theatre Collective in Jamaica. Sistren also has had to negotiate the peculiar relations of race and class in Jamaica as they impinge on the black woman; the near-institutionalization of the "baby-faada" system in which the aspirations of a large percentage of lower-class black women are crushed by the demands of too early motherhood, while involved males bear little or no legal responsibility; and the violence of American "deindustrialization" (back at home) in its aggressive exploitation—in foreign territories—of female (as cheap) labor and the creation of hate-filled gender-based competition in the working class.[11] And finally, in the context of mid-1970s black America, Ntozake Shange's choreopoem *for colored girls who have considered suicide / when the rainbow is enuf* literally precipitated a national debate on the place or placing of gender in theorizing black cultural identity.[12]

The three instances all retain the anti-Eurocentric thrust of Soyinka, Baraka and Walcott, but in ways that interrogate, extend, and re-vision their practices. In this circumstance, a productive critique of the three dramatists is best achieved by a detailed attention to an instance of the "new" practices: Ntozake Shange's.

Combat Breathing

> it's ours. alla ours. don't nobody own history/ cant nobody make
> ours but us
> my photographs are the contours of life unnoticed
> unrealized & suspect/ no buckwheat here
> no farina & topsy/ here we have the heat of our lives in our ordi-
> nariness we are most bizarre/
> prone to eccentricity/ even in our language . . .
>
> Ntozake Shange[13]

Shange's artistic practice shares with that of many African-American women the daring identification of what Cheryl A. Wall calls an "unwritten space" in African-American literary discourse, and the bold inscription in that space of an "Afro-American female self."[14] I borrow the preceding epigraph from the dramatist's characters Michael and Sean, in *a photograph*, as a remarkably close reading of the *phenomenon* of this literature: the bold rupture of the imprisoning walls of a dominated margin in which black women's lives have long been confined—"don't nobody own history"; the unapologetic assertion of difference—"most bizarre/ prone to eccentricity"; and the epistemic challenge of its representations, because they are of life previously "unnoticed/ unrealized and suspect," to conventional modes of seeing. "[H]ere we have the heat of our lives," Sean affirms, in a tone that recalls Hortense Spillers's when she writes of "the palpable and continuing urgency of black women writing themselves into history."[15]

Shange's drama decisively participates in the urgency. Her practice simultaneously critiques and democratizes the conjunctural space in which I locate Soyinka, Baraka, and Walcott. It is, at the same time, unrelenting in the common quest for an anti-imperialist identity. Shange's practice is able to "speak" simultaneously in so many "tongues" because of what Mae G. Henderson defines as "at once characteristic and suggestive about black women's writing": its "interlocutory, or dialogic character," borne out of an engagement with a profoundly heterogeneous space.[16] Thus it is that a task which appears insurmountable in the three dramatists—constructing a gender-informed cultural identity—is the point of departure for Shange's practice. This chapter's second epigraph explains the simultaneous engagement of this practice with the hegemonic Eurocentric discourse *and* the male-dominated Afrocentric counterdiscourses—in Henderson's perceptive term, the "ambiguously (non)hegemonic."

Shange, borrowing from Frantz Fanon on French colonialism in Algeria, describes the character of her intervention in the discourse of black cultural difference as "combat breathing":

> in everything i have ever written & everything i hope to write/ i have made use of what Frantz Fanon called "combat breath." although Fanon waz referring to francophone colonies, the schema he draws is sadly familiar: "there is no occupation of territory, on the other hand, and independence of persons on the other. It is the country as a whole, its history, its daily pulsation that are contested, disfigured, in the hope of final destruction. Under this condition, the individual's breathing is an observed, an occupied breathing. It is a combat breathing."[17]

"Combat breathing" is agonistic breathing. Harassed, pursued, and intimidated but nevertheless confounding all attempts to unravel the secrets of its resilience, combat breath is characteristically tactical. Neither are its contours carved in stone nor are its modulations predictable. A veritable weapon in the hands of the dominated against, in Shange's words, "the involuntary constrictions n amputations of their humanity,"[18] combat breath resists recuperation by the dominant by being a "hazard to definitions."[19] It confronts the oppressor as a "problem," "incomprehensible," utterly ambivalent and inaccessible.[20]

The brief piece in which Fanon writes of combat breath is included as an appendix to the essay "Algeria Unveiled," in his *A Dying Colonialism*. In examining the changing status of the *haik*, or veil, in the context of the Algerian revolution, the essay presents the dynamic character of the resistance of Algerian women to French colonialism. Originally worn in deference to the tradition of strict separation of the sexes, the veil was soon articulated as a mode of anticolonial resistance for the way it frustrates the colonizer's gaze and short-circuits *his* panoptic economy. During the anticolonial war, bombs, grenades, and explosives found functional residence under the veil. However, mutations in approach to the revolution later required an abandonment of the veil. The European city needed to be penetrated, but this could be done only by those who appeared to be European—a disguise that rendered the disguise of the veil obsolete. But when the colonial government decided to drag out Algerian women and symbolically unveil them "to the cries of '*Vive l'Algerie française!*,'" "spontaneously and without being told, the Algerian women who had long since dropped the veil once again donned the *haik*," denying legitimacy to the colonizer's discourse of *civilizing mission*. The Algerian women during the struggle thus constructed a "historic dynamism of the veil" in which the veil was "[r]emoved and reassumed again and again . . . manipulated, transformed into a technique of camouflage, into a means of struggle." In a situation of combat breathing, the veil was "stripped once and for all of its exclusively traditional dimension," profoundly altering relations between the sexes by opening it to questioning. The biforked struggle of the Algerian women in "breaking down the enemy system" and in "liquidating the old mystifications" within—a powerful performative thrust—is not unlike Shange's project of simultaneously challenging the hegemony of Western culture and interrogating the subdominant, male-centered discourse of black difference.[21]

Shange recalls in an interview a poetry reading session at which a man asked her why she never wrote about men. "It irked me," Shange reflects, "that someone would think that women were not an adequate subject. I really got much more involved with writing about women for that reason. I was determined that we were going to be viable and legitimate literary figures."[22] This is the determination Shange pitted against the blindness of the insights of the nationalist discourse of black self-refashioning. For while this discourse "exorcised a lot of demons" and "was a rite of passage" which "told us we could do anything we wanted,"[23] it is nevertheless regrettable "the flaw in the nationalists' dream": "they didn't treat women right."[24]

Trying to "treat women right" or make women "legitimate literary figures" obviously complicates the terms of the debate on black cultural identity, but it also specifically constitutes a great formal challenge to the black female dramatist. This is not because there is no recognizable tradition of African-American female dramatists to fall back upon for inspiration,[25] but because the demands of the moment are radically new horizons and previously unexplored and unconsidered domains. Besides, there is an additional burden for the female playwright committed to the dramaturgic appropriation of black performance forms. Cheryl Wall argues that women were "historically denied participation" in many of these forms, citing the example of speechifying, which, "whether in the pulpit or on the block, has been a mainly male prerogative."[26] And, of course, the usual and the biggest challenge of all: the overwhelming, unrelenting subjection of black America to the hegemonic Eurocentric theatrical norms, to the lure and reward of "artificial aesthetics":

> for too long now afro-americans in theater have been duped by the same artificial aesthetics that plague our white counterparts/ "the perfect play," as we know it to be/ a truly european framework for european psychology/ cannot function efficiently for those of us from this hemisphere.[27]

". . . those of *us* from this hemisphere"? Shange soon discovers that this phrase needs rephrasing. She does this in her essay "How I Moved Anna Fierling To The Southwest Territories, or, my personal victory over the armies of western civilization."[28] The essay was prompted by what she sees as the negative reactions of a white audience to the production of a Shakespeare play, *Coriolanus*, by a black and Latin troupe.

Shange queries the pervasive American rite of self-abasement at the altar of British culture, manifested in the expenditure of enormous resources "to recreate experiences that are not our own," meaning not American: "does a colonial relationship to a culture/ in this case Anglo-Saxon imperialism/ produce a symbiotic relationship or a parasitic one? if we perform the classics/ giving our culture some leeway in an adaptation/ which is the parasite?"[29] These questions are better interpreted as rhetorical, not because they are unanswerable but because their form and structure as questions are more useful to us than any answer they might yield. Shange the African-American decides momentarily to forget her specific hyphenatedness and assume the full American that she really is: "if *we* . . ."; ". . . *our* culture. . . ." But this is an obvious blind alley, for the peculiar hybrid character of America has condemned its constituent—especially, dominated—groups to a condition of perpetual hyphenation, refusing them even a momentary suture. When Shange comes to, only a searing *difference* stares her in the face. The very next question asks, "why aren't the talents & perspectives of contemporary third world artists touted in the same grand fashion successful revivals of dead white artists are?"[30] Joined with the previous two questions, the full force of Shange's deliberate, subversive "naïveté" comes into focus. She is simultaneously American and not-American. Thus her ". . . experiences that are not our own" rings with a cruel, ironic literality, for there are indeed Americans for whom the works of "dead white artists" recreate experiences that are *truly our own*, and for whom "Anglo-Saxon imperialism" is *not* that, and for whom whatever "third world" writers have to say would do little but recreate experiences that are *not our own*. And there is an even bitterer addition: that there are many Americans who would proudly claim "dead white artists" but would also claim their experience is short-changed if their dead white artists are performed by nonwhite troupes. Learning difference appears to be a painful process, and Shange strategically reconstitutes her "we" away from an amorphous, unhyphenated America:

> i cd feel as i clapped & shouted during curtain calls that it waz only the black folks who were clapping & shouting. the white people in the audience seemed more amazed that the black people had understood Shapespeare/ or that it waz possible to enjoy an entire evening when not a nigger danced/ let alone sang. I waz filled with an uncomfortable blend of excitement abt the actors, disdain for the audience, anger that we had to do this at all, & satisfaction that we had. i went to have a drink, to think, to talk to somebody abt the mess of my fortune to be born black & English- speaking.[31]

Shange as "black and English-speaking" is simultaneously African and American, and with a legitimate claim to the English literary and dramatic tradition. Her unspoken challenge in the quotation is how to recognize all her traditions without blurring their differences and the character of the relations between and among them, not unlike Alice Walker's move in her well-known essay "In Search of Our Mother's Gardens."[32] Shange can claim Shakespeare, but as her essay shows, the challenge is to know when subjectivity is obviously subjection. The white audience in Shange's narrative ignores the complex performative articulation involved in such negotiations in their amazement that blacks could understand Shakespeare.

Central to Shange's combat aesthetics is an affirmation of the very elements for which America has historically constructed the black as a minstrel and natural entertainer: music and dance. Shange's thrust is a reevaluation of this "peculiar" difference, appropriating it as a source of strength against the grain of its dominant reading as a sign of intellectual deficiency. The accent of this strength is unmistakably individual and collective. Shange, who studied dance with Raymond Sawyer, Ed Mock, and Halifu, writes that it is only with dance that "I discovered my body more intimately than I had imagined possible. With the acceptance of the ethnicity of my thighs & backside, came a clearer understanding of my voice as a woman & a poet."[33] Music and dance, as forms in perpetual motion—"pure solution"—have the potential to transgress institutionalized limits and open up zones of possibilities which, even if not realized or realizable, are capable of luring the dominated into the subversive realm of dream. "The freedom to move in space, to demand of my own sweat a perfection that could continually be approached, though never known, waz poem to me, my body & mind ellipsing, probably for the first time in my life."[34] It is through the idioms of music and dance that the "ladies" in *for colored girls* express and confront their fears, disappointments, frustrations, transforming them to hopes and determinations: music and dance as therapy. The lady in orange says:

        I dont wanna write
        in english or spanish
        i wanna sing   make you dance
        like the bata   dance   scream
        twitch hips with me cuz
        i done forget all abt words
        aint got no definition
        i wanna whirl
        with you[35]

When Dahlis, the young singer/dancer in *spell #7*, begins "a lyrical but pained solo," what her voice and movement accent is determined resistance:

            we will stand here
                . . .
            this is our space
            we are not movin[36]

In the hands of the dominated but rebellious poet, the slippery, unfixable forms, music and dance, become instruments for breaking down and reaching beyond the claustrophobic dominated space. For the *African-(/)American (/) woman*, reconstituting the tortuous history of the three fragments is no less one of such liberating moves:

> dance as explicated by Raymond Sawyer & Ed Mock insisted that everything African, everything halfway colloquial, a grimace, a strut, an arched back over a yawn, waz mine. I moved what waz my unconscious knowledge of being in a colored woman's body to my known everydayness. The depth of my past was made tangible to me in Sawyer's *Ananse*, a dance exploring the Diaspora to contemporary Senegalese music, pulling ancient trampled spirits out of present tense Afro-American Dance.[37]

For Shange then, song and dance are the African American's potent media for remembering the unsayable:

> what does it mean that blk folks cd sing n dance?
> why so we say that so much/ we dont know what we mean/
> i saw what that means/ good gal/ did i see/ like i cda
> walked on the water myself/ i cda clothed the naked & fed
> the hungry/ with what dance i saw tonite/ i don't mean dance
> i mean a closer walk with thee/ a race thru swamps that fall
> off in space/ i mean i saw the black people move the ground
> & set stars beneath they feet/ so what's this mean that
> black folks cd dance/ well/ . . .
> it dont mean we got rhythm/ it dont mean the slop or the hully
>   gully
> or this dance in houston callt "the white boy"/ it don't mean just
> what we do all the time/ it's how we remember what cannot be
>   said/
> that's why the white folks say it aint got no form/ what was the
>   form

of slavery/ what was the form of jim crow/ & how wd they
know . . . [38]

In Shange's theater, music and dance are not conceived as ornamental
elements added on to enrich the drama but as the very constitutive fabric
of the performance, setting and upsetting the pace, underscoring and
contradicting the mood, creating and destroying moods, showing the
form (the way it is) and the formlessness (the way it is is contingent,
alterable) of history.

What Shange, who regularly collaborates with musicians and dancers,
writes of her *spell #7* is applicable to most of her other pieces: that "music
functions as another character." "[w]e are an interdisciplinary culture,"
she says, and "we must use everything we've got":

> in the first version of BOOGIE WOOGIE LANDSCAPES i presented myself with the
> problem of having my person/ body, voice & language/ address the space as
> if i were a band/ a dance company & a theater group all at once. cuz a poet
> shd do that/ create an emotional environment/ felt architecture.[39]

And if the text is read rather than seen in performance, Shange makes
sure that the emphasis on dance is not missed. Explaining her anticon-
ventional punctuation and orthography and their inspirational sources in
the early Baraka and in Ishmael Reed, Shange tells of her fascination with
"the idea that letters dance" on the page, and the political and ideological
need that this could serve in "visual stimulation, so that reading becomes
not just a passive act and more than an intellectual activity, but demands
rigorous participation."[40]

As a poet who considers her "fortune" to be born black and English-
speaking a "mess," Shange demonstrates a problematic attitude to the
language similar to what we encounter in Soyinka, Baraka, and Walcott.
Fashioning a new self in the context of combat breathing certainly demands a reassessment of received tools. This is even more urgent in a
situation where the function English has been made to perform best is
the construction of a racist consensus and the legitimation of drudgery
and routine: "the straightjacket that the english language slips over the
minds of all americans." Accused by a reviewer of distorting and destroying the English language with her "verbal gymnastics," Shange unequivocally pleads guilty:

> i cant count the number of times i have viscerally wanted to attack deform n
> maim the language that i waz taught to hate myself in/ the language that
> perpetuates the notions that cause pain to every black child as he/she learns to
> speak of the world & the "self." yes/ being an afro-american writer is some-
> thing to be self- conscious abt/ & yes/ in order to think n communicate the
> thoughts n feelings i want to think n communicate/ i haveta fix my tools to
> my needs/ i have to take it apart to the bone/ so that the maligancies/ fall
> away/ leaving us space to literally create our own image.[41]

If it appears that Shange overstates her case, I think it is because of a peculiar bind in which she finds herself: she deforms English in order to be able to express herself. She is promptly arraigned for distorting the language, but she must defend herself in the same language, English, she had to distort in the first place to be able to say anything.

This kind of bind, not generally unfamiliar to dominated groups, closely approximates what Jean-François Lyotard calls the *différend*, "the case wherein the plantiff is divested of the means to argue and becomes for that reason a victim." If Shange cannot express or defend herself except in distorted English, then, of course, what better evidence can one have that she is guilty of distorting English? "A case of différend between two parties," says Lyotard, "takes place when the 'regulation' of the conflict that opposes them is done in the idiom of one of the parties while the wrong suffered by the other is not signified in that idiom." When Shange implies that conventional English does not allow her *to think n communicate the thoughts n feelings i want to think n communicate*, she testifies that in the différend, "something 'asks' to be put into phrases, and suffers from the wrong of not being able to be put into phrases right away" due to the inadequacy of the existing idiom for the victim. But this bind can be exploded and, toward this end, Shange says *i haveta fix my tools*. This is precisely Lyotard's suggestion, that the victim claim the right to "institute idioms which do not yet exist":

> To give the différend its due is to institute new addressees, new addressors, new significations, and new referents in order for the wrong to find an expression and for the plaintiff to cease being a victim. This requires new rules for the formation and linking of phrases. No one doubts that language is capable of admitting these new phrase families or new genres of discourse. Every wrong ought to be able to be put into phrases. A new competence (or "prudence") must be found.[42]

The "verbal gymnastics" is Shange's instituted new idiom against the "malignancies." It is a kind of counterorthography in which capitalization or the capital letter, the *central* exclusive marker of certain privileges, is the first victim. Capital letters, Shange says, are "boring to me."[43] What we have is a relegation of hierarchy, a *democratic* interaction of "lowercase"—as they are called—letters. Punctuation, the obsession of discursive rationalism in its bid to have everything under control, is pared down to a minimum. Of the ubiquitous, eccentric, exasperating virgules, I cite Houston A. Baker:

> Virgules, which are traditionally employed to separate alternatives such as *either/or*, are deployed to *summon* alternatives and to avoid closure. Rather than duality, Shange creates a plenitude of options. She produces a fluidity akin to a jazz solo. Her statement riffs on (without disconnecting itself from) the orchestrations of a standard grammar. To take apart the symbolic order "to the bone," is to riff within it and signify on it until it yields a signal image, creating aesthetic space.[44]

Like the virgules that create "a plenitude of options," music and dance, also important features of Shange's aesthetic space, are constitutively enemies of the totalizing perspective. They exist as *motion* and our appreciation of them does not depend on, in fact discourages, our having a complete grasp of their flow. We absorb them only as dispersed fragments that our perceptual apparatuses have collared and made available for contemplation.

This subversion of the transcendental vision appears to be an important principle informing Shange's dramaturgy. Her preference is generally for multiple protagonists and stories. Her stories are stitched together in no necessary particular order, and they remain as individual episodes whose status within the whole is unstable and contingent. "[T]he selection of poems chang[ed]," Shange writes of *for colored girls*, "dependent upon our audience & our mood."[45] In fact many of the "episodes" are written differently as individual poems, "collected" for the needs of performance or publication.[46] Inevitably, the narrative voices are also multiple, with the first-person voice vying with the distanced reportorial one. Sometimes, the latter's narrative authority is further split, between a narrating-saying voice and a demonstrating-acting body. Most of *spell #7* is constructed this way. Besides, the status of the performers, especially in *for colored girls*, is never stable, intermittently shifting identities as performer or as character in the numerous dramatized stories or pieces-within-piece. The improvisational mode is privileged, not only in terms of performers' actions and movements (stage direction is spare) but also in terms of thought and understanding (the broken sentences and fragmentary phrases). "I can't let you get away with thinking you know what I mean," Shange writes, "After all, I didn't mean whatever you can just ignore. I mean what you have to struggle with. . . ."[47] The route to meaning is strewn with hazards—disjunctions, disruptions, contradictions, juxtapositions—that structure her works.

But if Shange's is the dramaturgy of pastiche or collage, we must emphasize that it is not aimless or unanchored, produced as it is in the context of combat breathing. There is a deliberate orchestration, articulation, in the service of a particular politics, a politics committed to the challenge of what Shange describes as "the primacy of the dollar,"[48] and the myopia of the male-dominated counterhegemonic discourse of black cultural identity in not recognizing "black" as an articulated catachresis of healthy, constitutive differences including and especially gender. Shange's controversial choreographed poetry, or "choreopoem," *for colored girls*, is a remarkable instance of this combat performative articulation.

"A Layin on of Hands"

sing a black girl's song

. . .

sing the song of her possibilities

Shange[49]

Writing in the feminine. And on a colored sky. How do you in-
scribe difference without bursting into a series of euphoric narcissistic accounts of yourself and your own kind? Without indulging in a
marketable romanticism or in a naive whining about your condition? In other words, how do you forget without annihilating? Between the twin chasms of navel-gazing and navel- erasing, the
ground is narrow and slippery. None of us can pride . . . ourselves
on being sure-footed there.

Trin T. Minh-ha[50]

What unites the two epigraphs to this section is a contemplation of the
demands of inscribing female difference. Trin T. Minh-ha delineates a
dilemma which *for colored girls* boldly confronts. As a text that sets out
to right/write an erasure and burst a "conspiracy of silence"[51] (by singing "the song of her possibilities"), the danger of "euphoric narcissism," of "navel-gazing," is great indeed. But it *eloquently*, like many
other writings by black women, refuses to be crippled by the fear of this
danger. Forgetting or annihilation is out of the question for it, and it
celebrates without whining, without getting drowned in the sea of its
own mirror. It is able to do this because of the terrain it proposes and
occupies: a ground of unrelenting vigilance defined by Minh-ha as "narrow and slippery." The text accepts the stressful character of this performative turf and converts it into strength, for nothing else constitutes
a combat space.

for colored girls, Shange says in a way that gives voice to the individual
in the collective and the collective in the individual, presents "the words
of a young black girl's growing up, her triumphs & errors, our struggle
to become all that is forbidden by our environment, all that is forfeited
by our gender, all that we have forgotten."[52] The struggle is presented
in a vast tableau in which seven colored women, named after the colors
of the rainbow, detail the desperate and oppressive situations they have
gone through, sing requiems for innumerable instances of failed resistance, document their depths of despair, and galvanize to struggle for a
hopeful horizon. In the text's episodic, polyphonous structure, there appears to be a movement which is pursued with determination: the movement toward a triumph over the represented inequities—"she's been
dead for so long," so "sing the song of her life" and "let her be
born."[53] The progress of this movement, however, is not linear. There
is no evolutionary determinism. Just like social processes, the movement
is broken, discontinuous, momentarily lost sight of, mourned, and re-
connected again. Perhaps the status of the twenty poems constituting
the piece as individual constructs, distinct variations on a similar topic,
also contributes to this free, lose structure.

The opening poem, titled "dark phrases," is unique. It is not only autonomous but also structurally "mimics" or anticipates the whole of

which it happens to be a part. Narrated mainly by the lady in brown, the poem begins with "[h]arsh music" and "postures of distress" of the other women. This context is perhaps only too appropriate, for what is at issue is plucked life, arrested growth, fragmented existence:

> dark phrases of womanhood
> of never havin been a girl
> half-notes scattered
> without rhythm/ no tune
> distraught laughter fallin
> over a black girl's shoulder
> it's funny/ it's hysterical
> the melody-less-ness of her dance
> don't tell nobody don't tell a soul
> she's dancin on beer cans & shingles[54]

What we have here is a catalogue of pains—"half-notes," "distraught laughter"—attending black womanhood. Valiant individual attempts at alleviation most often end in failure, "interrupted solos" and "unseen performances." "[A]re we ghouls?," "children of horror?," the lady asks with rhetorical exasperation. The exasperation leads to silence as solution: "don't tell anybody don't tell a soul." The real problem, though, is not whether the black girl should or should not tell of her pains but that she *cannot* tell in her "distraught" circumstances, given the characteristic invisibility and inexpressibility of pain, as Elaine Scarry shows in *The Body in Pain*.[55] Though Scarry is not writing specifically about black women's pains, I find her observations relevant:

> Vaguely alarming yet unreal, laden with consequence yet evaporating before the mind because not available to sensory confirmation, unseeable classes of objects such as subterranean plates, Seyfert galaxies, and the pains occurring in other people's bodies flicker before the mind, then disappear.[56]

The inexpressibility of pain is an existential plight faced by black womanhood in Shange's text. The plight is underscored when all we get for the black woman's pains is the "inarticulate pre-language" of rhythmless tunes, "distraught laughter," and "hysterical" babbles:

> i can't hear anythin
> but maddening screams
> & the soft strains of death[57]

Pain "does not simply resist language," Scarry writes, "but actively destroys it, bringing about an immediate reversion to a state anterior to language, to the sounds and cries a human being makes before language is learned."[58] Pain lacks "referential content," yet as Scarry has demonstrated, expressing pain is the prelude to, and a condition for the task of ending it, for "the relative ease or difficulty with which any given phenomenon can be *verbally represented* also influences the ease or difficulty with which that phenomenon comes to be *politically represented*."⁵⁹

The enormous political implications of the inexpressibility of pain demand the invention of all kinds of avenues to bring pain into the realm
of language. "[D]on't tell nobody don't tell a soul" would not just do:
it is fully complicit with the pain-ful order. The poem/lady in brown
seems to realize this and changes tone. From a choking concatenation of
black women's pains and expressions of horror, the poem begins a calm,
methodical and determined attempt to will into existence a way of articulating the pains: artistic creativity–song:

> somebody/ anybody
> sing a black girl's song
> bring her out
> to know herself
> . . .
>
> sing her rhythms
> carin/ struggle/ hard times
> sing her song of life
> she's been dead so long
> she doesn't know the sound
> of her own voice
> her infinite beauty
> . . .
>
> sing the song of her possibilities
> . . .
>
> let her be born⁶⁰

Interestingly, Scarry arrives at a similar conclusion: art as one avenue in
which pain begins to enter the realm of shared discourse.⁶¹ The poem
ends in a lighter, hopeful mood as the ladies sing and dance to children's
tunes, appropriately after distancing themselves from the transcendentalist
"centralizing and inclusive" space of cities and metropolises.⁶²

This then is the movement of the poem "dark phrases": the "unmaking," in Scarry's term, of black womanhood, the pains attendant on the
subjected status of the black woman, and gradually an exploration and
discovery of the ways and means for self-(re)fashioning, for the "making"
of collective and individual selves. This is also the movement of the text
as a whole. Reflected in this structural pattern is the political project the
text sets for itself: "making" the black woman from and against her existing oppressed and degraded—"unmade"—condition. The poems "latent rapists," in which the slap Baraka's Black Man gives the Black
Woman in *Madheart* is brilliantly signified upon, "abortion cycle #1,"
and "no assistance" are moving testimonies to the unmaking of black
womanhood by "these men friends of ours" and their patriarchal hegemony. Of the male crimes represented in the text—rape, brutality, hypocrisy, insensitivity, irresponsibility, the construction of pregnancy and
abortion as exclusively women's problems—the women lament that, as
always, "we are left with the scars."⁶³

Ironically, and perhaps to make the narrative of unmaking more poignant, it is preceded by "graduation nite" and "now i love somebody more than," poems comparatively brighter and more animated in tone, projecting some hopeful adult future for the black woman. The graduating girl, for instance, tells us how "wonderful" her sexual initiation was; she did not *lose* her virginity but "*gave* it up" and the experience is so marvelous she "just cdnt stop grinnin." But this attempt to make oneself, to appropriate one's experience and therefore take grip of the world, is promptly undermined by the grave risks and dangers made so chillingly real by the poems "latent rapists" and "abortion cycle #1": the pain and humiliation of rape, unwanted pregnancy, and the psychological stress of abortion.

In spite of this, Shange's women do not shy away from making themselves. They are usually undaunted, even when faced with obvious defeat. Sechita, the dancer in Natchez, is not unaware of how her corporeality has been mapped by the dominant racist discourse on beauty but her way of "resistance" is precisely to confirm rather than challenge this discourse:

> the broken mirror she used to decorate her face/ made her forehead tilt backwards/ her cheeks appear sunken/ her sassy chin only large enuf/ to keep her full lower lip/ from growin into her neck/ sechita/ had learned to make allowances for the distortions.[64]

Of course, in spite of her ennobling history, "sechita/ goddess/ of love/ egypt/ 2nd millennium," she remains frozen within a space defined by the racist, dominant male gaze and its philistinic and prurient tastes: "sechita's legs slashed furiously thru the cracker nite/ & gold pieces hitting the makeshift stage/ her thighs/ they were aiming coins tween her thighs."[65]

In the poem "one," the woman in sequins and rhinestones is more or less another Sechita:

> she glittered in heat
> & seemed to be looking for rides
> when she waznt & absolutely
> eyed every man who waznt lame white or
> nodding out
> she let her thigh slip from her skirt
> crossing the street
> she slowed to be examined.[66]

Demonstrating a superb grasp of the contours of femininity and masculinity as dictated by her gendered society, she flaunts this knowledge back in society's face not necessarily by questioning but by performing her assigned role to the hilt. She is "a deliberate coquette" "who never did without" "what she wanted," and her undying want is "to be unforgettable," "a memory," "a wound," to "every man" "arrogant enough to want her." So she dresses and walks in the most seductive manner, attracting a man to her house for a full night's enjoyment. It is all, however, an impersonal transaction. She wakes up very early in the morning and drives the man away, then cries herself to sleep.[67] The acts of Sechita and the woman in rhinestones are the "interrupted solos" of self-making.

To underscore the overwhelming character of the destructive forces of unmaking, the next poem, "i used to live in the world," is a garish portrait of Harlem as an inhuman, stifling space for the black woman. Harlem is a "stagnant" "grey filth" full of "shit & broken lil whiskey bottles" "left to make me bleed." There is also human decay and danger as well: "ol men's bodies," "women hanging outta windows" "like ol silk stockings," "bad smells," and the ubiquitous danger of rape, mugging, or murder:

> praying wont no young man
> think i'm pretty in a dark mornin
> wdnt be good
> not good at all
> to meet a tall short black brown young man
> fulla his
> power
> in the dark

The black male–female relationship shown here violently undermines the black male–female solidarity in struggle so infectiously portrayed earlier in the poem "toussaint."[68] Harlem, the lady in blue says, is a place anathema or unconducive to being "a woman in the world," for it is little more than "six blocks of cruelty" "piled up on itself." The picture is bleak, but it is in this poem that a decisively different strategy of making, of resistance, is introduced. Another woman gives assistance to the woman being accosted and harassed by a man:

> never mind sister
> dont pay him no mind
> go go go go go go sister
> do yr thing
> never mind

Unlike the individualist "rebellions"—interrupted solos, unseen performances—of Sechita and the rhinestones woman, a gesture of collective solidarity surfaces here.[69]

The succeeding poems such as "pyramid" and the "no more love poems" series build on this sisterly solidarity and rejection of oppression. A major part of this task is the decision of the women to transform their pain into a political issue by individually and collectively verbalizing it publicly. The lady in orange sings "a requiem for myself," her former self that had suffered too long in silence, vowing now never again "to avoid my own face wet with my tears." The lady in purple asserts that

she is "no longer symmetrical & impervious to pain," so she will henceforth "lay open" all "those scars i had hidden wit smiles & good fuck-
ing." And each of the women says apologies from her man will no longer
keep her quiet; instead, as the lady in blue says, "I will raise my voice"
and "tell all yr secrets bout yrself to yr face," "loud."[70] This is a long
call from the black girl's "don't tell a soul." What the women commence
here is similar to what Deborah McDowell perceptively describes as present in many black women's writings, the "deromanticization" of the
"family romance": the myth of a homogeneous black "community" in
which men sit in kingly control, the "story of the Black Family cum Black
Community headed by the Black Male who does battle with an oppressive
White world."[71] The end of this romance clears the space for the emergence of the black female subject. The women, in what bell hooks calls
a gesture of liberation, are "talking back."[72]

Shange gives us one final unforgettable image of threats to black female
self-making in the person of Beau Willie Brown and his relationship with
Crystal: a relationship governed by horror at the extent of man's capacity
for unmaking—rape, intimidation, beatings, and finally the paradigmatic
limit of unmaking, murder of their two children. Crystal, the black
woman, is the disconsolate victim.

The story of Beau and Crystal, however, is far more complicated. Their
ghetto existence, repeatedly described as a life and a world where "there
waz no air," frightfully evokes the Harlem of "i used to live in the
world." Crystal has been Beau's "girl since she waz thirteen/ when he
caught her on the stairway" and raped her ("on the stairway," note a
class difference in crime: unlike some of the middle-class black men
shown, Beau could not afford, in pursuance of his dastardly goal, the
conceit of "elaborate mediterranean dinners"). Not wanting formally to
accept responsibility for his actions, he bluntly refuses to marry her, in
spite of the resulting child, and then another one. This explosively uncertain relationship and existence is further exacerbated by more pressures
from the society at large. Just like many of his type on the negative side
of privilege, Beau is forced to do precisely what he knows he should never
even be caught dead doing: defending privilege, which is how he per-
ceives fighting in the Vietnam War. The war, he convinces himself, is
another American imperialist war from which ghetto blacks, as victims of
American imperialism, should at the very least stay clear:

> he kept tellin crystal/
> any niggah wanna kill vietnamese children
> more n stay home
> & raise his own is sicker than a rabid dog

Yet he had to go and fight in the war and, of course, live his own pro-
phetic formulation: "he came home crazy as hell," more than shell-
shocked, as people say, a permanent resident in the scary, paranoid,

twilight zone between sanity and insanity. All his efforts at self-rehabilitation fail woefully:

> he tried to get veterans benefits to go to school & they kept right on puttin him in remedial classes/ he cdnt read wortha damn/ so beau cused the teachers of holdin him back & got himself a gypsy cab to drive/ but his cab kept breakin down/ & the cops was always messin wit him/ plus not gettin much bread/

Defeated by the white-dominated world, Beau resorts to the last and only advantage allowed him by this world, the advantage of his sex. Through this, he, a lower-class black man and a slave of whites, could himself have a slave: a co-slave, the poor black woman, the lowest on the social hierarchy. He turns fully inward (from the white world) to claim his "rights." First he must have his manhood fully recognized *and* authorized; thus he declares his intention to marry Crystal and "have a family," so that he would be regarded as "a man in the house." Besides, he figures a marriage could get him "some more veterans benefits." Crystal, of course, would be no such pawn in an egotistical calculation, but Beau wastes no opportunity in rewarding her refusal with beatings and cuts till she "most died." Defying a court order to stay away from Crystal and the two children of their relationship, Beau returns and devises an ingenious method of wringing a marriage promise from Crystal. He grabs the children as hostages and holds them out of the fifth-story window, threatening to drop them unless Crystal "say to alla the neighbors/ you gonna marry me/." But Crystal is too dazed to speak. "i cd only whisper," she whispers "& he dropped em."[73]

Shange follows this nightmarish scene with a supreme and touching presentation of a way out that she had suggested earlier, sisterly solidarity. This is in the final poem, "a laying on of hands," in which the seven ladies individually and collectively recognize what has been missing in their lives that makes them so helpless against the agents of unmaking: sisterhood in and for self-(re-)creation:

> a layin on of hands
> the holiness of myself released

Even the elements of nature celebrate the discovery, and Shange—as one other way of culturally locating her enterprise—succumbs to an animist abandon but paradoxically in a context that forcefully collocates the social (the concrete struggle of the women) and the metaphysical (the struggle constructed as a necessity, a necessity with a divine sanction), the material and the spiritual:[74]

> i sat up one nite walkin a boardin house
> screamin/ cryin/ the ghost of another woman
> who waz missin what i waz missin
> i wanted to jump up outta my bones
> & be done wit myself

> leave me alone
> & go on the wind
> it waz too much
> i fell into a numbness
> til the only tre i cd see
> took me up in her branches
> held me in the breeze
> made me dawn dew
> that chill at daybreak
> the sun wrapped me up swingin rose light everywhere
> the sky laid over me like a million men
> i waz cold/ i waz burning up/ a child
> & endlessly weavin garments for the moon
> wit my tears

This newfound and potent empowerment is expressed in the famous closing spiritual, "song of joy,"

> i found god in myself
> & i loved her/ i loved her fiercely

which the ladies, says the stage direction, first "sing to each other, then gradually to the audience." At the peak of the song, the ladies enter into a "closed tight circle," the forceful image of a creative solidarity impenetrable to life-denying forces, which ends the choreopoem.[75]

Writing about *for colored girls* as a unique feminist phenomenon, Andrea B. Rushing, in her essay "For Colored Girls, Suicide or Struggle," directs attention to Shange's unequaled mastery of "the grammar of black women's bodies." "[T]he black women in the audience," she says, "are dislocated into delight because we simply have not seen ourselves on stage like this": "we not only hear lines real black women speak delivered with acutely accurate inflections, we also see familiar strides and shrugs. . . ."[76] The criticisms of the choreopoem have been mainly directed at its "negative" representation of the black man in particular and black male–female relations in general.[77] What is being challenged is Shange's construction of a performative, gender-sensitive African-American cultural identity, her articulation of gender as the *nodal point* of her practice and critique. To this challenge, classically articulated in the *Black Scholar* debate, Shange undauntingly replied with two poems, "is not so gd to be born a girl" and "otherwise i would think it odd to have rape prevention month,"[78] published later as part of *boogie woogie landscapes*. It is, however, her essay "takin a solo" that directly addresses the politics of the accusations. Shange firmly rejects what she reads as being suggested to her: to assume the burden of "uplifting the race," a burden that implicitly precludes uncompromising "internal" critiques and thereby gestures toward expressive identity. This is how she voices her rejection:

> when i take my voice into a poem or a story/ i am trying desperately to give you that/ i am not trying to give you a history of my family/ the struggle of

black people all over the world or the fight goin on upstairs tween susie & matt/ i am giving you a moment/ like something that isnt coming back/ a something particularly itself/ like an alto solo in december in nashville in 1937.[79]

To defend herself, Shange latches onto the weapon of "singularity," which appears as abstractly conceived: she speaks not of the "race" but alone of herself and a poetic "moment" "particularly itself." What Shange has done is to duplicate in a different way the conservative, expressive formulations of her critics. Against their desire for the presentation of a harmonious collective, Shange proposes the alone individual. Yet this reading is only partially true and must contend with what Hortense Spillers discerningly identifies as a peculiar "standing-apart-from" which defines the attitude of black women's writing to literary tradition:

> "[T]radition" for black women's writing community is a matrix of literary *discontinuities* that partially articulate various periods of consciousness in the history of an African-American people. This point of paradox not only opens the future to the work to come, but also reminds us that *symbolic discontinuity* is the single rule of terministic behavior that our national literature has still to pursue. The day it does so, the reader and writer both will have laid sight on a territory of the literary landscape that we barely knew was possible."[80]

Shange, in defending her *difference*, uncompromisingly calls upon the authority of *experience*—"my voice," "singularity"—generally considered to be too subjective and expressive a category, yet we must specify that the experience of the *black female*, situated as "not only the 'Other' of the Same, but also as the 'other' of the other(s),"[81] is thoroughly polyphonic in composition.[82] This location remains a potentially forceful site of subversive difference, of oppositional "discontinuities," in Spillers's term. Shange herself misses this political character of her articulatory practice and lapses into a regrettable binarism when she accuses her detractors of playing *politics* with *art*:

> we assume a musical solo is a personal statement/ we think the poet is speakin for the world/ there's something wrong there, a writer's first commitment is to the piece itself. how the words fall & leap/ or if they dawdle & sit down fannin themselves. writers are dealing with language, not politics. that comes later. so much later. to think abt the politics of a poem before we think abt the poem is to put what is correct before the moment/[83]

A musical solo is no more a personal statement, or any less concerned about the world than is a poetic verse. A *writer's* first commitment is surely "to the piece itself," otherwise there would be no writing. But this commitment itself is shot through with politics, beginning with the politics of the conditions of possibility of the vocation of writing, of being a writer, of being a black, a woman, and a writer. On the relation between language and politics, we can only assume that for Shange herself, her proposition is already dated, coming as it does before the dramatist's eloquent treatise on "fixing" the English language. And it matters little whether we think about the politics of a poem before or after it is written. The politics of a writing, to put it vulgarly, is always already there, inscribed in the writing as much as it inscribes the writing, constituted even as it constitutes the writing. Interestingly, as we have seen, Shange's very own practice denies the conservative, *expressive* separation.

7

Subjectivities and Institutions

What the dramatic practices of Wole Soyinka, Amiri Baraka, Derek Walcott, and Ntozake Shange together show us is an empowering post-Afrocentric space, a space that calls to account and radically revises the colonialist, triumphalist narrative of European modernity.[1] The dramatists show us that the space, though possible, is a thoroughly embattled space, a guerrilla space that is constantly forced to shift and improvise terrains because it is still a dominated space. In showing us that the space and its attendant performative conception of cultural identity are possible, the question they ask, I think, is whether the space can really flourish without its own supporting structures, that is, within still Eurocentric *institutions*,[2] or what Abiola Irele calls the "dominant factor" of the "Western frame of reference"[3] in the current global political economy of the production and circulation of subjectivities. This is another way of retelling the too obvious fact that these institutions—language, genre, artistic value, the theater, Western-style education and its institutionalized modalities of what is or is not worth teaching and researching, publishing, grants and fellowships, and so on—still dictate in large measure the terms of the production, distribution, and even consumption of many kinds of cultural articulations of black subjectivity: whether of creative practice, as in the case of the dramatists, or critical discourse on such creations, as in the instance of studies like this.

Under this broad umbrella of institutional subordination, the theme of epistemological domination—whose origin I discussed as the colonialist "reformation of minds" and its intractable character, has remained a central concern of the dramatists.

While we can regard the suggested propositions of cultural identity as "black" because the dramatists are black, it is only too clear that they are indebted to Western categories of knowing. Language is the most obvious manifestation of this debt, though it is by no means confined to it. Can a "truly authentic" black cultural identity be symbolized in European languages and according to European modalities? That this is a significant question is underscored by the reality of another: Why is the language question an issue at all for African-American and Caribbean dramatists, whose languages bear no such radically disjunctive relations to English as is the case with Africans? What the foregoing questions translate to is this: Do we need an epistemological shift from the West? Perhaps the answer is unequivocally affirmative, yet this answer must face another question which I have borrowed from Mudimbe: "Is it possible to consider this shift outside of the very epistemological field [Western] which makes my question both possible and thinkable?"[4] After all, Soyinka, Baraka, Walcott, and Shange are trained and supremely versed in the Western literary and dramatic tradition. They *rediscovered* themselves and their different cultures through engagements with this tradition. This is why the epistemological shift we demand cannot be absolute. This is not a liberal or moral point; it is just that the absolutism, which would mean a present or future without a past, is unachievable.

This leads me to the important observation that the black quest for cultural identity examined in this study coincides with the break up of Empire and the birth of political decolonization and general critical interrogation of European cultural hegemony. I am empowered by this coincidence to specify its *essential* character thus: the quest is *simultaneously* a *scar* and a *mask*: a scar of conquest, and a mask of resistance. Blacks across the three continents studied are questing for cultural identity not because they are black but because they are black *and* dominated. Ultimately, this is where the *difference* of the identity/the *identity* of the difference lies. And this is where we must begin. This is what must inform our epistemological choices and inventions.[5] The question here, of course, is how to keep this insight in focus *theatrically*, that is, through and in performance.

If it could be argued that I have privileged "text" over "performance" in this study, I will insist that it is only apparent, for I do not consider whatever difference there is between the theater script and performance to be absolute. Following Michael Issacharoff in *Discourse as Performance*, I conceive the text as "*the place of inscription of virtual performance.*"[6] Indelibly inscribed in the very body of the text is the performative and its determinants. The text's priority in a text–performance continuum is not sacrosanct, for performance is also equally prior, given the inevitability with which it (in the guise of previous performances in the cultural repertoire of the dramatist) shapes the text's very articulation. "[T]he constant pointing within the dialogue to a non-described context," writes Keir Elam, "suggests that the dramatic text is radically conditioned by its performability. The written text, in other words, is determined by its very need for stage contextualization, and indicates throughout its allegiance to the physical conditions of performance, above all to the actor's body and its ability to materialize discourse within the space of the stage."[7]

The relationship between text and performance is hence a "complex of reciprocal constraints constituting a powerful *intertextuality*. Each . . . bears the other's traces, the performance assimilating those aspects of the written play which the performers choose to transcodify, and the dramatic text being 'spoken' at every point by the model performance—or the *n* possible performances—that motivate it."[8] Thus I placed Shange's emphasis on dance as the constitutive fabric of performance, Walcott's dramaturgic appropriation of Carnival, Baraka's stress on the performance of change and *action* of filmic fracture, and Soyinka's immersion in the ritual roots of theater at the foreground.

The lever, then, that promises to keep our epistemological choices and inventions relevant is the question that is universal in performance, expressed by Herbert Blau: "*[W]hat are we performing for?*"[9] It is a question with profound implications for *both* the means and ends of performance; for the relations between and among author, text-performance, stage, audience, and society. It is important to examine, in this respect, the attitudes of Soyinka, Baraka, Walcott, and Shange to the established institution of performance, to performance as an institution.

Elizabeth Burns, in her book *Theatricality*, identifies two main inseparable conventions of dramatic performance: *rhetorical*, relating to modes of interaction between performers and spectators, and *authenticating*, governing the relations between the characters in the play.[10] Rhetorical conventions—more appropriately termed *presentational* by Keir Elam[11]— are the "devices of exposition that enable the audience to understand the play. . . . They are the means by which the audience is persuaded to accept characters and situations whose validity is ephemeral and bound to the theatre." Authenticating conventions, on the other hand, ensure that the "modes of speech, demeanour and action that are explicit in the play . . . carry conviction and imply a connection with the world of human action of which the theatre is only a part." Authenticating conventions "suggest a total and external code of values and norms of conduct from which the speech and action of the play are drawn."[12]

There is far greater observance of these conventions of performance in the works of Wole Soyinka and Derek Walcott than in Ntozake Shange and Amiri Baraka. It is perhaps not a totally unrelated point that Soyinka and Walcott are also the more embroiled in what could be termed the practice and tensions of "high art," even when, as we mostly find in Walcott, the appropriation of popular elements is privileged. The recent Baraka, and Shange especially, on the other hand, are somewhat further outside the orbit of "play"(making) in the dominant institutionalized conception. Thus we would not find a *Motion of History* or *for colored girls* in the corpus of either Soyinka or Walcott. And this is not simply a matter of the influence of context, since we would easily find a *Lion and the Jewel* or *Ti-Jean and His Brothers* in the writings of other African-American dramatists like Alice Childress or August Wilson. If the whole "structural reality of theatre," including performance, is shot through with ideology, as Herbert Blau has argued,[13] then cultural identity as an articulatory practice requires that performance view its sanctioned props, "what we already know and believe," with active suspicion. The quest, I think, should be for "something in the grain of performance which will convulse the ideological field in which the enunciation of power invisibly prevails."[14] A ceaselessly self-critical performative identity demands nothing less.

Notes

Introduction

1. Ellison, "Some Questions and Some Answers" 263.

2. See Tomlinson's insightful study, *Cultural Imperialism*.

3. The double quotes signify that this name is a Western invention, though rarely acknowledged as such; it is a naming which "bespeaks a white subjectivity manipulating tropes." See Miller, *Blank Darkness* 9, 6–14.

4. Foucault, *The Archaeology* 229. For a helpful general study on discourse, see Macdonell, *Theories of Discourse*.

5. Terdiman, *Discourse/Counter-Discourse* 54.

6. "There is no 'discourse' in the sense that there is a classical system of tropes known as 'rhetoric'; there are only *discourses*, forming themselves according to the shape of their objects. To speak of a discourse is thus to express a critical attitude, a bias toward reducing utterances to their 'paper reality,' understanding them as contingent and overdetermined rather than necessary and immutable." Miller, *Blank Darkness* 61. Let us make the observation here that rather than "forming themselves according to the shape of their objects," it would be more rewarding to conceive discourse as forming the shape of their objects, insofar as shape is imperceivable outside of the way it is thought, inscribed.

7. Terdiman, *Discourse/Counter-Discourse* 38. We should probably speak of "discursive practice," to emphasize the materiality of discourse, its "incorporeal materialism," in Foucault's phrase. Discursive practices are "not purely and simply ways of producing discourse, they are embodied in technical processes, in institutions, in patterns for general behavior, in forms for transmission and diffusion, and in pedagogical forms which, at once, impose and maintain them." Foucault, *The Archaeology* 231; and his *Language, Counter-Memory* 200.

8. I know no group is more sensitive to the charges of being merely "reactive" rather than "active" than a dominated one. This issue came up on one or two occasions during presentations of material that appears in this book. The best response is a philosophical one. Since necessity never confronts one other than as that, necessity, the distinction between action and reaction becomes useful only for heuristic and specific purposes. This is why every action is a reaction and every reaction an action. My conception of the relation between action and reaction is a horizontal, not a vertical one. The West today is unthinkable outside of its reaction, since the fateful encounter, to Africa. The quest for "pure," autonomously motivated social action is a chimerical pursuit of the absolute; it does not even begin to address domination, much less resist it. As far as I know, Frederick Douglass did not lose sleep over the possible interpretation of his escape to freedom—as necessity—he saw it as necessity—as "merely" a "reaction" to the Western "action" of his enslavement. But this is not to say that the transatlantic slavery is not to be lamented as a forceful and exploitative incorporation of Africa into a specifically Western orbit and agenda. The gargantuan energy so far expended by blacks in physically and psychically taming the incorporation could certainly have been channeled to meeting necessities of a far less horrendous and cataclysmic nature. In issues such as this, our emphasis should be not so much on "difference" as the domination that is mapped on it and produces it as a *project*.

9. See Mlama, *Culture and Development*; Jeyifo, *Yoruba Popular Travelling Theatre*; Desai, "Theater as Praxis"; Special Section on Theatre for Development in Africa; Kidd, *The Popular Performing Arts*; Sistren, with Honor Ford-Smith, *Lionheart Gal*; van Graan, "International Models."

10. A striking illustration from Nigeria is the divergent representations of the 1946 fateful encounter between a Yoruba tradition (which demands the ritual suicide of the Elesin, Commander of the King's Stables, on the death of the King) and the British Colonial Administration. Soyinka in *Death and the King's Horseman* weaves a great tragic issue out of the failure of Elesin (partly because of his arrest by the colonial authority) to perform his task. However, in the hands of Baba Sala, Nigeria's foremost popular comedian, this is an occasion for great slapstick. His own Elesin not only flatly refuses to commit suicide but actually threatens to enlist the support of the colonizers against whoever insists that he conform to tradition. (Biodun Jeyifo related this performance to an audience of which I was a part.) Yet another interpretation by the popular tragedian Duro Ladipo is far closer to Soyinka's than to Baba Sala's, and it is conceived primarily as a tragedy. See Ladipo, *Oba Waja* (*The King Is Dead*).

11. Because the rhetoric of the collective ("culture") too often uncritically defines these discourses, I attempt to restore the basic individual–collective perpetual tension by italicizing that jarring locution, "cultural self"; despite protestations, no representative transparently represents a constituency.

Chapter 1

1. See Jeyifo, "The Reinvention of Theatrical Tradition" 242.

2. "To have been colonized was a fate with lasting, indeed grotesquely unfair results, especially after national independence had been achieved. Poverty, dependency, underdevelopment, various pathologies of power and corruption, plus of course notable achievements in war, literacy, economic development: this mix

of characteristics designated the colonized people who had freed themselves on one level but who remained victims of their past on another." Said, "Representing the Colonized" 207.

3. Fanon, *Black Skin, White Masks* 10.

4. Fanon, "Racism and Culture," *Toward the African Revolution* 31.

5. Foucault, *The Archaeology* 219.

6. See Jeyifo, "Reinvention" 242–43.

7. Bourdieu, *Outline of a Theory of Practice* 171–83.

8. Foucault, *The Archaeology* 225–26 on the "fellowships of discourse."

9. See Mudimbe, *The Invention of Africa* 1–23; Miller, *Blank Darkness* 3–65; Gates, *"Race," Writing, and Difference* 1–20; Cesaire, *Discourse*; and Hammond and Jablow, *The Myth of Africa*. On the construction of Eurocentrism, see Amin, *Eurocentrism*; and Bernal, *Black Athena* 1–73.

10. Fanon, *The Wretched of the Earth* 36.

11. Some scholarly commentaries on blackface minstrelsy I found useful include Lott, *Love and Theft*; Jeyifo, *Masks of Otherness*; Boskin, *Sambo*; Toll, *Blacking Up*; Nathan, *Dan Emmett and the Rise of Early Negro Minstrelsy*; Belcher, "The Place of the Negro"; Wittke, *Tambo and Bones*; and Rice, *Monarchs of Minstrelsy*. With particular reference to black participation, see Sampson, *Blacks in Blackface*.

12. Jeyifo, *Masks of Otherness* 65.

13. Toll, *Blacking Up* 30, v.

14. F. P. Gaines, *The Southern Plantation: A Study in the Development and Accuracy of a Tradition* (1925), cited in Wittke, *Tambo and Bones* 7.

15. Jeyifo, *Masks of Otherness* 1.

16. Boskin, *Sambo* 16.

17. Toll, *Blacking Up* 66.

18. See the following historical and critical studies: Bigsby, *A Critical Introduction to Twentieth-Century American Drama*; Craig, *Black Drama of the Federal Theatre Era*; Abramson, *Negro Playwrights in the American Theatre: 1925–1959*; Mitchell, *Black Drama*; Isaacs, *The Negro in the American Theatre*; Bond, *The Negro and the Drama*; and Burke, *The Philosophy of Literary Form*.

19. Shange, "unrecovered losses/ black theater traditions," Foreword, *Three Pieces* xiii.

20. Hill, *The Trinidad Carnival* 11. See also Hill's excellent historical account of the Eurocentric stage in Jamaica, *The Jamaican Stage, 1655-1900*.

21. Hill, *Trinidad Carnival* 10.

22. Hill, *Trinidad Carnival* 17, 16, for all the citations in this paragraph.

23. Hill, *Trinidad Carnival* 14, 25, for the citations in this paragraph.

24. See, as further instances of the Eurocentric discourse in the Caribbean, Beckwith, *Black Roadways*; Wright, *Revels in Jamaica*; and Baxter, *The Arts of an Island*.

25. Finnegan, *Oral Literature in Africa* 500.

26. Finnegan, *Oral Literature in Africa* 500, 516 (emphasis added), 501, 500.

27. Finnegan, *Oral Literature in Africa* 516.

28. Kirby, "Indigenous African Theatre" 22. For expressions of similar position, see De Graft "Roots in African Drama and Theatre" 77–80; Rotimi, "The Drama in African Ritual Display"; Echeruo, "The Dramatic Limits of Igbo Ritual" 136–48; and Dhlomo, "Nature and Variety of Tribal Drama."

29. Further examples of the Eurocentric discourse include Graham-White, *The Drama of Black Africa*; Havemeyer, *The Drama of Savage Peoples*; British Drama League, "Native African Drama."

30. See, respectively, these two studies of the movement in general, and of a contemporary leading figure of the troupes in particular: Joel Adedeji, "The Alarinjo Theatre"; Jeyifo, *The Yoruba Popular Travelling Theatre of Nigeria*; and Ebun Clark, *Hubert Ogunde*,

31. Said, *Orientalism* 202–3.

32. Amilcar Cabral, "Identity and Dignity in the Context of the National Liberation Struggle," *Return to the Source* 58.

33. Langston Hughes, "Note on Commercial Theatre" 190.

34. Clarence Muse, blurb on the cover of Hill, *The Theater of Black Americans*.

35. This is Bourdieu's concept, explained as "systems of durable, transposable *dispositions*, structured structures predisposed to function as structuring structures, that is, as principles of the generation and structuring of practices and representations which can be objectively 'regulated' and 'regular' without in any way being the product of obedience to rules, objectively adapted to their goals without presupposing a conscious aiming at ends or an express mastery of the operations necessary to attain them and, being all this, collectively orchestrated without being the product of the orchestrating action of a conductor." *Outline of a Theory* 72.

36. Terdiman, *Discourse/Counter-Discourse* 14.

37. Terdiman, *Discourse/Counter-Discourse* 56, 15–16.

38. See Olaniyan, "Discussing Afrocentrism." One of the very visible proponents of Afrocentrism in the United States is Molefi K. Asante. See his *The Afrocentric Idea* and *Afrocentricity*.

39. Matthews, "The Value of Race Literature" 170–85; 184, 171, 185, 175, 176.

40. Matthews, "The Value of Race Literature" 183–84, 173–74, 178–83. See also Soyinka, "And after the Narcissist" 53, 56; Hountondji, *African Philosophy*; and Cabral, *Return to the Source*. For sympathetic accounts of negritude, see Finn, *Voices of Negritude*; and Irele, *The African Experience in Literature and Ideology* 67–124.

41. Most of the plays that won the contests were not pageants by any stretch of the imagination. Marita Bonner's *The Purple Flower* (1928), one of the most experimental of the plays, is expressionist. For a brief account of Du Bois's famous pageant, *The Star of Ethiopia* (1913), see Samuel A. Hay, *African American Theatre* 78–80.

42. On Du Bois's stated terms of the debate on representation and the various responses, see the following issues of *Crisis*: 31 (February 1926): 165, (March 1926): 219–20, (April 1926): 278–78; 32 (May 1926): 35–36, (June 1926): 71–73, (August 1926): 193–94, (September 1926): 238–39; and 33 (November 1926): 28–29. Over forty years later, this symposium was revived by Henry Louis Gates, Jr., perhaps a comment on its continuing pertinence, in spite of changed circumstances. See the responses published in two 1987 issues of *Black American Literature Forum*, 21.1–2 and 21.3. For Du Bois's formulation of the four principles, see "Krigwa Players Little Negro Theatre." See also his related essay, "Criteria of Negro Art." For a detailed review of Du Bois's aesthetic writings, see Turner, "W. E. B. Du Bois and the Theory of a Black Aesthetic."

43. Julia Peterkin, a "sympathetic" respondent to Du Bois's national debate, wrote: "I write about Negroes because they represent human nature obscured by

so little veneer; human nature groping among its instinctive impulses and in an environment which is tragically primitive and often unutterably pathetic." *The Crisis* 32 (September 1926): 239.

44. Hughes, "The Negro Artist and the Racial Mountain" 177, 178–79.

45. Alain Locke, Introduction, Locke and Gregory, *Plays of Negro Life*. The introduction has no pagination. Most of the twenty plays in are collection by white authors. The next two anthologies implicitly critique this fact. The plays were written by blacks and contained materials essentially of "racial upliftment" designed for schools. "Why does not the Negro dramatize his own life and bring the world to him?" Carter G. Woodson queried in the introduction to one of them (*Plays and Pageants*), "Paul Green, Eugene O'Neill, and Marc Connelly cannot do it. They see that the thing is possible, and they are trying to do it; but at best they misunderstand the Negro because they cannot think black." Richardson, *Plays and Pageants from the Life of the Negro* iii; and Richardson and Miller, *Negro History in Thirteen Plays*. For a discussion of these anthologies, see Sanders, *The Development of Black Theater in America*. In his obviously "political" conception of drama, Woodson is in good company with Du Bois—against Locke. Hay in his *African American Theatre* (Introduction and Chapters 1 and 2) has done a useful survey of the influence of this ideological division on subsequent African-American dramatic/theatrical production.

46. Senghor, "The African Apprehension of Reality" 29–34. For an illuminating commentary on Senghor's proposition, see Hountondji, "Reason and Tradition" 141–42.

47. Cited in Jeyifous, "Black Critics and Black Theatre" 39.

48. Amiri Baraka, with his usual acerbic wit, characterizes this as "the guilt of the overintegrated," in his account of his cultural nationalist days. *The Autobiography of LeRoi Jones* 255.

49. For some illuminating insight into this period of productive flux that appropriately left little as sacrosanct from critical inspection, see Gitlin, *The Sixties*; Carlisle, *The Roots of Black Nationalism*; Allen, *Black Awakening in Capitalist America*; Cruse, *The Crisis of the Negro Intellectual* and *Rebellion or Revolution?*; and Essien-Udom, *Black Nationalism*. On theater, see Mance Williams, *Black Theatre in the 1960s and 1970s*.

50. LeRoi Jones and Larry Neal, *Black Fire*; *The Drama Review* 12 (Summer 1968); Gayle, *Black Expression*, and also *The Black Aesthetic*.

51. Quoted in Jeyifous, "Black Critics and Black Theatre" 41.

52. See, for instance, Harrison, *The Drama of Nommo*; and Molette and Molette, *Black Theater*.

53. Benston, "The Aesthetic of Modern Black Drama" 62.

54. For a valuable introduction to the Black Consciousness Movement and antiapartheid resistance, see Fatton, *Black Consciousness in South Africa*.

55. Kavanagh, *Theatre and Cultural Struggle in South Africa* 161–68, has tried to distill a Black Consciousness dramatic-cultural theory from the manifestoes of the various groups and from conference releases and fragmented propositions on culture by many of the movement's activists. See also Larlham, *Black Theater, Dance and Ritual in South Africa* 75–92; Coplan, *In Township Tonight!* 203–29. Hauptfleisch and Steadman's *South African Theatre*, introduces four different theater traditions in South Africa, Black, English, Alternative, and Afrikaans.

56. See Kavanagh, *Theatre and Cultural Struggle* 162–63. See also Steve Biko,

"Black Consciousness and the Quest for a True Humanity," *I Write What I Like* 96.

57. Kavanagh, *Theatre and Cultural Struggle* 166.

58. See Fugard, *Notebooks: 1960–1977*; Jeyifo, "The Reductive 'Two-hander' Dramaturgy of Athol Fugard: Aspects of the Art and Society Dialectic," *The Truthful Lie* 98–104. Ndlovu's, ed., *Woza Afrika! An Anthology of South African Plays* is a recent anthology of black and interracial South African drama.

59. Enekwe, "Myth, Ritual and Drama in Igboland"; Adedeji, "Alarinjo: The Traditional Yoruba Travelling Theatre," "Traditional Yoruba Theater," and "A Yoruba Pantomime"; Ogunba, "Traditional African Festival Drama"; Lesohai, "Black South African Theatre"; Kennedy, *In Search of African Theatre*; John P. Clark, *The Example of Shakespeare*; Traore, *Black African Theatre and Its Social Functions*; Gotrick, *Apidan Theatre and Modern Drama*; Schipper, *Theatre and Society in Africa*; Soyinka, *Art, Dialogue and Outrage* and *Myth, Literature and the African World*; Owomoyela, *Visions and Revisions*; and Enekwe, *Igbo Masks*.

60. Soyinka, *Art, Dialogue and Outrage* 192, 194, 195.

61. Walcott, "What the Twilight Says" 37, 34–35.

62. Hill, *Trinidad Carnival* 4, 69–113, 114–15. For a more detailed review of these positions, see Omotoso, *The Theatrical into Theatre* 46–61. See also Hill, *The Jamaican Stage, 1655-1900*.

63. See Taylor, *The Narrative of Liberation* 160.

64. Dollimore, "The dominant and the deviant" 190. See also Derrida, *Positions* 41–42.

65. Fanon, *Black Skin, White Masks* 10, 29.

66. Fanon, *Black Skin, White Masks* 29. This is also the position elaborated decades later by Derrida, in his argument that "[t]he invention of the other is not opposed to that of the same, its difference beckons toward another coming about . . . the one that allows the coming of a still unanticipatable alterity and for which no horizon of waiting as yet seems ready, in place, available. Yet it is necessary to prepare for it; for to allow the coming of the entirely other, passivity, a certain kind of resigned passivity for which everyone comes down to the same, is not suitable." Derrida, "Psyche: Inventions of the Other" 55.

67. Jeyifo, "The Reinvention of Theatrical Tradition" 247.

68. Fabre, *Drumbeats, Masks and Metaphor* 1.

69. For a few other instances of the articulation of the post-Afrocentric, see Harris, *The Wombs of Space*; Glissant, *Caribbean Discourse*; Wynter, "One Love—Rhetoric or Reality?"; Kavanagh, *Theatre and Cultural Struggle in South Africa*; Jeyifo, *The Truthful Lie*; Etherton, *The Development of African Drama*; Osofisan, *Beyond Translation*; DeVeaux, "The Tapestry"; Wallace, *Black Macho and the Myth of the Superwoman*; Gates, *The Signifying Monkey*; Baker, *Blues, Ideology*; Benston, *Baraka: The Renegade and the Mask*.

Chapter 2

1. Mudimbe, *The Invention of Africa* 2.

2. I prefer to state the problematic this way rather than simply repeat the well-worn phrase that is often substituted for concrete specification, "ideological struggle." For useful speculation on this realm, which I have drawn upon, see Marx, *A Contribution to the Critique of Political Economy* and *The German Ideology*; Gramsci, *Selections from the Prison Notebooks* 12–14; Althusser, "Ideology

and Ideological State Apparatuses"; Woodson, *The Mis-Education of the Negro*, and Cabral, *Unity and Struggle* 138–54.

3. With certain modifications, I have found useful Foucault's concept of "power." "Power," he says, is "a mode of acting upon the action of others;" a "total structure of actions brought to bear upon possible actions . . . a way of acting upon an acting subject or acting subjects by virtue of their acting or being capable of action." To the extent that I am dealing with the dispossession of subjectivity resulting from the Europe–Africa encounter, as testified to by the exertions of the anti-Eurocentric discourses, this conception is apt. The exertions are thus seen as struggles against *subjection*, a nonviolent field of power relations Foucault distinguishes from *domination* and *exploitation*—both involving some measure of direct violence in their operation. (Note the parallels to Mudimbe's tripartite colonizing structure.) Foucault's "power" assumes a context in which a hierarchical distinction among the three realms of power relations, based on which (or which combination) is dominant or subordinate at a given point in time, could be useful. This explains his inference that "subjection" (and hence the struggles against it) is in the ascendant today in the West, rather than the other two virulent forms. He gives as a reason a "new political structure" that has been developing in the the West since the sixteenth century. I read the effect of this political structure as the creation on a world scale of a sort of *center* and *periphery*. The West locates itself in the former and "transfers" the more extreme power relations, "domination" and "exploitation," to the latter, with continued gain to it. Foucault's "power" assumes this center. I am, however, dealing with *both* regions, specifically with the periphery and the process of its becoming peripheral; I am dealing with a periphery where "subjection" presupposes, exists side by side, and goes apace with "domination" and "exploitation"—where gestures such as "dreadlocks" or "afro"; "wa Thiong'O" instead of "James," "Baraka" in place of "Jones"; or "black aesthetic" rather than "white aesthetic" (all of them aspects of a refusal of subjection), reverberate to, connect with, and implicate "domination" and "exploitation." All citations are from Foucault's essay "The Subject and Power" 221, 220, 212, 213.

4. Rabinow, "Representations Are Social Facts" 260.

5. This is also the impulse, for instance, behind "ethnophilosophy" in Africa, and also the massive indigenization of Christianity currently going on in the continent. Mudimbe has done an astute survey of these issues in Chapters 2, 3 and 5 of *The Invention of Africa*. See also Hountondji, *African Philosophy: Myth and Reality*, and his "Scientific Dependence in Africa."

6. Cabral, *Unity and Struggle* 140–49; Raymond Williams, *Marxism and Literature* 11–20.

7. Clifford, *The Predicament of Culture* 344.

8. "Philosophically, then, the kind of language, thought, and vision that I have been calling Orientalism very generally is a form of radical realism; anyone employing Orientalism, which is the habit for dealing with questions, objects, qualities, and regions deemed Oriental, will designate, name, point to, fix what he is talking or thinking about with a word or phrase, which then is considered either to have acquired, or more simply to be, reality." "[T]he figures of speech associated with the Orient . . . are all declarative and self-evident; the tense they employ is the timeless eternal; they convey an impression of repetition and strength. . . . For all these functions it is frequently enough to use the copula *is*." Said, *Orientalism* 72. See also Radhakarishnan, "Ethic Identity and Post-

Structuralist Differance" 203; Laclau and Mouffe, *Hegemony and Socialist Strategy* 119; Bhabha, "Representation and the Colonial Text."

9. Hobsbawn and Ranger, *The Invention of Tradition*; and Wagner, *The Invention of Culture*.

10. Mann, *The Sources of Power*.

11. Clifford, *Predicament* 338.

12. I recall here Chinua Achebe's fine intervention: "In the nature of things, the work of the western writer is automatically informed by universality. It is only others who must strive to achieve it. As though universality were some distant bend in the road you must take if you travel far enough in the direction of America or Europe." *Morning Yet on Creation Day* 9.

13. H. Dieterlen and F. Kohler on the Sotho of South Africa in a book published by the French Missionary Society in 1912. Quoted in Graham-White, *The Drama of Black Africa* 8.

14. See Heilpern, *The Conference of the Birds*. Charges of "Orientalism" have been leveled against some of Brook's productions—see Dasgupta, "The Mahabharata: Peter Brook's "Orientalism.""

15. Said, *Orientalism* 7.

16. Said, "Orientalism Reconsidered" 15; Foucault, "Truth and Power," *Power/Knowledge* 133.

17. Chinweizu, Jemie, and Madubuike, *Toward the Decolonization of African Literature* 4. For interesting "confessions" of position shifts by formerly committed cultural nationalists, see Baker, *Afro-American Poetics* 166–78; LeRoi Jones/Amiri Baraka, *Autobiography*; Larry Neal, "The Black Contribution to American Letters." See also the salient critique of Black Power and black cultural nationalism by Adolph Reed: "Black Particularity Reconsidered."

18. Stephen Henderson, "Saturation: Progress Report on a Theory of Black Poetry" 14. See also his *Understanding the New Black Poetry* 1–69. See Houston Baker's illuminating discussion of Henderson in the context of the Black Arts Movement, *Blues, Ideology* 71–87.

19. Fanon, *The Wretched of the Earth* 212–13; and his "West Indians and Africans," *Toward the African Revolution* 27.

20. See also Dathorne, *Dark Ancestor: The Literature of the Black Man in the Caribbean*.

21. Fanon, "Racism and Culture," *Toward the African Revolution* 44.

22. Satya P. Mohanty, "Us and Them: On the Philosophical Bases of Political Criticism" 13, 14. See also Mitter, "Can We Ever Understand Alien Cultures?" 21–24.

23. Graham-White, *The Drama of Black Africa*.

24. Homi K. Bhabha, in a consideration of similar issues, writes: "What is denied is any knowledge of cultural otherness as differential *sign*, implicated in specific historical and discursive conditions, requiring construction in different practices or reading. The place of otherness is fixed in the west as a subversion of western metaphysics and is finally appropriated by the west as its limit-text, anti-west." "The Other Question: Difference, Discrimination and the Discourse of Colonialism" 151.

25. Hountondji, *African Philosophy* 159–64.

26. Anderson, *Imagined Communities*; and Denys Hay, *Europe: The Emergence of an Idea*.

27. Etherton, *The Development of African Drama* 22–42; and Jeyifo, *The Truthful Lie* 8.

28. Hountondji, *African Philosophy* 161. In formulating the performative "model," I have also benefited substantially from Laclau and Mouffe, *Hegemony and Socialist Strategy*.

29. Hall, "Race, Articulation and Societies Structured in Dominance" 325. See also his "On Postmodernism and Articulation." 45–60.

30. Laclau and Mouffe, *Hegemony and Socialist Strategy* 109.

31. I think Derrida aptly describes this principle when he puts forward the idea of a theoretical "jetty" which would be "*destabilizing* and *devastating*," a "jetty" that "destabilizes the conditions of the possibility of objectivity, the relationship to the object, everything that constitutes and institutes the assurance of subjectivity in the indubitable presence of the cogito, the certainty of self-consciousness, the original project, the relation to the other determined as egological intersubjectivity, the principle of reason and the system of representation associated with it and hence everything that supports a modern concept of theory as objectivity." "Some Statements and Truisms" 86.

32. "The practice of articulation," says Laclau and Mouffe, "consists in the construction of nodal points which partially fix meaning; and the partial character of this fixation proceeds from the openness of the social, a result in its turn of the constant overflowing of every discourse by the infinitude of the field of discursivity." *Hegemony and Socialist Strategy* 113; 193, 112.

33. Let me give a hypothetical instance to make this point less abstract. If we argue that the effectiveness of the NAACP today is severely waning, then perhaps it is time to challenge and revise "civil rights" as the organization's continuing nodal point.

34. "The genre has always in all genres been able to play the role of order's principle: resemblance, analogy, utility and difference, taxonomic classification, organization and genealogical tree, order of reason, order of reasons, sense of sense, truth of truth, natural light and sense of history." Derrida, "The Law of Genre" 228.

35. See Raymond Williams, *Marxism and Literature* 181–83; 187–88; and Cohen, "Do Postmodern Genres Exist?" 242–43.

36. Wellek and Warren, *Theory of Literature* 234.

37. I cite this classic formulation: "There is no incontrovertible reason why the Greek example must be repeated everywhere else. Nor is there any compulsive necessity to describe drama entirely in terms of the proscenium stage and its conventions. Why must drama be seen from the point of view of a distinct stage and auditorium, of actors and the audience? Is there any particular reason, except that of meeting the specifically practical pressures of the present age, why an enactment should last only two or three hours instead of six months? Is the sense of organic unity which we assume in the modern theatre and its conventions not possible on an extended scale among a people whose sensibilities are trained to absorb more diffused ritual and symbolic significances of action? Is a broad communal canvas not more suitable for painting more inclusive social and emotional action than the mere mouse-tongue platform called the modern stage?" Obiechina, "Literature: Traditional and the Modern" 393. For a useful study that traces a mode across Pan-Africa, see Euba, *Archetypes, Imprecators, and Victims of Fate*.

38. Anthony Appiah, "An Evening with Wole Soyinka." For a useful book-

length study of Soyinka on tragedy, see Katrak, *Wole Soyinka and Modern Tragedy*.

39. Raymond Williams, *Marxism and Literature* 183.

40. Baraka, *Raise Race Rays Raze* 15; Milner, "Black Theater—Go Home!"

41. Fanon: "To speak means to be in a position to use a certain syntax, to grasp the morphology of this or that language, but it means above all to assume a culture, to support the weight of a civilization." *Black Skin, White Masks* 17–18; see also Gauri Viswanathan's insightful study, *Masks of Conquest*.

42. "I know of no company or corporation," says Constance Clayton, a school superintendent in Philadelphia, who is a black woman, "which hires you on the basis of your ability to speak Black English." And in fact, she adds, "I have yet to find Black English as being beneficial in filling out a job application." Quoted in McCrum, Cran, and MacNeil, *The Story of English* 230.

43. "Because any language that can command attention is an 'authorized language', invested with the authority of a group, the things it designates are not simply expressed but also authorized and legitimated." Bourdieu, *An Outline of a Theory* 170.

44. See what is only a few significant interventions in the language question in African literature: Special Issue: The Language Question; Ngugi wa Thiong'O, *Decolonising the Mind*, and *Barrel of a Pen: Resistance to Repression in Neo-Colonial Kenya* 77–100; Irele, *The African Experience* 43–65; Achebe, *Morning Yet on Creation Day* 52–62; Kwame A. Appiah, "Topologies of Nativism," *In My Father's House* 47–72; Wali, "The Dead-End of African Literature?"; Okara, "African Speech . . . English Words."

45. See McCrum, Cran, and MacNeil, *The Story of English* 195–234; and Smitherman, *Talkin and Testifyin*.

46. Brathwaite, *History of the Voice* 13. See also Amon S. Saakana's discussion of language in the Caribbean, *The Colonial Legacy in Caribbean Literature* 44–52.

47. Ngugi, *Decolonising the Mind*; Shange, "How I Moved Anna Fierling To The Southwest Territories, or, my personal victory over the armies of western civilization," *See No Evil* 354–38; Soyinka, "Ethics, Ideology and the Critic" and "Language as Boundary," *Art, Dialogue and Outrage* 132–45; Walcott, "The Muse of History."

48. Ashcroft, Griffiths, and Tiffin, *The Empire Writes Back* 7–8, 195–97.

49. I am thinking of this testament by Maya Angelou, the accomplished African-American woman writer: "In the classroom we all learned past participles, but in the streets and in our homes the Blacks learned to drop s's from plurals and suffixes from past-tense verbs. . . . We learned to slide out of one language and into another without being conscious of the effort. At school, in a given situation, we might respond with 'That's not unusual.' But in the street, meeting the same situation, we easily said, 'It be's like that sometimes.'" Cited in Levine, *Black Culture and Black Consciousness* 154.

50. Mudimbe, *The Invention of Africa* 186.

51. Pecheux, *Language, Semantics and Ideology* 156–59.

Chapter 3

1. Soyinka, *Death and the King's Horseman* 10, 11.

2. Soyinka, *Myth, Literature* viii.

3. Soyinka, *Myth, Literature* ix, vii.

4. Soyinka, *Myth, Literature* x, ix, x.

5. Soyinka, *Myth, Literature* xi.

6. Soyinka, *Myth, Literature* x.

7. It goes without saying that Soyinka's "African world" is derived primarily from Yoruba metaphysics and is not a synthesis representing all African cultural traditions. Nor is such a synthesis necessary before a proposition in any of the traditions can be legitimately described as "African." Anthony Appiah once took Soyinka to task for passing his local, culture-specific rationalizations as "African," thereby suggesting a "metaphysical and mythic unity" of African peoples. "Soyinka and the Philosophy of Culture" 259. As Biodun Jeyifo has argued, Appiah's critique is "academicist to the extent that its cutting edge is exclusively *methodological* without moving into the realm of cultural praxis." Jeyifo continued: "[T]he point has to be made that if the ultimate question of a philosophy of culture is its relevance to the present and future prospects of Africa or, in other words, its relevance to the African revolution and the consciousness it fosters in our societies, then a construct based on the tradition of *any* African peoples would do as long as it met that criterion and is thus applicable to all of Africa." "What Is the Will of Ogun?" 177.

8. Soyinka, *Myth, Literature* xii.

9. Anthony Appiah, "An Evening with Wole Soyinka" 782.

10. Soyinka, *Myth, Literature* 37–38.

11. Soyinka, *Myth, Literature* 44, 37.

12. Soyinka, *Myth, Literature* 49, 38.

13. Jeyifo, "Wole Soyinka and the Tropes of Disalienation" xviii.

14. Soyinka, *Myth, Literature* Chapter 1.

15. Soyinka, *Myth, Literature* 1–36, 140–60. See also the author's poetic evocation of Ogun and his primal adventure in the title poem of *Idanre and Other Poems* 61–85.

16. Soyinka, *Myth, Literature* 1–36, 140–60.

17. Soyinka, *Myth, Literature* 144, 144, 42, 30–31.

18. Soyinka, *Myth, Literature* 13.

19. Soyinka, *Myth, Literature* 140. If identity is always relative, meaning a German could know himself better through a Yoruba, and vice versa, why the phrase "ironic truths"? The passion and eloquence of Soyinka in marking the African worldview from the European sometimes results in a language that appears absolute, but we invariably arrive at an "ironic truth." Soyinka's "irony" is the type that Ross Chambers calls "appropriative," an irony that hides nothing but "signals that it is part of an open-ended historical process" of interrelationships and cross-influences. "Irony and the Canon" 23.

20. Soyinka, *Myth, Literature* 158, 159. See also Soyinka's dramatic revision of Greek tragedy by way of Euripides, *The Bacchae of Euripides*. For an introduction to the rich, multiple heritage of this play, see Sotto, *The Rounded Rite*.

21. Soyinka, *Myth, Literature* 14.

22. Soyinka, *Myth, Literature* 141.

23. Soyinka, "Who's Afraid of Elesin," *Art, Dialogue* 128.

24. Soyinka, *Death and the King's Horseman* 75.

25. Soyinka, "Author's Note," *Death and the King's Horseman* n.p.

26. See Jeyifo's reading of these departures, *The Truthful Lie* 27–28; and Soyinka's reply, "Who's Afraid of Elesin," *Art, Dialogue* 126–29.

27. Soyinka, *Death and the King's Horseman* 14.

28. Soyinka, *Death and the King's Horseman* 9, stage direction. Emphasis added.

29. Soyinka, *Death and the King's Horseman* 10.

30. Soyinka, *Death and the King's Horseman* 13, 14.

31. Soyinka, *Death and the King's Horseman* 18.

32. Soyinka, *Death and the King's Horseman* 20, 22.

33. Soyinka, *Death and the King's Horseman* 23.

34. Nietzsche, *The Birth of Tragedy* 36–46.

35. Nietzsche, *The Birth of Tragedy* 46.

36. Soyinka, *Myth, Literature* 147, 148.

37. Soyinka, *Death and the King's Horseman* 27.

38. Soyinka, *Death and the King's Horseman* 40, 41, 45.

39. Soyinka, *Myth, Literature* 38–39.

40. Soyinka writes of the human "desire 'to put off Death', 'to come to terms with Death', to 'communalise' Death so as to make it more bearable for the individual, 'to humour Death'. . . . My suspicion is that this need to communally contain Death will always be there." "Who's Afraid of Elesin," *Art, Dialogue* 127.

41. Soyinka, *Myth, Literature* 146.

42. Soyinka, *Myth, Literature* 146.

43. Soyinka, *Death and the King's Horseman* 20.

44. Ready, "Through the Intricacies" 715.

45. To Nietzsche's reading that "illusion" is the "original act of the naive artist and at the same time of all Apollonian culture" (*The Birth of Tragedy* 33), Soyinka poses the Obatalan difference as "inner essence." The creation which follows or commences with the act of creativity is not an illusion which is a copy of something. Yoruba classical art is not "identical" but "'essential'. It is not the idea (in religious arts) that is transmitted into wood or interpreted in music or movement but a quintessence of inner being, a symbolic interaction of the many aspects of revelations (within a universal context) with their moral apprehension." Soyinka argues that Ogun's charge into the "chthonic realm," that is, the quintessential creative process with all its perils, is not, as European representations put it, the "fictive" pool from which art is fashioned: "In our journey to the heart of Yoruba tragic art which indeed belongs in the Mysteries of Ogun and the choric ectasy of revellers, we do not find that the Yoruba, as the Greek did, 'built for his chorus the scaffolding of a fictive chthonic realm and placed thereon fictive nature spirits . . .' on which foundation, claims Nietzsche, Greek tragedy developed: in short, the principle of illusion. Yoruba tragedy plunges straight into the 'chthonic realm', the seething cauldron of the dark world will and psyche, the transitional yet inchoate matrix of death and becoming. Into this universal womb once plunged and emerged Ogun, the first actor, disintegrating within the abyss. His spiritual reassemblage does not require a 'copying of actuality' in the ritual re-enactment of his devotees, any more than Obatala does in plastic representation, in the art of Obatala." *Myth, Literature* 141, 142.

46. Ready, "Through the Intricacies" 715.

47. Soyinka, *Death and the King's Horseman* 18.

48. Soyinka, *Myth, Literature* 36.

49. Soyinka, *Death and the King's Horseman* 75.

50. Soyinka, *Death and the King's Horseman* 29, 30, 31.

51. Soyinka, "Who's Afraid of Elesin," *Art, Dialogue* 128.

52. I have benefited from Milton Fisk, *Ethics and Society*
53. Soyinka, *Death and the King's Horseman* 50.
54. Soyinka, *Death and the King's Horseman* 51.
55. Soyinka, *Death and the King's Horseman* 64.
56. Soyinka, *Death and the King's Horseman* 15.
57. Soyinka, *Death and the King's Horseman* 54. I am relating this, in an ironically illuminating way, to the charge of "obscurantism" commonly leveled against Soyinka's use of English (see Chinweizu, Jemie, and Madubuike, "Towards the Decolonization of African Literature"). Soyinka announces what few critics have recognized as his *working* answer to the vexed question of the position of English in African literature, a clue to his own richly challenging and peculiar deployment of that language: "[W]hen we borrow an alien language to sculpt or paint in, we must begin by co-opting the entire properties in our matrix of thought and expression. We must stress such a language, stretch it, impact and compact, fragment and reassemble it with no apology, as required to bear the burden of experiencing and of experiences, be such experiences formulated or not in the conceptual idioms of that language." "Aesthetic Illusions," *Art, Dialogue* 107. Compare this "manifesto" with a critic's perception in a review of a U.K. production of *The Road* in 1965: "Every decade or so, it seems to fall to a non-English dramatist to belt new energy into the English tongue. The last time was when Brendan Behan's 'The Quare Fellow' opened at Theatre Workshop. Nine years later, in the reign of Stage Sixty at the same loved Victorian building at Stratford East, a Nigerian called Wole Soyinka has done for our napping language what brigand dramatists from Ireland have done for centuries: booted it awake, rifled its pockets and scattered the loot into the middle of next week." Penelope Gilliatt, "A Nigerian Original," *The Observer*, 19 September, 1965: 25. Cited in Gibbs, *Critical Perspectives on Wole Soyinka* 106.
58. Soyinka, *Death and the King's Horseman* 64.
59. Soyinka, *Death and the King's Horseman* 54.
60. Soyinka, *Death and the King's Horseman* 69.
61. See, for instance, Johnson, *The History of the Yorubas* 326–27, 330–31, 396–99.
62. Soyinka, *Death and the King's Horseman* 58, 67. The "colonial factor" is so deeply implicated as to deny Wole Ogundele's claim that it is "no more than . . . a historical mirror which reflects the moribund and impotent state of native ethics at this time in history." See his essay, "*Death and the King's Horseman*: A Poet's Quarrel with His Culture" 58. The specific character of the stasis and impotence cannot be totally severed from the colonial encounter, as Ogundele himself persuasively shows earlier in the essay in his comments about the power of the new colonial "cosmic order" (50). A cause cannot simply at the same time be a reflector.
63. Soyinka, *Death and the King's Horseman* 56.
64. "The native intellectual nevertheless sooner or later will realize that you do not show proof of your nation from its culture but that you substantiate its existence in the fight which the people wage against the forces of occupation. No colonial system draws its justification from the fact that the territories it dominates are culturally non-existent. You will never make colonialism blush for shame by spreading out little -known cultural treasures under its eyes." Fanon, *The Wretched of the Earth* 223.
65. Johnson, *The History of the Yorubas* 396–98. I think this is also the argu-

ment of Adebayo Williams that "what Soyinka achieved in *Death and the King's Horseman* was to counterpose the dominant culture of the ancient Oyo Kingdom against the equally hegemonic culture of the white invaders." "Ritual and the Political Unconsciousness" 77.

66. See Senghor, *The Foundation of "Africanite" or "Negritude" and "Arabite," The Mission of the Poet*, and *Prose and Poetry*.

67. Soyinka, "The Future of West African Writing"; "From a Common Back Cloth: A Reassesment of the African Literary Image" (1963), *Art, Dialogue* 7–14; and "And after the Narcissist?"

68. Soyinka, "Future," cited in Chinweizu, Jemie, and Madubuike, *Toward the Decolonization of African Literature* 201. *A Dance of the Forests* is in *Collected Plays 1*. See my detailed discussion of the play in "Dramatizing Postcoloniality."

69. Soyinka, interview with Biodun Jeyifo, "Introduction," *Six Plays* xiii.

70. Faced with bitter but mostly mistaken critiques of his position, Soyinka returns to Negritude, in an attempt to come to terms with it both in the similarity of goals and in the great divergence of means. "Our opposition to negritude . . . is based on self-acceptance," he writes, "a hard-eyed self-examination, not self-denial." Soyinka, "The African World and the Ethnocultural Debate" 36. He identifies the vision of Negritude as the "restitution and re-engineering of a racial psyche, the establishment of a distinct human entity and the glorification of its long-suppressed attributes," and warns that this vision "should never be underestimated or belittled." The sad point, however, is that negritude adopts an overly simplified route toward realizing its goal: "Its re-entrenchment of black values was not preceded by any profound effort to enter into this African system of values. It extolled the apparent. Its reference points took far too much colouring from European ideas even while its Messiahs pronounced themselves fanatically African. In attempting to refute the evaluation to which black reality had been subjected, Negritude adopted the Manichean tradition of European thought and inflicted it on a culture which is most radically anti-Manichean." *Myth, Literature* 126, 127.

71. See, for instance, interview with Biodun Jeyifous, *Transition* 42 (1973): 62.

72. Soyinka, "Cross-Currents: The 'New African' after Cultural Encounters," and "The External Encounter: Ambivalence in African Arts and Literature," *Art, Dialogue* 183–84 and 239–42, respectively.

73. Davies, "Maidens, Mistresses and Matrons."

74. Stratton, "Wole Soyinka: A Writer's Social Vision."

75. See the following abbreviated list: Jeyifo, *Soyinka Demythologized* and *The Truthful Lie* 11–22, 23–45; Osofisan, "Ritual and the Revolutionary Ethos" and "Drama and the New Exotic"; Ogunbiyi, "A Study of Soyinka's *Opera Wonyosi*" 3–14; and Hunt, "Two African Aesthetics." Some of Soyinka's trenchant responses—"Who's Afraid of Eleson Oba?" "The Autistic Hunt; or, How to Marximize Mediocrity," and "The Critic and Society: Barthes, Leftocracy and Other Mythologies"—appear in *Art, Dialogue* 110–31, 279–314, and 146–78 respectively.

76. Soyinka, "Who's Afraid of Elesin," *Art, Dialogue* 120.

77. Soyinka, "Drama and the Idioms of Liberation: Proletarian Illusions" (published as "Drama and the Revolutionary Ideal" in 1975), *Art, Dialogue* 54, 60. Soyinka's *The Bacchae* is an eloquent statement of this belief.

78. Osofisan, "Ritual and the Revolutionary Ethos" 73, 75.

79. Soyinka, "Who's Afraid of Elesin," *Art, Dialogue* 120–23.

80. Osofisan, "Ritual and the Revolutionary Ethos" 75–76. A note of caution here. This debate took place in the 1970s. My guess is that Osofisan today would not be unwilling to qualify some of his claims, given the recent self-rewriting of similar views earlier held by Biodun Jeyifo, another major participant in the debate and Osofisan's friend, colleague, and intellectual collaborator.

81. Soyinka, "Who's Afraid of Elesin," *Art, Dialogue* 123, 124.

82. Soyinka, "Who's Afraid of Elesin," *Art, Dialogue* 114.

83. For an incisive introduction to this issue, see Jeyifo, "Femi Osofisan as Literary Critic and Theorist."

84. Osofisan, "Ritual and the Revolutionary Ethos" 78.

85. Soyinka, "Who's Afraid of Elesin," *Art, Dialogue* 119.

86. Jeyifo, *Soyinka Demythologized* 7–8, 9.

87. Jeyifo, *Soyinka Demythologized* 53. See also Jeyifo's review of Soyinka's *Myth, Literature*, "Some Corrective Myths for the Misguided Native and the Arrogant Alien."

88. Soyinka, "Who's Afraid of Elesin," *Art, Dialogue* 110; "The Critic and Society," *Art, Dialogue* 170.

89. Soyinka, "Who's afraid of Elesin," *Art, Dialogue* 110.

90. Soyinka, "The Critic and Society," *Art, Dialogue* 169.

91. Jeyifo, *Truthful Lie* 9.

92. Jeyifo, "What Is the Will of Ogun" 174, 176. The seminal essay in this regard, one which will most likely set the tone of Soyinka criticism in the coming years, is, however, Jeyifo's introduction to *Art, Dialogue*, "Wole Soyinka and the Tropes of Disalienation," viii–xxxii.

93. Jeyifo, "Wole Soyinka" xx–xxi. On the antinomian character of Soyinka's constructs, Jeyifo writes: "It has been Soyinka's ideological and theoretical struggle in virtually all [his] essays to argue . . . in effect that the 'African World', in its ideational systems and ideological superstructures, is both essentialist and non-essentialist: a willed aporia as much as a verifiable construct. And we might remark . . . that Soyinka's aporetic arguments find powerful theoretical supports in some of the most influential works on philosophy of culture in Africa, notably W. E. Abraham's *The Mind of Africa* and Paulin J. Hountondji's *African Philosophy: Myth and Reality*. When Abraham writes: 'Essentialist views have themselves changed from era to era. One may even say that it is they which place a cachet on their eras', we recognise not only the same aporia of Soyinka's theoretical discourse but also the very source of this factor—a theoretical anxiety to affirm archaic, autochthonous insights and yet be at one with the march of human thought and progress. In this respect, aporia may well be the master trope for a society, like contemporary Africa, wracked by profound antipodal impulses and rapid, vertiginous transformations." xxviii-xxix.

94. Jeyifo, "What Is the Will" 180.

Chapter 4

1. If you relate this tale to Baraka he would probably laugh at its heavy ornamental coating but admit a "kernel of truth" beneath and above it. See Melhem, "Amiri Baraka (LeRoi Jones)" 226–27.

2. This is a principal analytic tool I am bringing to bear on the appreciation of Baraka, mandated by the unusual character of his relations to the ruling norms

of literary discourse. I am aware that curiosity is generally read as an attribute of negative value but, as Michel Foucault argues in a recuperative move, curiosity "evokes 'care'; . . . the care one takes of what exists and what might exist; a sharpened sense of reality, but one that is never immobilized before it; a readiness to find what surrounds us strange and odd; *a certain determination to throw off familiar ways of thought and to look at the same things in a different way,* a passion for seizing what is happening now and what is disapppearing; *a lack of respect for the traditional hierarchies of what is important and fundamental.*" See "The Masked Philosopher," *Politics, Philosophy, Culture* 328. Emphases added.

3. Baraka tries an explanation for this state of things: "I think it's basically because my work . . . has been—most people know it principally as political. And so it's different if you have a political professor who is essentially a professor and is political in that sense. But . . . you have somebody who people identify primarily as a political activist and only secondarily as a writer . . ." Melhem, "Amiri Baraka (LeRoi Jones)" 226.

4. Lloyd W. Brown, *Amiri Baraka* 166, 164, 168.

5. Sollors, *Amiri Baraka/LeRoi Jones* 237, 246.

6. Walcott, "The Theatre of Abuse."

7. Greg Tate, "Growing Up in Public" 41. For similar criticisms, see also Andrews, "The Marxist Theater of Amiri Baraka," and David L. Smith, "Amiri Baraka and the Black Arts of Black Art."

8. Early, "The Case of Leroi Jones/Amiri Baraka" 346–47; William J. Harris, *The Poetry and Poetics of Amiri Baraka* 122–24.

9. McClintock, " 'Azikwelwa' (We Will Not Ride)" 240.

10. Hogue, *Discourse and the Other* 1–47.

11. Hogue, *Discourse and the Other* 31.

12. Lindenberger, *The History in Literature* xix. See also, for discussions of value as socially and historically contingent, Barbara H. Smith, *Contingencies of Value;* Dubois and Durand, "Literary Field and Classes of Texts"; Lauter, "History and the Canon"; Eagleton and Fuller, "The Question of Value"; and Eagleton, *Criticism and Ideology.*

13. Lindenberger, *The History in Literature* 19.

14. Foucault, "The Masked Philosopher," *Politics, Philosophy, Culture* 327.

15. Fanon, *Black Skin, White Masks* 176.

16. Raymond Williams, *Problems in Materialism and Culture* 47–48.

17. Cited in Harris, *The Poetry and Poetics of Amiri Baraka* 2.

18. Cornel West, interview with Anders Stephanson, *Universal Abandon?* 281, 277.

19. LeRoi Jones, "The Changing Same (R&B and the New Black Music."

20. Cited in Jessica B. Harris, "The National Black Theatre" 283–84.

21. In a not too dissimilar context, Peter Stallybrass and Allon White have written: "[T]he top attempts to reject and eliminate the bottom for reasons of prestige and status only to discover not only that it is some way frequently dependent upon that low-Other (in the classic way that Hegel describes in the master–slave section of *Phenomenology*), but also that the top *includes* that low symbolically, as a primary eroticized constituent of its own fantasy life. The result is a mobile conflictual fusion of power, fear and desire in the construction of subjectivity: a psychological dependence upon precisely those Others which are being rigorously opposed and excluded at the social level. It is for this reason that what is *socially* peripheral is so frequently *symbolically* central. . . . The low-Other

is despised and denied at the level of political organization and social being whilst it is instrumentally constitutive of the shared imaginary repertoires of the dominant culture." *The Politics and Poetics of Transgression* 5–6.

22. Harris, *The Poetry and Poetics of Amiri Baraka* 13.

23. Harris, *The Poetry and Poetics of Amiri Baraka* 13–33.

24. Benston, *Baraka: The Renegade and the Mask* xvii.

25. From *The Dead Lecturer* in *Three Books* 10, 79.

26. See the chapter titled "Black Brown Yellow White," *The Autobiography of LeRoi Jones* 42–47.

27. Baraka, *The Autobiography of LeRoi Jones* 44.

28. "The brown was like a reserve, an exit or quick passage to somewhere else. You look up you could be getting a scholarship somewhere or shaking Joe Louis' and Sandy Saddler's hand or being introduced by Willie Bryant as a bright Negro child, or reciting the Gettysburg Address in a Boy Scout suit down at the Old First Church, where George Washington was and most black people wasn't." Baraka, *The Autobiography of LeRoi Jones* 45.

29. Interview with Judy Stone, "If It's Anger . . . Maybe that's Good." Cited in Lacey, *To Raise, Destroy, and Create* 1.

30. Interview with Judy Stone, cited in Lacey, *To Raise, Destroy, and Create* 2.

31. Baraka, *The Autobiography of LeRoi Jones* 118.

32. See the chapter "Error Farce" in Baraka, *The Autobiography of LeRoi Jones* 94–123.

33. For detailed and useful accounts of Baraka's activities and friendships, and the decisive influences on him in Greenwich Village, see Sollors, *Amiri Baraka/LeRoi Jones* 11–35; Harris, *The Poetry and Poetics of Amiri Baraka* 34–66; and Baraka, *The Autobiography of LeRoi Jones* 124–201.

34. Helmut Kreuzer, cited in Sollors, *Amiri Baraka/LeRoi Jones* 18.

35. Sollors, *Amiri Baraka/LeRoi Jones* 21.

36. Melhem, "Amiri Baraka (LeRoi Jones)" 250.

37. Cited in Lacey, *To Raise, Destroy, and Create* 3.

38. Baraka, cited in Harris, *The Poetry and Poetics of Amiri Baraka* 6

39. Cited in Sollors, *Amiri Baraka/LeRoi Jones* 29.

40. Cited in Sollors, *Amiri Baraka/LeRoi Jones* 32.

41. LeRoi Jones, *The Moderns* 343–44.

42. Sollors, *Amiri Baraka/LeRoi Jones* 32.

43. It is noteworthy that these techniques survive Baraka's various ideological shifts, manipulated at every stage to answer new demands. See, for instance, the poetry section of the recent collection of poetry and music criticism, *The Music: Reflections on Jazz and Blues.*

44. Baraka, *The Autobiography of LeRoi Jones* 187, 186.

45. LeRoi Jones, *The Baptism and The Toilet* 15.

46. Taylor Mead, "Drama Mailbag: Again the Readers Argue LeRoi Jones," *New York Times*, 14 December 14, section 2:15. Cited in Sollors, *Amiri Baraka/LeRoi Jones* 107.

47. Sollors, *Amiri Baraka/LeRoi Jones* 28.

48. Baraka, *The Autobiography of LeRoi Jones* 163.

49. Baraka, *The Autobiography of LeRoi Jones* 166.

50. LeRoi Jones, "Cuba Libre," *Home: Social Essays* 42–43.

51. Baraka, *The Autobiography of LeRoi Jones* 165.

52. Jones, *Home: Social Essays* 20.

53. Barthes, "Whose Theater? Whose *Avant-Garde?*" 68.

54. Jones, *Home: Social Essays* 65.

55. Jones, *Home: Social Essays* 93.

56. Baraka's extensive critical explorations of black music include the historical and theoretical study *Blues People*; a collection of reviews of the 1960s jazz avant-garde, *Black Music*; and more contemporary reflections, *The Music*. For a detailed discussion of Baraka's musical aesthetics as developed in the first two books, see Benston, *Baraka: The Renegade and the Mask* 69–96.

57. Jones, "The Myth of a 'Negro Literature,'" *Home: Social Essays* 105, 106, 110, 111, 114, 112, 109.

58. For an insightful discussion of the play's circulating identity between naturalism and the avant-garde, see Benston, *Baraka: The Renegade and the Mask* 151–57.

59. LeRoi Jones, *Dutchman* 12.

60. Jones, *Dutchman* 19.

61. Jones, *Dutchman* 18.

62. Jones, *Dutchman* 30.

63. Jones, *Dutchman* 34.

64. Jones, *Dutchman* 35.

65. Baraka, "Black Art," *Selected Poetry* 107.

66. Jones, *The Slave* 51, 55.

67. A popular quote commonly attributed to Fidel Castro: This earth is ours / And the air / And the sky / We will defend them! Cited in Wole Soyinka, *The Man Died* 183.

68. Jones, The *Slave* 75.

69. Jones, "The Revolutionary Theatre," *Home: Social Essays* 210, 211, 214, 212, 213.

70. Jones, "The Revolutionary Theatre," *Home: Social Essays* 212, 211, 214–15.

71. Imamu Amiri Baraka (LeRoi Jones), "Work Notes—'66" *Raise Race Rays Raze* 15.

72. Hettie Jones's interesting account of their relationship is far more detailed than Baraka's in *The Autobiography of LeRoi Jones*. See her *How I Became Hettie Jones*. Baraka subsequently married a black woman, Sylvia Wilson, now Amina Baraka.

73. See Baraka's cultural nationalist manual, *A Black Value System*, a popularization of the "Kawaida" doctrine of Maulana Karenga, founder and leader of the cultural nationalist organization US. See Karenga, *Kawaida Theory*.

74. Baraka, *The Autobiography of LeRoi Jones* 267.

75. See also Hudson, *From LeRoi Jones to Amiri Baraka* 181–82.

76. See Benston's sensitive treatment of many of these much-maligned plays. *Baraka: The Renegade and the Mask* 209–42.

77. See Benston's useful comments on the drama's "modernist assault on representation in which *performance* connotes a revolutionary liberation from all prior codes." "Being There" 438.

78. Baraka, *Slave Ship*, in *The Motion of History* 132.

79. Stefan Brecht, "LeRoi Jones' *Slave Ship*" 217.

80. Baraka, *Slave Ship* 133.

81. Baraka, *Slave Ship* 142.

82. Baraka, *Slave Ship* 133, 135, 136, 141, 142, 143, 144. Wole Soyinka, writing on a performance of this play, comments on the effectiveness of one of the techniques it employed for the social registration of African-American identity: "When Imamu Baraka . . . instructs his actors to go around the theatre to touch and shake hands with members of the black audience and leave out the white, he is using the concept of audience involvement in a truthful, relevant, and, in this case, deliberate personality dissociating sense. I read the reaction of a white critic in the audience who declared that after seeing the play itself, watching the catalog of dehumanization of the black man, and emphathizing with it on a level which he had never before suspected, it was a shock to him to find literally that the play, and his ordeal, was not over, that he had to experience yet another level of his unsuspected rejection. He, in spite of these feelings of identification which had been fed into him from the universality of suffering, found that his emotive identification existed only for him and was not necessarily reciprocal in itself with the essential truths of the evening. The suffering humanity not only rejected him but by so doing questioned and raised doubts in his mind that he was a member of the human race at all, this not alone by the actual business of the selective handshakes afterwards but by its finality, the fact that it was a culminating metaphor of that emotive temperature which had been aroused. It was not, wrote the critic, simply a question of guilt. The charge which was lodged in his mind was that he was not a member of the human race, that this doubt had been achieved by the theatrical contraction of the entire human race into the sum of anguish and courage presented upon that stage. The world outside of it was wiped out in that microcosmic totality of ritual. Now this is a rational exploitation of audience participation, selective, unforced, perfectly posed contextually." "Drama and the Idioms of Liberation," *Art, Dialogue* 55.

83. Baraka, "Black Woman," *Raise Race Rays Raze* 147, 148, 152, 153. Very little is original in Baraka's essay. The subtending "master text" is Maulana Karenga's: "What makes a woman appealing is femininity but she can't be feminine without being submissive. The role of the woman is to inspire her man, educate their children and participate in social development. Equality is false; it's the devil's concept. Our concept is complementary. Complementary means you complete or make perfect that which is imperfect." Cited in Allen, *Black Awakening in Capitalist America* 168–69. I have benefited from the following readings of the repressive, sexist character of black nationalism: White, "Africa on My Mind"; and hooks, *Ain't I a Woman: Black Women and Feminism* 87–117.

84. LeRoi Jones, *Madheart*, in *Four Black Revolutionary Plays: All Praises to the Black Man* 81–83. See Sandra L. Richards's fine discussion of this play in her article "Negative Forces and Positive Non-Entities."

85. Baraka, "Nationalism Vs PimpArt," *Raise, Race, Rays, Raze* 130.

86. Baraka, "7 Principles of US: Maulana Karenga & the Need for a Black Value System," *Raise, Race, Rays, Raze* 138.

87. Cited in Sollors, *Amiri Baraka/LeRoi Jones* 221–22.

88. Cited in Sollors, *Amiri Baraka/LeRoi Jones* 222, 225–26. For a detailed background to Baraka's politics at this time, see McCartney, *Black Power Ideologies* 166–80.

89. Baraka, "Toward Ideological Clarity" 29, 30, 27, 32, 33. Baraka has not abandoned the naive cultural nationalist thesis of a black nation within the United States. For a critique of this thesis, see West, "Marxist Theory and the Specificity of Afro-American Oppression" 19–20.

90. Baraka, *The Autobiography of LeRoi Jones* 327.

91. Baraka, "Revolutionary Culture & the Future of PanAfrikan Culture," (Newark, N.J., June 19–27, 1974). Cited in Sollors, *Amiri Baraka/LeRoi Jones* 227.

92. Baraka, *Selected Poetry* 238, 236–37.

93. Baraka, *The Motion of History* 13.

94. Baraka, *The Motion of History* 57.

95. Baraka, *The Motion of History* 118.

96. Baraka, *The Motion of History* 21.

97. Baudry, "Ideological Effects of the Basic Cinematographic Apparatus" 294.

98. Murray, "Screening the Camera's Eye" 118.

99. Baraka, *The Motion of History* 89–90.

100. Baraka, *The Motion of History* 13.

101. Andrews, "The Marxist Theatre of Amiri Baraka" 143.

102. Baraka, *The Motion of History* 23, 22.

103. Baraka, *The Motion of History* 121.

104. Baraka, *The Motion of History* 121.

105. See Bertolt Brecht, "Writing the Truth: Five Difficulties" 146.

106. Baraka, *The Motion of History* 120.

107. Henry Louis Gates, Jr., misses this point when, in a review of Baraka's *The Autobiography of LeRoi Jones,* he reads the dramatist's changes as betrayals of previously held positions and acolytes gathered along the way: "Each of Mr. Baraka's lives has its own flavor of language, its own distinct style. He draws upon style as a correlative of his changing spots; reading his book is like listening to albums by Coleman Hawkins, Charlie Parker, James Brown, then late John Coltrane, a remarkable stylistic achievement. It is the serial lives depicted here, however, and the acts of betrayal that connect them, that make his autobiography problematical indeed. . . . One must wonder at the costs of those who, at any given phase, have been his true believers." "Several Lives, Several Voices."

108. Harris, "The National Black Theatre" 88–89. If it is no longer easy to recognize the "real" cultural nationalist Teer in my appropriation of her, I plead guilty—to opening up in different directions and to different possibilities her profoundly suggestive but exclusivist black line. For a brief critique of her group's surrender to the sexist discourse of black nationalism, see Wallace, *Invisibility Blues* 19–20.

109. Baraka, *The Autobiography of LeRoi Jones* 328. Emphasis added.

Chapter 5

1. Walcott, *Collected Poems* 11, 350.

2. Knight and Palmer, "The Caribbean" 1.

3. Knight and Palmer, "The Caribbean" 1.

4. Brathwaite, "Timehri" 29.

5. In addition to Knight and Palmer, see, on sociopolitical and cultural conditions in the Caribbean, two collections of essays: Mintz and Price, *Caribbean Contours,* and Henry and Stone, *The Newer Caribbean: Decolonization, Democracy, and Development.*

6. Walcott, "The Muse of History" 1.

7. Walcott, "The Sea Is History," *Collected Poems* 364.

8. Walcott, "The Sea Is History" 366.

9. Walcott, "The Star-Apple Kingdom," *Collected Poems* 392.

10. See Rodman, *Tongues of Fallen Angels* 252–53.

11. Walcott, "Homage to Gregorias," *Collected Poems* 212, 211.

12. "The judges of normality are present everywhere. We are in the society of the teacher-judge, the doctor-judge, the educator-judge, the 'social worker'-judge; it is on them that the universal reign of the normative is based; and each individual, wherever he may find himself, subjects to it his body, his gestures, his behaviour, his aptitudes, his achievements. The carceral network, in its compact or disseminated forms, with its systems of insertion, distribution, surveillance, observation, has been the greatest support, in modern society, of the normalizing power." Foucault, *Discipline and Punish* 304.

13. Cited by Rodman, *Tongues of Fallen Angels* 253.

14. Walcott, "What the Twilight Says" 12, 13, 13, 13, 12 (in order of citation). See also Walcott's early play on the Haitian Revolution, *Henri Christophe*. For a brief historical account of the subject dramatized in this play, see Geggus, "The Haitian Revolution," and the insightful study by James, *The Black Jacobins*.

15. Walcott, "What the Twilight Says" 11.

16. Walcott, "Crusoe's Journal," *Collected Poems* 93.

17. Walcott, "What the Twilight Says" 13.

18. Walcott, "Homage to Gregorias," *Collected Poems* 195.

19. Walcott, "What the Twilight Says" 4.

20. Walcott, "What the Twilight Says" 31.

21. Walcott, "The Caribbean: Culture or Mimicry" and "The Muse of History." See also the early short article, "Necessity of Negritude" (1964) as well as *Another Life, Omeros* (1990), *Remembrance, Remembrance and Pantomime: Two Plays* (1980), and *The Last Carnival, Three Plays* (1986), all published in New York by Farrar, Straus and Giroux.

22. Walcott, "The Muse of History" 2, 6, 7, 2, 2, 5, 2–3 (in order of citation). Socioculturally specific labels, especially when about to cross borders, must be used reflexively, but it is impossible not to note a very close parallel between Walcott here and Michel Foucault's postmodern critique of origin and the subject of history in his important essay "Nietzsche, Genealogy, History." "The lofty origin [Walcott's detestable history-as-time] is no more than a 'metaphysical extension which arises from the belief that things are most precious and essential at the moment of birth,'" Foucault writes, quoting from Nietzsche's *The Wanderer and His Shadow*. "We tend to think this is the moment of their greatest perfection," he continues, "where they emerged dazzling from the hands of a creator or in the shadowless light of a first morning. The origin always precedes the Fall. It comes before the body, before the world and time; it is associated with tne gods, and its story is always sung as a theogony." *Language, Counter-Memory* 143; 139–64. It seems to me that the experience defined as "postmodern," in terms of its emphasis on self-reflexivity and the relative and contingent decentered subject, is not peculiar to the metropole but is also *the* very constitutive feature of most anti-Eurocentric discourses. Their quintessentially relativist character, which I discussed in chapter 2, is fundamentally against the impulse to dominate. As I have suggested elsewhere, these discourses actually *precede* postmodernism in their articulation of a decentered subjectivity: "Their major weapon has always been different but equal: we are not heathens, we have our own religions and deities; we are not barbaric, we have our own cultures, etc. Let me quickly say

that this is not necessarily out of any altruism on the part of these counter-discourses—in fact, the dream is always to take over the master's house, not to dismantle it. Witness the result of political nationalism in most erstwhile colonized countries—but out of a structural *lack* in their composition. Born in the flaming kiln of history, they emerge with a permanently scarred 'psyche.' They are born already aware of difference, thus they are denied the luxury and comfort of Lacan's 'mirror phase,' that phase of growth in which 'we'—both corporeal and discursive bodies—imagine ourselves not only as the center of the universe but the universe itself. The moment of birth, normally unknown and unrememberable for others, becomes for these subordinate discourses witnessed and unforgettable. They are thus doomed to constantly acknowledge their own contingent character, unlike Eurocentrism whose image of itself as *essential* was little challenged for centuries. This is why counter-discourses can only dream (futilely suturing the lack) but can never yarn grand narratives. Anti-colonial Afrocentric nationalist discourses reached this ironically liberating and anti-expansionist insight since its birth in the early decades of this century, an insight which is only now being discovered by current poststructuralist thought." "Discussing Afrocentrism" 4. This is also similar to the insight in Philip B. Harper's recent fine book, *Framing the Margins: The Social Logic of Postmodern Culture*. Rei Terada tries to address the question of postmodernism and Walcott's poetic practice in the epilogue to the book *Derek Walcott's Poetry: American Mimicry*.

23. Walcott, "The Antilles: Fragments of Epic Memory" 28; 26ff

24. Walcott, "The Muse of History" 2.

25. On Black Power in the Caribbean, see the other essays in Coombs, *Is Massa Day Dead?*; Pantin, *Black Power Day*; Nettleford, *Identity, Race and Protest in Jamaica*; Palmer, "Identity, Race, and Black Power in Independent Jamaica"; and Rodney, *The Groundings with My Brothers*.

26. Edward K. Brathwaite, "Jazz and the West Indian Novel," *Bim* 44 (January–June 1967). Cited in Maxwell, "Towards a Revolution in the Arts" 19–20. Brathwaite is generally regarded as the West Indies's second leading poet, after Walcott. Some of his works include *Rights of Passage* (1967), *Masks* (1968), *Islands* (1969)—the three published as *The Arrivants: A New World Trilogy*—and more than seven other volumes to date. See also his essay "The Love Axe (1): Developing a Caribbean Aesthetic 1962–1974."

27. Rohlehr, *Pathfinder: Black Awakening in The Arrivants of Edward Kamau Brathwaite* 111–12.

28. Walcott, "The Muse of History" 3–4.

29. Walcott, "The Muse of History" 19, 22.

30. Walcott denounces them as "the dividers" who "pronounce their measure / of toms, of traitors, of traditionals and Afro-Saxons," who "measure each other's sores / to boast who has suffered most." *Collected Poems* 270. See also 350: "I had no nation now but the imagination. / After the white man, the niggers didn't want me / when the power swing to their side. / The first chain my hands and apologize, "History"; / the next said I wasn't black enough for their pride."

31. Walcott, "What the Twilight Says" 9, and "The Muse of History" 19.

32. Walcott, "The Muse of History" 4, 2, 1, 5.

33. Walcott, "The Muse of History" 16–17, 17.

34. Walcott, "What the Twilight Says" 26.

35. Walcott, "The Caribbean: Culture or Mimicry" 6.

36. Walcott, "The Muse of History" 12–13.

37. Walcott, "The Muse of History" 5, 24, 26.
38. Walcott, "What the Twilight Says" 13.
39. Walcott, "Meanings" 48.
40. Walcott, "Meanings" 48, 47; "The Kabuki—Something to Give to Our Theatre" 14. See also Walcott's discussion of West Indian musicals and dance, "Patterns to Forget."
41. Walcott, "The Theatre of the Streets."
42. Walcott, "Problems of Exile." For Walcott's intimation of his earlier respect and the waning of that respect for calypso, see "We Are Still Being Betrayed" 16.
43. Walcott, "Patterns to Forget."
44. See Maxwell, "Towards a Revolution in the Arts" 21.
45. I discussed this play in some detail in "Dramatizing Postcoloniality."
46. Walcott, "The Caribbean: Culture or Mimicry" 9–10.
47. Walcott, "What the Twilight Says" 35, 7.
48. Walcott, "National Theatre Is the Answer."
49. Walcott, "Meanings" 51.
50. Walcott, "What the Twilight Says" 9. There is some measure of self-reference here beyond the literary: the explosive issue of "race" in the Caribbean. Whereas in the United States the mythical "one drop" is denied and therefore the mulatto is by force of law black, the West Indian mulatto is by no means black in the popular imagination, an imagination propped up by the historically higher social privilege accorded the mulatto, so that since the wave of independence, the color of native aristocracy and economic power has turned predominantly "brown." Walcott, a brown man—"red nigger," he likes to say—but by no means an aristocrat, has Dutch, African, and English ancestries, holds a British passport, and had a middle-class upbringing. See Hirsch, "An Interview with Derek Walcott" 285. For some useful studies of "race" in the Caribbean, see M. G. Smith, *Culture, Race, and Class in the Commonwealth Caribbean*; Lowenthal and Comitas, *Consequences of Class and Color: West Indian Perspectives*; and Raymond T. Smith, "Race and Class in the Post-Emancipation Caribbean."
51. In Walcott, *Dream on Monkey Mountain and Other Plays.*
52. Walcott, *Dream* 237.
53. Walcott, *Dream* 215, 225, 226, 227, 217.
54. "Discourse always requires a speaking position (a position from which power-knowledge is exercised) and a spoken subject (a position brought into existence through the exercise of power-knowledge)." Silverman, *"Histoire d'O:* The Story of a Disciplined and Punished Body" 66–67.
55. Walcott, *Dream* 280, 279, 216, 217.
56. Walcott, *Dream* 236, 216, 281, 280.
57. Walcott, *Dream* 222, 223.
58. Walcott, *Dream* 219, 226.
59. Foucault, *Discipline and Punish* 202–3.
60. Walcott, *Dream* 280.
61. Walcott, *Dream* 236, 227, 236, 227, 236, 236.
62. Walcott, *Dream* 226, 228, 240, 241–42, 285, 242, 287.
63. Walcott, *Dream* 305. Walcott writes of "Makak's trip back to Africa where he found the tribes slaughtering each other (Ibos were being slaughtered by their Nigerian brothers while I wrote the play: a familiar human tragedy, of course, for

civil wars are going on all over the world). Makak recognizes that human cruelty is raceless." Cited by Rodman, *Tongues of Fallen Angels* 249.

64. Walcott, *Dream* 308–11, 311.

65. Walcott, *Dream* 312–5, 250–55, 265–69.

66. See Dollimore, "The Dominant and the Deviant" 190.

67. Walcott, *Dream* 316, 318–19, 320.

68. Cited by Rodman, *Tongues of Fallen Angels* 240, 249.

69. Fido, "Value Judgements on Art" 110.

70. Walcott, *Dream* 321–26.

71. See Hill, "The Emergence of a National Drama in the West Indies" 31–32.

72. Walcott, "What the Twilight Says" 37, 8–9.

73. Cited by Rodman, *Tongues of Fallen Angels* 240.

74. See Walcott, "We Are Still Being Betrayed" 14.

75. Walcott, "We Are Still Being Betrayed" 14.

76. See Hirsch, "Interview with Derek Walcott" 286- 87; Walcott, "Musings on Art" 115. See also Hamner, "Conversation with Derek Walcott" 417.

77. I emphasize "dramatic" because the language of Walcott's poetry largely approproximates the standard English. Walcott explains this disparity by arguing that while dramatic characterization demand a sense of *real people talking*, his own education and development demand something else of his poetic persona: "I couldn't pretend that my voice was the voice of the St. Lucia peasant or fisherman. So for the poetry to be true, it had to be accurate, quietly accurate in terms of the sound of my own voice." Hirsch, "Interview with Walcott" 287, 286.

78. Ciccarelli, "Reflections Before and After Carnival: An Interview with Derek Walcott" 303.

79. Walcott, *Dream* 250, 304, 322.

80. Walcott, in Ciccarelli, "Reflections," 306–7, 306.

81. Walcott, "What the Twilight Says" 10.

82. Walcott, "Poetry—Enormously Complicated Art."

83. Walcott, *Dream* 208.

84. Walcott, Introduction to *Ti-Jean* in Programme Brochure, Jamaica Season of Plays, April 1973. Cited by Nettleford, *Caribbean Cultural Identity* 33–34. See Grotowski, *Towards a Poor Theatre*.

85. Walcott, Introduction to *Ti-Jean*, in Nettleford, *Caribbean Cultural Identity* 36–37.

86. Michael Issacharoff defines a "definite reference" as a "mention in the dialogue (or in the didascalia) of a person, place, or thing that exists either in the real world or in a particular coherent fictional universe." "How Playscripts Refer: Some Preliminary Considerations" 86.

87. Walcott, "Meanings" 48.

88. Walcott, *Dream* 215–26, 216, 250, 248, 231–56.

89. Walcott, *Dream* 279.

90. Weiss, "Ideology and the Problem of Style" 20. See Merleau-Ponty, *Signs* 91.

91. "Though, theoretically speaking, it would seem that hybridity functions as the ultimate decentering of all identity regimes, in fact and in history hybridity is valorized on the basis of a stable identity, such as European hybridity, French hybridity, American hybridity, etc. So which hybridity are we talking about? It would be most disingenuous to use 'hybridity' as a theoretical sleight of hand to

exorcise the reality of unequal histories and identities." Radhakrishnan, "Postcoloniality and the Boundaries of Identity" 753.

92. Walcott, "The Muse of History" 15.

93. Walcott, "What the Twilight Says" 18.

Chapter 6

1. White, "Africa on My Mind" 82.

2. Mae Gwendolyn Henderson, "Speaking in Tongues" 120.

3. Hountondji, *African Philosophy: Myth and Reality* 154.

4. Anderson, *Imagined Communities* 16.

5. White, "Africa on My Mind" 84.

6. Cited in Ogundipe-Leslie, "Women in Nigeria" 119–21. Let us change the scene of enactment and compare this poem to the spurious theory justifying black male dominance in the civil rights movement advanced by Robert Staples during the 1979 Black Sexism Debate in *The Black Scholar*: "When Ms. Wallace talks about black men denying women meaningful positions in civil rights organizations, she is on a sounder ground. She would, also, have been a more objective writer had she placed the issue in historical context. During the Sixties there was a general consensus—among men and women—that black men would hold the leadership positions in the movement. The reasoning behind this philosophy was that black women had held up their men for too long and it was time for the men to take charge . . . the rationale was the trickle down theory: that by enabling black men to advance, the entire black family would be uplifted." "The Myth of Black Macho" 27; 24–32. As Audre Lorde, one of the many respondents, argued, Staples's position was no more than another instance of "the Great American Disease [which] has been always to blame the victim for the oppressor's victimization." "The Great American Disease" 18.

7. Ogundipe-Leslie, "Women in Nigeria," 121.

8. hooks, *Ain't I a Woman* 87–117.

9. I have borrowed insights from Hearn, *The Gender of Oppression* xi–xiv.

10. See the first major production of the group written by Ngugi wa Thiong'O and Ngugi wa Mirii, *I Will Marry When I Want* (*Ngaahika Ndeenda* 1977) (London: Heinemann, 1982). The second, *Maitu Njugira* (1982) (*Mother, Sing for Me*), is unpublished. See also Ngugi's account of the role of women in the group, "Women in Cultural Work: The Fate of Kamiriithu People's Theater in Kenya," *Barrel of a Pen* 39–51; and Ingrid Bjorkman's study, *Mother, Sing for Me*.

11. See Sistren, with Honor Ford-Smith, ed., *Lionheart Gal*; Ford-Smith, "Sistren: Exploring Women's Problems through Drama" and "Sistren at Work."

12. See "The Black Sexism Debate" and Shange, *for colored girls*.

13. Shange, *a photograph: lovers in motion*, in *Three Pieces* 80, 108.

14. Wall, "Response" 187, 188.

15. Spillers, "Cross-Currents, Discontinuities" 249.

16. Henderson, "Speaking in Tongues" 118.

17. Shange, "unrecovered losses," in *Three Pieces* xii. See also Fanon, *A Dying Colonialism* 65.

18. Shange, "unrecovered losses" xiii.

19. Shange, *boogie woogie landscapes*, in *Three Pieces* 115.

20. Fanon, *A Dying Colonialism* 64.

21. Fanon, *A Dying Colonialism* 62, 63, 61, 63.

22. Cited in Wallace, *Invisibility Blues* 133–34.

23. Shange, cited in Wallace, *Invisibility Blues* 134. Perhaps part of the nationalist influence on Shange is her assumption of African names (Ntozake: "she who comes with her own things," and Shange: "one who walks like a lion") in place of her given Paulette Williams. She explains in an interview: "I had a violent, violent resentment of carrying a slave name; poems and music come from the pit of myself and the pit of myself wasn't a slave." Cited in Janet Brown, *Feminist Drama* 115.

24. Shange, cited in Hogue, *Discourse and the Other* 62.

25. See Elizabeth Brown-Guillory's discussion of Shange in the context of African-American women dramatists, especially Alice Childress and Lorraine Hansberry, *Their Place on the Stage*. See also Murray, "Facing the Camera's Eye: Black and White Terrain in Women's Drama."

26. Wall, "Response" 188.

27. Shange, "unrecovered losses" ix.

28. Shange, "How I Moved Anna Fierling To The Southwest Territories, or, my personal victory over the armies of western civilization," *See No Evil* 34–38.

29. Shange, "How I Moved" 35.

30. Shange, "How I Moved" 35.

31. Shange, "How I Moved" 35.

32. Alice Walker, "In Search of Our Mother's Gardens," *In Search of Our Mother's Gardens* 231–43.

33. Shange, preface, *for colored girls* xi.

34. Shange, *for colored girls* xi.

35. Shange, *for colored girls* 14–15.

36. Shange, *spell #7: geechee jibara quick magic trance manual for technologically stressed third world people*, in *Three Pieces* 11.

37. Shange, *for colored girls* xi.

38. Shange, *Sassafrass, Cypress & Indigo* 166–68.

39. Shange, "unrecovered losses" in *Three Pieces* xi, x.

40. Claudia Tate, ed., "Ntozake Shange," interview, *Black Women Writers at Work* 163.

41. Shange, "unrecovered losses," in *Three Pieces* xii.

42. Lyotard, *The Differend* 9, 13.

43. Tate, "Ntozake Shange" 163.

44. Baker, *Workings of the Spirit* 171.

45. Shange, *for colored girls* xiii.

46. Tate, "Ntozake Shange" 152–54.

47. Tate, "Ntozake Shange" 163.

48. Shange, "How I Moved" 37.

49. Shange, *for colored girls* 4–5.

50. Minh-ha, *Woman, Native, Other* 28.

51. Tate, *Black Women Writers at Work* 159.

52. Shange, *for colored girls* xv.

53. Shange, *for colored girls* 4, 5.

54. Shange, *for colored girls* 3.

55. Scarry, *The Body in Pain* 3–11.

56. Scarry, *The Body in Pain* 4.

57. Shange, *for colored girls* 3, 4.

58. Scarry, *The Body in Pain* 4.
59. Scarry, *The Body in Pain* 5, 12.
60. Shange, *for colored girls* 4–5.
61. Scarry, *The Body in Pain* 10.
62. Mitchell, "'A Laying on of Hands'" 231.
63. Shange, *for colored girls* 18, 19, 17–22.
64. Shange, *for colored girls* 24.
65. Shange, *for colored girls* 25.
66. Shange, *for colored girls* 31.
67. Shange, *for colored girls* 31–35.
68. Shange, *for colored girls* 25–30.
69. Shange, *for colored girls* 36–39.
70. Shange, *for colored girls* 43, 44, 54.
71. McDowell, "Reading Family Matters" 78.
72. bell hooks, *Talking Back* 9.
73. Shange, *for colored girls* 55, 19, 55–56, 57, 60. The scene is atrocious enough, and I guess this was what Robert Staples meant by saying that "[w]atching a performance one sees a collective appetite for black male blood." "The Myth of Black Macho" 26. By this parochial reading, he actually lost an ally in the dramatist who took meticulous care to "historicize" Beau Willie Brown and thus implicate the larger white-dominated racist society (a perspective Staples would prefer) in what he did—the intersection of race and gender—though not as an exoneration.
74. In the essay "Conflicting Impulses in the Plays of Ntozake Shange," Sandra L. Richards sees in what I call Shange's animism a "will to divinity" which is at odds with her combat breath (74, 76–78). I conceive the spiritual in Shange not as a refuge for the characters away from the pains of the social but as a veritable part of the combat space.
75. Shange, *for colored girls* 62, 63, 64. Carolyn Mitchell writes incisively of the life-affirming thrust of this ending: "To claim the right 'to be' is to confront antilife forces. This self-affirmation is the first step toward spiritual affirmation. The rainbow represents the promise of a whole life, and Shange reveals her unique vision, for she draws a new covenant when she alters the gender of God, finding 'her' in self, and declaring love for 'her.' This 'mother' god will certainly heal her battered daughters. For this reason, too, Crystal's loss of her children is significant; the rules of patriarchy which allow mother and children to be held hostage must be rewritten." "'A Laying of Hands'" 239. Compare, of course, Robert Staples's own anxious, positivistic reading: "At the end of the play, what I especially find unsettling, is Shange's invitation to black women to love themselves. This seems, to me, to be no less than an extension of the culture of Narcissism. She does not mention compassion for misguided black men or a love of child, family and community. It all seems so strange, exhorting black women to go it alone. They, many of them, are already alone. That is their main complaint: black men have deserted them." "The Myth of Black Macho" 26.
76. Rushing, "For Colored Girls" 540, 544–45.
77. See "The Black Sexism Debate."
78. *The Black Sexism Debate* 28–30.
79. Shange, "taking a solo," *See No Evil* 32.
80. Spillers, "Cross-Currents, Discontinuities" 251.
81. Henderson, "Speaking in Tongues" 118.

82. The path-breaking study here, of course, is Hortense J. Spillers's "Mama's Baby, Papa's Maybe: An American Grammar Book."
83. Shange, "takin a solo" *See No Evil* 31.

Chapter 7

1. See Bhabha, "'Race,' Time and the Revision of Modernity," and Gilroy, *The Black Atlantic* 1- 42.
2. I have benefited from Herbert Lindenberger's discussion of institutions in *The History in Literature.*
3. Irele, "The African Scholar" 63.
4. Mudimbe, *The Invention of Africa* 186.
5. Paulin J. Hountondji incisively makes a similar point in "Reason and Tradition": "The problem . . . as regards our attitude towards our collective heritage, is how to respond to the challenge of cultural imperialism without imprisoning ourselves in an imaginary dialogue with Europe, how to re-evaluate our cultures without enslaving ourselves to them, how to restore the dignity of our past, without giving room to a passeistic attitude. Instead of blindly condemning our traditions on behalf of reason, or rejecting the latter on behalf of the former, or making an absolute of the internal rationality of these traditions, it seems more reasonable to me to try and know our traditions as they were, beyond any mythology and distortion, not merely for the purpose of self-identification or justification, but in order to help us meet the challenges and problems of today." 142–143.
6. Issacharoff, *Discourse as Performance* 4.
7. Elam, *The Semiotics of Theatre* 209.
8. Elam, *The Semiotics of Theatre* 209.
9. Blau, *The Eye of Prey: Subversions of the Postmodern* 177.
10. Burns, *Theatricality* 28–39.
11. Elam, *The Semiotics of Theatre* 90.
12. Burns, *Theatricality* 31, 32.
13. Blau, "Ideology and Performance" 447.
14. Blau, "Ideology and Performance" 458, 450.

Bibliography

Amiri Baraka/LeRoi Jones

"The Changing Same (R&B and the New Black Music)." *The Black Aesthetic.* Ed. Addison Gayle, Jr. New York: Doubleday, 1971. 118–31.

"Toward Ideological Clarity." *Black World* 24.1 (1974): 24–33; 84–95.

"Why I Changed My Ideology: Black Nationalism and Socialist Revolution." *Black World* 24.9 (1975): 30–42.

A Black Value System. Newark, N.J.: Jihad Publications, 1969.

Black Fire: An Anthology of Afro-American Writing. Ed. LeRoi Jones and Larry Neal. New York: William Morrow, 1968.

Black Magic: Collected Poetry 1961–1967. New York: Bobbs-Merrill, 1969.

Black Music. New York: William Morrow, 1968.

Bloodrites. Black Drama Anthology. Ed. Woodie King and Ron Milner. New York: New American Library, 1971. 25–31.

Blues People: Negro Music in White America. New York: William Morrow, 1963.

Confirmation: An Anthology of African-American Women. Ed. Amiri Baraka and Amina Baraka. New York: William Morrow, 1983.

Daggers and Javelins: Essays, 1974–1979. New York: Quill, 1984.

Dutchman and The Slave. New York: William Morrow, 1964.

Four Black Revolutionary Plays: All Praises to the the Black Man (Experimental Death Unit #1; A Black Mass; Great Goodness of Life; Madheart). New York: Bobbs-Merrill, 1969.

Home: Social Essays. New York: William Morrow, 1966.

Junkies Are Full of (Shhh. . . .). Black Drama Anthology. Ed. Woodie King and Ron Milner. New York: New American Library, 1971. 11–23.

Kawaida Studies: The New Nationalism. Chicago: Third World Press, 1972.

Preface to a Twenty Volume Suicide Note. New York: Totem Press, 1961.

Raise Race Rays Raze: Essays Since 1965. New York: Random House, 1969.

Selected Plays and Prose. New York: William Morrow, 1979

Selected Poetry. New York: William Morrow, 1979.

The Autobiography of LeRoi Jones. New York: Frundlich Books, 1984.

The Baptism and The Toilet. New York: Grove Press, 1967.

The Moderns: An Anthology of New Writing in America. Ed. New York: Corinth Books, 1963.

The Motion of History and Other Plays (includes *Slave Ship: A Historical Pageant* [1967], and *S-1*). New York: William Morrow, 1978.

The Music: Reflections on Jazz and Blues. New York: William Morrow, 1987.

Three Books: The System of Dante's Hell, The Dead Lecturer, Tales. New York: Grove Press, 1975.

Ntozake Shange

for colored girls who have considered suicide/ when the rainbow is enuf. New York: Macmillan, 1977.

nappy edges. New York: St. Martin's Press, 1978.

Sassafrass, Cypress & Indigo. New York: St. Martin's Press, 1982.

See No Evil: Prefaces, Essays & Accounts 1976–1983. San Francisco: Momo's Press, 1984.

Three Pieces: spell #7: geechee jibara quik magic trance manual for technologically stressed third world people; a photograph: lovers in motion; boogie woogie landscapes. New York: St. Martin's Press, 1981.

Wole Soyinka

"And after the Narcissist?" *African Forum* 1.4 (1966): 53–64.

"Ethics, Ideology and the Critic." *Criticism and Ideology*. Ed. K. H. Petersen. Uppsala: Scandinavian Institute of African Studies, 1988, 26–54.

"The African World and the Ethnocultural Debate." *African Culture: Rhythms of Unity*. Ed. Molefi K. Asante and Kariamu W. Asante. Westport, Conn.: Greenwood Press, 1985. 13–38.

"The Future of West African Writing." *The Horn* 4.1 (1960): 10–16.

A Play of Giants. London: Methuen, 1984.

A Shuttle in the Crypt. New York: Hill and Wang, 1972.

Ake: Years of Childhood. New York: Random House, 1982.

Art, Dialogue and Outrage: Essays on Literature and Culture. Ibadan, Nigeria: New Horn Press, 1988.

Collected Plays 1: A Dance of the Forests, The Swamp Dwellers, The Strong Breed; The Road; and The Bacchae of Euripides. Oxford: Oxford UP, 1973.

Collected Plays 2: The Lion and the Jewel; Kongi's Harvest; The Trials of Brother Jero; Jero's Metamorphosis; and Madmen and Specialists. Oxford: Oxford UP, 1973.

Death and the King's Horseman. London: Methuen, 1975.

Idanre and Other Poems. 1967. New York: Hill and Wang, 1968.

Mandela's Earth and Other Poems. New York: Random House, 1988.

Myth, Literature and the African World. Cambridge: Cambridge UP, 1976.

Ogun Abibiman. London: Rex Collings, 1976.

Opera Wonyosi. Bloomington: Indiana UP, 1981.

Requiem for a Futurologist. London: Rex Collings, 1985.

Six Plays (The Trials of Brother Jero, Jero's Metamorphosis, Camwood on the Leaves, Death and the King's Horseman, Madmen and Specialists, Opera Wonyosi). London: Methuen, 1984.

The Bacchae of Euripides: A Communion Rite. 1973. New York: W. W. Norton, 1974.

The Man Died: Prison Notes. 1972. Ibadan, Nigeria: Spectrum Books, 1985.

Derek Walcott

"Anthologies." *Sunday Guardian* 3 July 1966: 6.

"Any Revolution Based on Race Is Suicidal." Interview with Raoul Pantin. *Caribbean Contact* August 1973: 14+.

"Kaiso, Genius of the Folk." *Sunday Guardian* 9 February 1964: 13.

"Meanings." *Savacou* 2 (1970): 45–51.

"Musings on Art, Life, and the Island of St. Lucia." *House and Garden* August 1984: 15+.

"National Theatre Is the Answer." *Trinidad Guardian* 12 August 1964: 4.

"Necessity of Negritude." 1964. *Critical Perspectives on Derek Walcott.* Ed. Robert D. Hamner. Washington, D.C.: Three Continents Press, 1993. 20–23.

"New Novel by Dawes Sticks to Formula." *Sunday Guardian* 11 September 1960: 5.

"Parody of the Protest Formula." *Sunday Guardian* 23 August 1964: 4.

"Patterns to Forget." *Trinidad Guardian* 22 June 1966: 5.

"Playing the Old Race Game." *Sunday Guardian* 29 November 1964: 21.

"Poetry—Enormously Complicated Art." *Trinidad Guardian* 18 June 1962: 3.

"Problems of Exile." *Trinidad Guardian* 13 July 1966: 5.

"The Antilles: Fragments of Epic Memory." Nobel Lecture. *The New Republic* 28 December 1992: 28+.

"The Caribbean: Culture or Mimicry?" *Policy: Journal of Interamerican Studies and World Affairs* 16.1 (1974): 3–13.

"The Kabuki—Something to Give to Our Theatre." *Sunday Guardian* 16 February 1964: 14.

"The Muse of History: An Essay." *Is Massa Day Dead? Black Moods in the Caribbean.* Ed. Orde Coombs. New York: Anchor Books, 1974. 1–27

"The Theatre of Abuse." *Sunday Guardian* 3 January 1965: 4.

"The Theatre of the Streets." *Sunday Guardian* 9 February 1964: 4.

"Time to Separate Politics from Good Verse." *Trinidad Guardian* 17 March 1966: 5.

"Tribal Flutes." *Sunday Guardian Magazine* 19 March 1967: 2.

"We Are Still Being Betrayed." Interview with Raoul Pantin. *Caribbean Contact* July 1973: 14+.

"What the Twilight Says: An Overture." *Dream on Monkey Mountain and Other Plays.* New York: Farrar, Straus and Giroux, 1970. 3–40.

Collected Poems: 1948–1984. New York: Noonday Press, 1986.

Dream on Monkey Mountain and Other Plays (The Sea at Dauphin; Ti-Jean and His Brothers, Malcochon, or The Six in the Rain). New York: Farrar, Straus and Giroux, 1970.

Drums and Colours. Caribbean Quarterly. Special Issue, March–June 1961.
Henri Christophe: A Chronicle in Seven Scenes. Kingston, Jamaica: UWI Extra-Mural Department, 1949.
Remembrance and Pantomime: Two Plays. New York: Farrar, Straus and Giroux, 1980.
The Arkansas Testament. New York: Farrar, Straus and Giroux, 1987.
The Joker of Seville and O Babylon! Two Plays. New York: Farrar, Straus and Giroux, 1978.
Three Plays: The Last Carnival; Beef, No Chicken; A Branch of the Blue Nile. New York: Farrar, Straus and Giroux, 1986.

General

Abramson, Doris E. *Negro Playwrights in the American Theatre: 1925–1959.* New York: Columbia UP, 1969.
Achebe, Chinua. *Morning Yet on Creation Day: Essays.* London: Heinemann, 1975.
Adedeji, Joel A. "A Yoruba Pantomime: An Appraisal of Captain Clapperton's Account of a Yoruba Theatrical Performance." *Ibadan* 29 (1971): 63–66.
Adedeji, Joel A. "Alarinjo: The Traditional Yoruba Travelling Theatre." *Drama and Theatre in Nigeria: A Critical Sourcebook.* Ed. Yemi Ogunbiyi. Lagos: Nigeria Magazine, 1981. 221–247.
Adedeji, Joel A. "The Alarinjo Theatre: The Study of a Yoruba Thearical Art Form from its Earliest Beginnings to the Present Time." Ph.D. Diss. University of Ibadan, 1969.
Adedeji, Joel A. "Traditional Yoruba Theater." *African Arts* 3.1 (1969): 60–63.
Allen, Robert L. *Black Awakening in Capitalist America: An Analytic History.* New York: Anchor Books, 1970.
Althusser, Louis. "Ideology and Ideological State Apparatuses (Notes towards an Investigation)." *Lenin and Philosophy and Other Essays.* Trans. Ben Brewster. New York: Monthly Review Press, 1971. 127–185.
Amin, Samir. *Eurocentrism.* Trans. Russell Moore. New York: Monthly Review Press, 1989.
Amuta, Chidi. *The Theory of African Literature: Implications for Practical Criticism.* London: Zed Books, 1989.
Anderson, Benedict. *Imagined Communities: Reflections on the Origin and Spread of Nationalism.* London: Verso, 1983.
Andrews, W. D. E. "The Marxist Theater of Amiri Baraka." *Comparative Drama* 18.2 (1984): 137–161.
Anon. "How Far Are Derek Walcott and Edward Brathwaite Similar?. . ." *Busara* 6.1 (1974): 90–100.
Appiah, Anthony. "Soyinka and the Philosophy of Culture." *Philosophy in Africa: Trends and Perspectives.* Ed. P. O. Bodunrin. Ile-Ife, Nigeria: U of Ife P, 1985. 250–263.
Appiah, Anthony. Moderator. "An Evening with Wole Soyinka." *Black American Literature Forum* 22.4 (1988): 777–85.
Appiah, Kwame A. *In My Father's House: Africa in the Philosophy of Culture.* New York: Oxford UP, 1992.
Archer, Leonard B. *Black Images in American Theatre: NAACP Protest Campaigns.* Brooklyn, N.Y.: Pageant-Poseidon, 1973.

Asante, K. Molefi. *The Afrocentric Idea*. Philadelphia: Temple UP, 1987.

Asante, K. Molefi. *Afrocentricity: The Theory of Social Change*. Buffalo: Amulefi, 1980.

Asante, K. Moleti, and K. W. Asante, eds. *African Culture: The Rhythms of Unity*. Westport, Conn.: Greenwood Press, 1985.

Ashcroft, Bill, Gareth Griffiths, and Helen Tiffin. *The Empire Writes Back: Theory and Practice in Post-Colonial Literatures*. New York: Routledge, 1989.

Baker, Houston A., Jr. *Afro-American Poetics: Revisions of Harlem and the Black Aesthetic*. Madison: U of Wisconsin P, 1988.

Baker, Houston A., Jr. *Blues, Ideology, and Afro-American Literature: A Vernacular Theory*. Chicago: U of Chicago P, 1984.

Baker, Houston A., Jr. *Workings of the Spirit: The Poetics of Afro-American Women's Writing*. Chicago: U of Chicago P, 1991.

Baker, Houston A., Jr., and Patricia Redmond, eds. *Afro-American Literary Study in the 1990s*. Chicago: U of Chicago P, 1989.

Barthes, Roland. "Whose Theater? Whose *Avant- Garde*?" *Critical Essays*. Trans. Richard Howard. Evanston, Ill.: Northwestern UP, 1972. 67–70.

Baudry, Jean-Louis. "Ideological Effects of the Basic Cinematographic Apparatus." *Narrative, Apparatus, Ideology: A Film Theory Reader*. Ed. Philip Rosen. New York: Columbia UP, 1986. 286–298.

Baxter, Ivy. *The Arts of an Island: The Development of the Culture and of the Folk and Creative Arts in Jamaica, 1494–1962*. Metuchen, N.J.: Scarecrow Press, 1970.

Beckwith, Martha W. *Black Roadways: A Study of Jamaican Folk Life*. Chapel Hill: U of North Carolina P, 1929.

Belcher, Fanin A., Jr. "The Place of the Negro in the Evolution of the American Theatre." Ph.D. Diss. Yale U, 1945.

Benston, Kimberly W. *Baraka: The Renegade and the Mask*. New Haven: Yale UP, 1976.

Benston, Kimberly W. "Being There: Performance as Mise-en-Scène, Abscene, Obscene, and Other Scene." *PMLA* 107.3 (1992): 434–49.

Benston, Kimberly W. "Facing Tradition: Revisionary Scenes in African-American Literature." *PMLA* 105.1 (1990): 98–109.

Benston, Kimberly W. "The Aesthetic of Modern Black Drama: From *Mimesis* to *Methexis*." *Theater of Black Americans: A Collection of Critical Essays*. 1980. Ed. Errol Hill. New York: Applause Theatre Book Publishers, 1987. 61–78.

Bernal, Martin. *Black Athena: The Afroasiatic Roots of Classical Civilization, vol.1: The Fabrication of Ancient Greece 1785–1985*. New Brunswick, N.J.: Rutgers UP, 1987.

Bhabha, Homi. "'Race,' time and the revision of modernity." *The Location of Culture*. New York: Routledge, 1994. 236–56.

Bhabha, Homi K. "Representation and the Colonial Text: A Critical Exploration of Some Forms of Mimeticism." *The Theory of Reading*. Ed. Frank Gloversmith. New York: Barnes and Noble, 1984. 93–122.

Bhabha, Homi K. "The other question: difference, discrimination and the discourse of colonialism." *Literature, Politics and Theory: Papers from the Essex Conference 1976–84*. Ed. F. Barker et al. New York: Methuen, 1986. 148–172.

Bigsby, C. W. E. *A Critical Introduction to Twentieth-Century American Drama, Vol. 1: 1900–1940.* Cambridge: Cambridge UP, 1982.

Biko, Steve. *I Write What I Like.* San Francisco: Harper and Row, 1978.

Bjorkman, Ingrid. *Mother, Sing for Me: People's Theatre in Kenya.* London: Zed Books, 1989.

Black American Literature Forum 21.1–2 (1987), and 21.3 (1987).

Blau, Herbert. "Ideology and Performance." *Theatre Journal* 35 (1983): 441–60.

Blau, Herbert. *The Eye of Prey: Subversions of the Postmodern.* Bloomington: Indiana UP, 1987.

Bond, Fredrick W. *The Negro and the Drama.* Washington, D.C.: Associated Publishers, 1940.

Bonner, Marita. *The Purple Flower.* 1928. *Black Female Playwrights: An Anthology of Plays before 1950.* Ed. Kathy A. Perkins. Bloomington: Indiana UP, 1990. 191–99.

Boskin, Joseph. *Sambo: The Rise and Demise of an American Jester.* New York: Oxford UP, 1986.

Bourdieu, Pierre. *Outline of a Theory of Practice.* Trans. Richard Nice. Cambridge: Cambridge UP, 1977.

Brathwaite, Edward. "Timehri." *Is Massa Day Dead? Black Moods in the Caribbean.* Ed. Orde Coombs. New York: Anchor Books, 1974. 29–42.

Brathwaite, Edward K. *History of the Voice: The Development of Nation Language in Anglophone Caribbean Poetry.* London: New Beacon Books, 1984.

Brathwaite, Edward K. *The Arrivants: A New World Trilogy.* Oxford: Oxford UP, 1973.

Brathwaite, Edward K. "The Love Axe (1): Developing a Caribbean Aesthetic 1962–1974." *Reading Black: Essays in the Criticism of African, Caribbean, and Black American Literature.* Ed. Houston A. Baker. Cornell U ASRC Monograph Series 4, 1976. 20–36.

Brecht, Bertolt. "Writing the Truth: Five Difficulties." Appendix A. *Galileo.* English version by Charles Laughton. New York: Grove Press, 1966. 133–150.

Brecht, Stefan. "LeRoi Jones' *Slave Ship.*" *TDR* 14.2 (1979): 212–219.

Breslin, Paul. "I Met History Once, But He Ain't Recognize Me: The Poetry of Derek Walcott." *Tri-Quarterly* 68 (1987): 168–83.

British Drama League. "Native African Drama: An Enquiry." *Drama* 2.2 (1932): 27–29.

Brown, Janet. *Feminist Drama: Definitions and Critical Analysis.* Metuchen, N.J.: Scarecrow Press, 1979.

Brown, Lloyd W. *Amiri Baraka.* Boston: Twayne, 1980.

Brown, Stewart, Ed. *The Art of Derek Walcott.* Bridgend, Mid Glamorgan, Wales: Seren Books, 1991.

Brown-Guillory, Elizabeth. *Their Place on the Stage: Black Women Playwrights in America.* Westport, Conn.: Greenwood Press, 1988.

Burke, Kenneth. *The Philosophy of Literary Form.* 1941. Berkeley: U of California P, 1973.

Burns, Elizabeth. *Theatricality: A Study of Convention in the Theatre and in Social Life.* London: Longman, 1972

Cabral, Amilcar. *Return to the Source: Selected Speeches.* New York: Monthly Review Press, 1973.

Cabral, Amilcar. *Unity and Struggle: Speeches and Writings.* Trans. M. Wolfers. London: Heinemann, 1980.

Carlisle, Rodney. *The Roots of Black Nationalism.* Port Washington, N.Y.: Kennikat Press, 1975.

Cesaire, Aime. *Discourse on Colonialism.* Trans. Joan Pinkham. New York: Monthly Review Press, 1972.

Chinweizu. "Prodigals, Come Home!" *Okike* 4 (1973): 1–12.

Chinweizu. *The West and the Rest of Us: White Predators, Black Slavers and the African Elite.* New York: Vintage, 1975.

Chinweizu, O. Jemie, and I. Madubuike. "Gibbs's Gibberish." *Research in African Literatures* 17.1 (1986): 48–52.

Chinweizu, Onwuchekwa Jemie, and Ikechukwu Madubuike, *Toward the Decolonization of African Literature.* Enugu; Nigeria: Fourth Dimension, 1980.

Chinweizu, Onwuchekwa Jemie and Ikechukwu Madubuike. "Towards the Decolonization of African Literature." *Okike* 6 (1974): 11–27.

Ciccarelli, Sharon L. "Reflections Before and After Carnival: An Interview with Derek Walcott." *Chant of Saints: A Gathering of Afro-American Literature, Art, and Scholarship.* Ed. M. S. Harper and R. Stepto. Urbana: U of Illinois P, 1979. 296–309.

Clark, Ebun. *Hubert Ogunde: The Making of Nigerian Theatre.* Oxford: Oxford UP, 1980.

Clark, John P. *The Example of Shakespeare.* Evanston, Ill.: Northwestern UP, 1970.

Clifford, James. *The Predicament of Culture: Twentieth Century Ethnography, Literature and Art.* Cambridge, Mass.: Harvard UP, 1988.

Clifford, James, and G. E. Marcus, eds. *Writing Culture: The Poetics and Politics of Ethnography.* Berkeley: U of California P, 1986.

Cohen, Ralph. "Do Postmodern Genres Exist?" *Genre* 20.3–4 (1987): 241–58.

Coombs, Orde, ed. *Is Massa Day Dead? Black Moods in the Caribbean.* New York: Anchor Books, 1974.

Coplan, David B. *In Township Tonight! South Africa's Black City Music and Theatre.* New York: Longman, 1985.

Craig, E. Q. *Black Drama of the Federal Theatre Era.* Amherst: U of Massachusetts P, 1980.

Crow, Brian. "Soyinka and His Radical Critics: A Review." *Theatre Research International* 12.1. 61–73.

Cruse, Harold. *Rebellion or Revolution?* New York: William Morrow, 1968.

Cruse, Harold. *The Crisis of the Negro Intellectual.* New York: William Morrow, 1968.

Dasgupta, Gautam. "The Mahabharata: Peter Brook's "Orientalism."" *Performing Arts Journal* 10.3 (1987): 9–16.

Dathorne, O. R. *Dark Ancestor: The Literature of the Black Man in the Caribbean.* Baton Rouge: Louisiana State UP, 1981.

Davies, Carole Boyce "Maidens, Mistresses and Matrons: Feminine Images in Selected Soyinka Works." *Ngambika: Studies of Women in African Literature.* Ed. Carole B. Davies and Anne Adams Graves. Trenton, N.J.: Africa World Press, 1986. 75–88.

Davies, Carole Boyce, and Elaine S. Fido, eds. *Out of the Kumbla: Caribbean Women and Literature.* Trenton, N.J.: Africa World Press, 1990.

De Graft, J. C. "Roots in African Drama and Theatre." *African Literature Today* 8 (1976): 1–25.

Derrida, Jacques. *Positions.* Trans. Alan Bass. Chicago: U of Chicago P, 1981.

Derrida, Jacques. "Psyche: Inventions of the Other." Trans. C. Porter. *Reading De Man Reading.* Ed. Lindsay Waters and Wlad Godzich. Minneapolis: U of Minnesota P, 1989. 25–65.

Derrida, Jacques. "Some Statements and Truisms About Neologisms, Newisms, Postisms, Parasitisms, and Other Small Seismisms." *The States of "Theory": History, Art, and Critical Discourse.* Ed. David Carroll, 63–94. New York: Columbia UP, 1990, 63–94.

Derrida, Jacques. "The Law of Genre." *Glyph* 7 (1980): 202–32.

Desai, Gaurav. "Theater as Praxis: Discursive Strategies in African Popular Theater." *African Studies Review* 33.1 (1990): 65–92.

DeVeaux, Alexis. "The Tapestry." *9 Plays by Black Women.* Ed. M. B. Wilkerson. New York: New American Library, 1986. 139–95.

Dhlomo, H. I. E. "Nature and Variety of Tribal Drama." *Bantu Studies* 13 (1939). 33–48.

Dollimore, Jonathan. "The Dominant and the Deviant: A Violent Dialectic." *Critical Quarterly* 28.1–2 (1986): 179–192.

Du Bois, W. E. B. "Criteria of Negro Art." *Crisis* 32 (1926): 290–97.

Du Bois, W. E. B. "Krigwa Players Little Negro Theatre: The Story of a Little Theatre Movement." *Crisis* 32 (1926): 134–36.

Du Bois, W. E. B. *The Souls of Black Folk.* 1903. New York: Vintage Books, 1990.

Dubois, Jacques, and Pascal Durand. "Literary Field and Classes of Texts." *Literature and Social Practice.* Ed. P. Desan, P. P. Ferguson, and W. Griswold. Chicago: U of Chicago P, 1989. 137–153.

Eagleton, Terry. *Criticism and Ideology: A Study in Marxist Literary Theory.* London: Verso, 1978.

Eagleton, Terry, and Peter Fuller. "The Question of Value: A Discussion." *New Left Review* 142 (1983): 76–90.

Early, Gerald. "The Case of Leroi Jones/Amiri Baraka." *Salmagundi* 70–71 (1986): 343–52.

Echeruo, Michael J. C. "The Dramatic Limits of Igbo Ritual." *Drama and Theatre in Nigeria: A Critical Sourcebook.* Ed. Yemi Ogunbiyi. Lagos: Nigeria Magazine, 1981. 136–148.

Elam, Keir. *The Semiotics of Theatre and Drama.* London: Methuen, 1980.

Ellison, Ralph. *Shadow and Act.* 1964. New York: Vintage, 1972.

Ellison, Ralph. "Some Questions and Some Answers." 1958. *Shadow and Act.* 1964. New York: Vintage, 1972. 261–272.

Enekwe, Ossie. *Igbo Masks: The Oneness of Ritual and Theatre.* Lagos: Nigeria Magazine, 1987.

Enekwe, Ossie. "Myth, Ritual and Drama in Igboland." *Drama and Theatre in Nigeria: A Critical Sourcebook.* Ed. Yemi Ogunbiyi. Lagos: Nigeria Magazine, 1981. 149–63.

Essien-Udom, E. U. *Black Nationalism.* New York: Dell, 1964.

Etherton, Michael. *The Development of African Drama.* London: Hutchinson, 1982.

Euba, Femi. *Archetypes, Imprecators, and Victims of Fate: Origins and Developments of Satire in Black Drama.* New York: Greenwood Press, 1989.

Fabre, Genevieve. *Drumbeats, Masks and Metaphor: Contemporary Afro-American Theatre*. Trans. Melvin Dixon. Cambridge, Mass.: Harvard UP, 1983.

Fanon, Frantz. *A Dying Colonialism*. Trans. Haakon Chevalier. New York: Grove Press, 1967.

Fanon, Frantz. *Black Skin, White Masks*. Trans. C. L. Markmann. New York: Grove Press, 1967.

Fanon, Frantz. *The Wretched of the Earth*. Trans. Constance Farrington. New York: Grove Press, 1968.

Fanon, Frantz. *Toward the African Revolution: Political Essays*. Trans. H. Chevalier. New York: Grove Press, 1969.

Fatton, Robert, Jr. *Black Consciousness in South Africa: The Dialectics of Ideological Resistance to White Supremacy*. Albany: Stat U of New York P, 1985.

Feuser, Willfried F. "Wole Soyinka: The Problem of Authenticity." *Black American Literature Forum* 22.3 (1988): 555–75.

Fido, Elaine S. "Finding a Way to Tell It: Methodology and Commitment in Theatre about Women in Barbados and Jamaica." *Out of the Kumbla: Caribbean Women and Literature*. Ed. Carole B. Davies and Elaine S. Fido. Trenton, N.J.: Africa World Press, 1990. 331–43.

Fido, Elaine Savory. "Value Judgements on Art and the Question of Macho Attitudes: The Case of Derek Walcott." *Journal of Commonwealth Literature* 21.1 (1986): 109–19.

Finn, Julio. *Voices of Negritude*. New York: Quartet Books, 1988.

Finnegan, Ruth. *Oral Literature in Africa*. Nairobi: Oxford UP, 1970.

Fisk, Milton. *Ethics and Society: A Marxist Interpretation of Value*. New York: New York UP, 1980.

Ford-Smith, Honor. "Sistren at Work." *Carib* 4 (1986): 55–61.

Ford-Smith, Honor. "Sistren: Exploring Women's Problems through Drama." *Jamaica Journal* 19.1 (1986): 2–12.

Foucault, Michel. *Discipline and Punish: The Birth of the Prison*. Trans. Alan Sheridan. New York: Vintage Books, 1979.

Foucault, Michel. *Language, Counter-Memory, Practice: Selected Essays and Interviews*. Trans. D. F. Bouchard and S. Simon. Ithaca, N.Y.: Cornell UP, 1977.

Foucault, Michel. *Politics, Philosophy, Culture: Interviews and Other Writings 1977–1984*. Trans. A. Sheridan et al. New York: Routledge, 1988.

Foucault, Michel. *Power/Knowledge: Selected Interviews and Other Writings 1972–1977*. Ed. C. Gordon. New York: Pantheon Books, 1980.

Foucault, Michel. *The Archaeology of Knowledge and the Discourse on Language*. Trans. A. M. S. Smith. New York: Pantheon Books, 1972.

Foucault, Michel. "The Subject and Power." Afterword. *Michel Foucault: Beyond Structuralism and Hermeneutics*. Ed. H. Dreyfus and P. Rabinow. 208–26. Chicago: U of Chicago P, 1982.

Fugard, Athol. *Notebooks: 1960–1977*. Ed. M. Benson. London: Faber and Faber, 1983.

Gates, Henry L., Jr. "Several Lives, Several Voices," *The New York Times Book Review* 11 March, 1984: 11–12.

Gates, Henry L., Jr. *The Signifying Monkey: A Theory of Afro-American Literature*. New York: Oxford UP, 1988.

Gates, Henry L., Jr. ed. *"Race," Writing, and Difference*. Chicago: U of Chicago Press, 1985.

Gates, Henry L., Jr. ed. *Reading Black, Reading Feminist: A Critical Anthology.*
New York: Meridian, 1990.

Gayle, Addison, Jr., ed. *Black Expression.* New York: Weybright & Talley, 1969.

Gayle, Addison, Jr., ed. *The Black Aesthetic.* New York: Anchor Books, 1972.

Geertz, Clifford. *The Interpretation of Cultures.* New York: Basic Books, 1973.

Geggus, David. "The Haitian Revolution." *The Modern Caribbean.* Ed. Franklin
W. Knight and Colin A. Palmer. Chapel Hill: U of North Carolina P,
1989. 21– 50.

Gibbs, James. " 'Larsony' with a Difference: An Examination of a Paragraph from
Toward the Decolonization of African Literature." *Research in African Literatures* 17.1 (1986): 39–47.

Gibbs, James, ed. *Critical Perspectives on Wole Soyinka.* Washington, D.C.: Three
Continents Press, 1980.

Gilroy, Paul. *The Black Atlantic: Modernity and Double Consciousness.* Cambridge,
Mass.: Harvard UP, 1993.

Gitlin, Todd. *The Sixties: Years of Hope, Days of Rage.* New York: Bantam Books,
1987.

Glissant, Edouard. *Caribbean Discourse.* Trans. J. M. Dash. Charlottesville: UP
of Virginia, 1989.

Goddard, Horace I., ed. *A Common Tongue: Interviews with Cecil Abrahams,
John Agard, John Hearne, and Wole Soyinka.* St. Laurent, Quebec: A F O
Enterprises, 1986.

Gotrick, Kacke. *Apidan Theatre and Modern Drama.* Stockholm: Almqvist and
Wiksell, 1984.

Graham-White, Anthony. *The Drama of Black Africa.* New York: Samuel French,
1974.

Gramsci, Antonio. *Selections from the Prison Notebooks.* Ed. and trans. Q. Hoare
and G. N. Smith. New York: International Publishers, 1971.

Grotowski, Jerzy. *Towards a Poor Theatre.* New York: Simon and Schuster, 1968.

Gugelberger, Georg M., ed. *Marxism and African Literature.* Trenton, N.J.: Africa World Press, 1986.

Hall, Stuart. "On Postmodernism and Articulation: An Interview with Stuart
Hall." Ed. Lawrence Grossberg. *Journal of Communication Inquiry* 10
(1986): 45–60.

Hall, Stuart. "Race, Articulation and Societies Structured in Dominance." *Socio-
logical Theories: Race and Colonialism.* Ed. UNESCO. Paris: UNESCO,
1980. 305–345.

Hammond, Dorothy, and Alta Jablow. *The Myth of Africa.* New York: Library of
Social Science, 1977.

Hamner, Robert. "Conversation with Derek Walcott." *World Literature Written
in English* 16.2 (1977): 409–20.

Hamner, Robert D. *Derek Walcott.* Boston: Twayne, 1981.

Harper, Philip B. *Framing the Margins: The Social Logic of Postmodern Culture.*
New York: Oxford UP, 1994.

Harris, Jessica B. "The National Black Theatre: The Sun People of 125th Street."
In *The Theatre of Black Americans: A Collection of Critical Essays.* 1980.
Ed. Errol Hill. New York: Applause Theatre Book Publishers, 1987. 283–
91.

Harris, William J. *The Poetry and Poetics of Amiri Baraka: The Jazz Aesthetic.*
Columbia: U of Missouri P, 1985.

Harris, Wilson. *The Wombs of Space: The Cross-Cutural Imagination*. Westport, Conn.: Greenwood Press, 1983.

Harrison, Paul C. *The Drama of Nommo*. New York: Grove Press, 1972.

Hauptfleisch, Temple, and Ian Steadman, eds. *South African Theatre: Four Plays and an Introduction*. Pretoria: Haum Educational Publishers, 1984.

Havemeyer, Loomis. *The Drama of Savage Peoples*. 1916. New York: Haskell House, 1966.

Hay, Denys. *Europe: The Emergence of an Idea*. Edinburgh: Edinburgh UP, 1957.

Hay, Samuel A. *African American Theatre: A Historical and Critical Analysis*. Cambridge: Cambridge UP, 1994.

Hearn, Jeff. *The Gender of Oppression: Men, Masculinity, and the Critique of Marxism*. New York: St. Martin's Press, 1987.

Hegel, G. W. F. *The Philosophy of History*. New York: Willey, 1900.

Heilpern, John. *The Conference of the Birds: The Story of Peter Brook in Africa*. London: Faber and Faber, 1977.

Henderson, Mae Gwendolyn. "Speaking in Tongues: Dialogics, Dialectics, and the Black Woman Writer's Literary Tradition." *Reading Black, Reading Feminist: A Critical Anthology*. Ed. Henry L. Gates, Jr. New York: Meridian, 1990. 116–42.

Henderson, Stephen. "Saturation: Progress Report on a Theory of Black Poetry." *Black World* 24 (1975): 4–17.

Henderson, Stephen. *Understanding the New Black Poetry: Black Music and Black Speech as Poetic References*. New York: William Morrow, 1973. 1–69.

Henry, Paget, and Carl Stone, eds. *The Newer Caribbean: Decolonization, Democracy, and Development*. Philadelphia: Institute for the Study of Human Issues, 1983.

Hill, Errol. "The Emergence of a National Drama in the West Indies." *Caribbean Quarterly* 18.4 (1972): 9–40.

Hill, Errol. *The Jamaican Stage, 1655–1900: Profile of a Colonial Theatre*. Amherst: U of Massachusetts P, 1992.

Hill, Errol. *The Trinidad Carnival: Mandate for a National Theatre*. Austin: U of Texas P, 1972.

Hill, Errol, ed. *The Theater of Black Americans: A Collection of Critical Essays*. 1980. New York: Applause Theatre Book Publishers, 1987.

Hirsch, Edward. "An Interview with Derek Walcott." *Contemporary Literature* 20.3 (1979): 279–292.

Hobsbawn, Eric, and Terence Ranger, eds. *The Invention of Tradition*. Cambridge: Cambridge UP, 1983.

Hogue, W. L. *Discourse and the Other: The Production of the Afro-American Text*. Durham, N.C.: Duke UP, 1986.

hooks, bell. *Ain't I a Woman: Black Women and Feminism*. Boston: South End Press, 1981.

hooks, bell. *Yearning: Race, Gender, and Cultural Politics*. Boston: South End Press, 1990.

Hountondji, Paulin. *African Philosophy: Myth and Reality*. Trans. H. Evans. London: Hutchinson, 1977.

Hountondji, Paulin. "Scientific Dependence in Africa." *Research in African Literatures* 21.3 (1990): 5–15.

Hountondji, Paulin J. "Reason and Tradition. *Philosophy and Cultures*. Ed. H. O. Oruka and D. A. Masolo. Nairobi: Bookwise Limited, 1983. 142–143.

Hudson, Theodore R. *From LeRoi Jones to Amiri Baraka: The Literary Works.* Durham, N.C.: Duke UP, 1973.

Hughes, Langston. "Note on Commercial Theatre." *Selected Poems of Langston Hughes.* 1959. New York: Knopf, 1983. 190.

Hughes, Langston. *The Big Sea.* New York: Knopf, 1940.

Hughes, Langston. "The Negro Artist and the Racial Mountain." *The Black Aesthetic.* Ed. Addison Gayle, Jr. New York: Doubleday, 1971. 175–181.

Hunt, Geoffrey. "Two African Aesthetics: Wole Soyinka vs Amilcar Cabral." 1978. *Marxism and African Literature.* Ed. Georg M. Gugelberger. Trenton, N.J.: Africa World Press, 1986. 64–93.

Irele, Abiola. *The African Experience in Literature and Ideology.* London: Heinemann, 1981.

Irele, Abiola. "The African Scholar." *Transition* 51 (1990): 56–69.

Isaacs, E. J. R. *The Negro in the American Theatre.* New York: Theatre Arts, 1947.

Issacharoff, Michael. *Discourse as Performance.* Stanford, Calif.: Stanford UP, 1989.

Issacharoff, Michael. "How Playscripts Refer: Some Preliminary Considerations." *On Referring in Literature.* Ed. A. Whiteside and M. Issacharoff. Bloomington: Indiana UP, 1987. 84–94.

Jahn, Janheinz. *Neo-African Literature: A History of Black Writing.* Trans. O. Coburn and U. Lehrburger. New York: Grove Press, 1969.

James, C. L. R. *The Black Jacobins: Toussaint L'Ouverture and the San Domingo Revolution.* 1963. New York: Vintage Books, 1989.

Jeyifo, Biodun. "Femi Osofisan as Literary Critic and Theorist." *Perspectives on Nigerian Literature 1700 to the Present,* Vol. 2. Ed. Yemi Ogunbiyi. Lagos: Guardian Press, 1988. 228–232.

Jeyifo, Biodun. *Masks of Otherness and Negation: Theatrical Images of Blacks in America.* Unpublished ms. Revised version of "Theatre and Drama and the Black Physical and Cultural Presence in America: Essays in Interpretation." Ph.D. Dissertation, New York University, 1975.

Jeyifo, Biodun. "Some Corrective Myths for the Misguided Native and the Arrogant Alien." *Positive Review* 1 (1978): 15–16.

Jeyifo, Biodun. *Soyinka Demythologized: Notes on a Materialist Reading of A Dance of the Forests, The Road and Kongi's Harvest.* 1974. Ife Monographs on Literature and Criticism. Department of Literature in English, U of Ife, 1984.

Jeyifo, Biodun. "The Reinvention of Theatrical Tradition: Critical Discourses on Interculturalism in the African Theatre." *The Dramatic Touch of Difference: Theatre, Own and Foreign.* Ed. Erika Fischer-Lichte, J. Riley, and M. Gissenwehrer. Tübingen: Gunter Narr Verlag, 1990. 239–251.

Jeyifo, Biodun. *The Truthful Lie: Essays in a Sociology of African Drama.* London: New Beacon Books, 1985.

Jeyifo, Biodun. *The Yoruba Popular Travelling Theatre of Nigeria.* Lagos: Nigeria Magazine, 1984.

Jeyifo, Biodun. "What Is the Will of Ogun?" *Perspectives on Nigerian Literature: 1700 to the Present,* Vol.1. Ed. Yemi Ogunbiyi. Lagos: Guardian Books, 1988. 169–185.

Jeyifo, Biodun. "Wole Soyinka and the Tropes of Disalienation." Introduction. *Art, Dialogue and Outrage: Essays on Literature and Culture.* By Wole Soyinka. Ibadan, Nigeria: New Horn Press, 1988. vii–xxxii.

Jeyifous, Abiodun. "Black Critics and Black Theatre in America." *TDR* 18.3 (1974): 34–45.

Johnson, Samuel. *The History of the Yorubas.* 1921. London: Routledge & Kegan Paul, 1969.

Jones, Hettie. *How I Became Hettie Jones.* New York: E. P. Dutton, 1990.

July, Robert W. *An African Voice: The Role of the Humanities in African Independence.* Durham, N.C.: Duke UP, 1987.

Karenga, Maulana. *Kawaida Theory: An Introductory Outline.* Inglewood, Calif.: Kawaida Publications, 1980.

Katrak, Ketu H. *Wole Soyinka and Modern Tragedy: A Study of Dramatic Theory and Practice.* Westport, Conn.: Greenwood Press, 1986.

Kavanagh, Robert. *Theatre and Cultural Struggle in South Africa.* London: Zed Books, 1985.

Kennedy, Scott. *In Search of African Theatre.* New York: Charles Scribner's Sons, 1973.

Kidd, Ross. *The Popular Performing Arts, Non-Formal Education and Social Change in the Third World: A Bibliography and Review Essay.* The Hague: Centre for the Study of Education in Developing Countries, 1982.

Kirby, E. T. "Indigenous African Theatre." *TDR* 18:4 (1974): 22–35.

Knight, Franklin W. and Colin A. Palmer. "The Caribbean: A Regional Overview." *The Modern Caribbean.* Ed. Franklin W. Knight and Colin A. Palmer. Chapel Hill: U of North Carolina P, 1989. 1 -19.

Lacey, Henry C. *To Raise, Destroy, and Create: The Poetry, Drama, and Fiction of Imamu Amiri Baraka.* Troy, N.Y.: Whitston, 1981.

Laclau, Ernesto, and Chantal Mouffe. *Hegemony and Socialist Strategy: Towards a Radical Democratic Politics.* London: Verso, 1985.

Lacoue-Labarthe, Philippe. *Typography: Mimesis, Philosophy, and Politics.* Cambridge, Mass.: Harvard UP, 1989.

Ladipo, Duro. *Oba Waja (The King Is Dead). Three Yoruba Plays: Oba Koso, Oba Moro, Oba Waja.* English adaptations by Ulli Beier. Ibadan, Nigeria: Mbari Publications, 1964. 54–72.

Lamming, George. "Caribbean Literature: The Black Rock of Africa." *African Forum* 1 (1966): 32–52.

Larlham, Peter. *Black Theater, Dance and Ritual in South Africa.* Ann Arbor, Mich.: UMI Research Press, 1985.

Lauter, Paul. "History and the Canon." *Social Text* 12 (1985): 94–101.

Lesohai, B. L. "Black South African Theatre." *Theatre in Africa.* Ed. O. Ogunba and A. Irele. Ibadan, Nigeria: Ibadan UP, 1978. 115–130.

Levine, Lawrence W. *Black Culture and Black Consciousness: Afro-American Folk Thought from Slavery to Freedom.* New York: Oxford UP, 1977.

Lindenberger, Herbert. *The History in Literature: On Value, Genre, Institutions.* New York: Columbia UP, 1990.

Locke, Alain, and Montgomery Gregory, eds. *Plays of Negro Life: A Source-Book of Native American Drama.* New York: Harper and Brothers, 1927.

Lorde, Audre. "The Great American Disease." *The Black Scholar* May–June 1979: 17–20.

Lott, Eric. *Love and Theft: Blackface Minstrelsy and the American Working Class.* New York: Oxford UP, 1993.

Lowenthal, David, and Lambros Comitas, eds. *Consequences of Class and Color: West Indian Perspectives.* New York: Anchor Books, 1973.

Lyotard, Jean-François. *The Differend: Phrases in Dispute.* Trans. Georges Van Den Abbeele. Minneapolis: U of Minnesota P, 1988.

Macdonell, Dianne. *Theories of Discourse: An Introduction.* Oxford: Basil Blackwell, 1986.

Macebuh, Stanley. "Poetics and the Mythic Imagination." *Transition / Chi'Indaba.* 50/1 (1975): 79–84.

Mann, Michael. *The Sources of Power, Vol. I: A History of Power from the Beginning to AD 1760.* Cambridge: Cambridge UP, 1986.

Marx, Karl. *A Contribution to the Critique of Political Economy.* New York: International Publishers, 1970.

Marx, Karl. *The German Ideology.* London: Lawrence & Wishart, 1974.

Matthews, Victoria Earle. "The Value of Race Literature." Address delivered at the First Congress of Colored Women of the United States. Boston, 30 July 1895. In *Massachusetts Review* 27.2 (1986): 170–85.

Maxwell, Marina. "Towards a Revolution in the Arts." *Savacou* September 1970: 19–32.

McCartney, John T. *Black Power Ideologies: An Essay in Afro-American Political Thought.* Philadelphia: Temple UP, 1992

McClintock, Anne. " 'Azikwelwa' (We Will Not Ride): Politics and Value in Black South African Poetry." *Politics and Poetic Value.* Ed. Robert von Hallberg. Chicago: U of Chicago Press, 1987. 225–51.

McCrum, Robert, William Cran, and Robert MacNeil. *The Story of English.* New York: Elisabeth Sifton Books, 1986.

McDowell, Deborah E. "Reading Family Matters." *Changing Our Words: Essays on Criticism, Theory, and Writing by Black Women.* Ed. Cheryl A. Wall. New Brunswick, N.J.: Rutgers UP, 1989. 75–97.

Melhem, D. H., ed. "Amiri Baraka (LeRoi Jones): Revolutionary Traditions." *Heroism in the New Black Poetry: Introductions and Interviews.* Lexington: UP of Kentucky, 1990. 215–63.

Merleau-Ponty, Maurice. *Signs.* Trans. Richard C. McCleary. Evanston, Ill.: Northwestern UP, 1964.

Miller, Christopher L. *Blank Darkness: Africanist Discourse in French.* Chicago: U of Chicago P, 1985.

Miller, Christopher L. *Theories of Africans: Francophone Literature and Anthropology in Africa.* Chicago: U of Chicago P, 1990.

Milner, Ronald. "Black Theater—Go Home!" *The Black Aesthetic.* Ed. Addison Gayle, Jr. New York: Doubleday, 1971. 306–312.

Minh-ha, Trin T. *Woman, Native, Other: Writing Postcoloniality and Feminism.* Bloomington: Indiana UP, 1989.

Mintz, Sidney W., and Saly Price, eds. *Caribbean Contours.* Baltimore: Johns Hopkins UP, 1985.

Mitchell, Carolyn. " 'A Laying on of Hands': Transcending the City in Ntozake Shange's *for colored girls who have considered suicide/ when the rainbow is enuf.*" *Women Writers and the City: Essays in Feminist Literary Criticism.* Ed. Susan M. Squier. Knoxville: U of Tennessee P, 1984.

Mitchell, Loften. *Black Drama: The Story of the American Negro in the Theatre.* New York: Hawthorn Books, 1967.

Mitter, Partha. "Can we ever understand alien cultures? some epistemological concerns relating to the perception and understanding of the Other." *Comparative Criticism* 9 (1987): 3–34.

Mlama, Penina M. *Culture and Development: The Popular Theatre Approach in Africa.* Uppsala: Scandinavian Institute of African Studies, 1991.

Mohanty, Chandra T., Ann Russo, and Lourdes Torres, eds. *Third World Women and the Politics of Feminism.* Bloomington: Indiana UP, 1991.

Mohanty, Satya P. "Us and Them: On the Philosophical Bases of Political Criticism." *Yale Journal of Criticism* 2.2 (1989): 1–31.

Molette, Carlton W., and Barbara J. Molette. *Black Theater: Premise and Presentation.* Bristol, IN: Wyndham Hall Press, 1986.

Mudimbe, V. Y. *The Invention of Africa: Gnosis, Philosophy, and the Order of Knowledge.* Bloomington: Indiana UP, 1988.

Murray, Timothy. "Facing the Camera's Eye: Black and White Terrain in Women's Drama." *Reading Black, Reading Feminist: A Critical Anthology.* Ed. Henry L. Gates, Jr. New York: Meridian, 1990. 155–73.

Murray, Timothy. "Screening the Camera's Eye: Black and White Confrontations of Technological Representation." *Modern Drama* 28.1 (1985): 110–24.

Nathan, Hans. *Dan Emmett and the Rise of Early Negro Minstrelsy.* Norman: U of Oklahoma P, 1962.

Ndlovu, Duma, ed. *Woza Afrika! An Anthology of South African Plays.* New York: George Braziller, 1986.

Neal, Larry. "The Black Contribution to American Letters: Part II: The Writer as Activist—1960 and After." *The Black American Reference Book.* Ed. Mabel Smythe. Englewood Cliffs, N.J.: Prentice-Hall, 1976. 767–790.

Nettleford, Rex. *Caribbean Cultural Identity: The Case of Jamaica.* Los Angeles: Center for Afro-American Studies and Latin American Center Publications, UCLA, 1978.

Nettleford, Rex M. *Identity, Race and Protest in Jamaica.* New York: William Morrow, 1972.

Ngugi wa Thiong'O. *Barrel of a Pen: Resistance to Repression in Neo-Colonial Kenya.* Trenton, N.J.: Africa World Press, 1983.

Ngugi wa Thiong'O. *Decolonising the Mind: The Politics of Language in African Literature.* London: James Currey, 1986.

Nietzsche, Friedrich. *The Birth of Tragedy and the Genealogy of Morals.* Trans. Francis Golffing. New York: Doubleday, 1956.

Obiechina, E. N. "Literature: Traditional and Modern." *The Nsukka Environment.* Ed. G. E. K. Ofomata. Enugu: Fourth Dimension Publishers, 1978. 376 -398.

Ogunba, Oyin. "Traditional African Festival Drama." *Theatre in Africa.* Ed. O. Ogunba and A. Irele. Ibadan, Nigera: Ibadan UP, 1978. 3–26.

Ogunba, Oyin, and Abiola Irele. Eds. *Theatre in Africa.* Ibadan, Nigeria: Ibadan UP, 1978.

Ogunbiyi, Yemi. "A Study of Soyinka's *Opera Wonyosi.*" *Nigeria Magazine* 128–29 (1979): 3–14.

Ogundele, Wole. "*Death and the King's Horseman*: A Poet's Quarrel with His Culture." *Research in African Literatures* 25.1 (1994): 47–60.

Ogundipe-Leslie, 'Molara. "Women in Nigeria." *Women in Nigeria Today.* Ed. WIN. London: Zed Books, 1985. 119–31.

Okara, Gabriel. "African Speech . . . English Words." *Transition* 10 (1963): 16.

Olaniyan, Tejumola. "Discussing Afrocentrism: A Seminar led by Tejumola Olaniyan." *Passages: A Chronicle of the Humanities* (Program of African Studies, Northwestern U), no. 3 (1992): 4–5, 16.

Olaniyan, Tejumola. "Dramatizing Postcoloniality: Wole Soyinka and Derek Wal-
    cott." *Theatre Journal* 44 (1992): 485–499.
Omotoso, Kole. *The Theatrical into Theatre: A Study of the Drama and Theatre
    of the English-Speaking Caribbean.* London: New Beacon Books, 1982.
Osofisan, Femi. *Beyond Translation.* Ife Monographs on Literature and Criticism,
    3rd ser., no. 1, 1985.
Osofisan, Femi. "Drama and the New Exotic: The Paradox of Form in Modern
    African Theatre." Department of Modern European Languages Seminar,
    University of Ife, 19 April 1978.
Osofisan, Femi. "Ritual and the Revolutionary Ethos: The Humanistic Dilemma
    in Contemporary Nigerian Theatre." 1976. *Okike* 22 (1982): 72–81.
Owomoyela, Oyekan. *Visions and Revisions: Essays on African Literatures and
    Criticism.* New York: Peter Lang, 1991.
Palmer, Colin A. "Identity, Race, and Black Power in Independent Jamaica." *The
    Modern Caribbean.* Ed. Franklin W. Knight and Colin A. Palmer. Chapel
    Hill: U of North Carolina P, 1989. 111–28.
Pantin, Raoul. *Black Power Day: The 1970 February Revolution.* Santa Cruz, Trin-
    idad and Tobago: Hatuey Productions, 1990.
Pecheux, Michel. *Langauge, Semantics and Ideology.* Trans. Harbans Nagpal. New
    York: St. Martin's Press, 1982.
Peters, Erskine. "Some Tragic Propensities of Ourselves: The Occasion of Nto-
    zake Shange's 'For Colored Girls Who Have Considered Suicide/ When
    the Rainbow Is Enuf.'" *Journal of Ethnic Studies* 6.1 (1978): 79–85.
Rabinow, Paul. "Representations Are Social Facts: Modernity and Postmodernity
    in Anthropology." *Writing Culture: The Poetics and Politics of Ethnogra-
    phy.* Ed. J. Clifford and G. E. Marcus. Berkeley: U of California P, 1986.
    234–61.
Radhakarishnan, R. "Ethnic Identity and Post-Structuralist Differance." *Cultural
    Critique* 6 (1987): 199–220.
Radhakrishnan, R. "Postcoloniality and the Boundaries of Identity." *Callaloo*
    16.4 (1993): 750– 71.
Ready, Richard M. "Through the Intricacies of 'The Fourth Stage' to an Appre-
    hension of *Death and the King's Horseman.*" *Black American Literature
    Forum* 22.4 (1988): 711–21.
Reed, Adolph. "Black Particularity Reconsidered." *Telos* 39 (1979): 71–93.
Rice, Edward Le Roy. *Monarchs of Minstrelsy, from "Daddy" Rice to Date.* New
    York: Kenny, 1911.
Richards, Sandra L. "Conflicting Impulses in the Plays of Ntozake Shange." *Black
    American Literature Forum* 17.2 (1983): 73–78.
Richards, Sandra L. "Negative Forces and Positive Non-Entities: Images of
    Women in the Dramas of Amiri Baraka." *Theatre Journal* 34.2 (1982):
    233- 40.
Richardson, Willis, ed. *Plays and Pageants from the Life of the Negro.* Washington,
    D.C.: Associated Publishers, 1935.
Richardson, Willis, and May Miller, eds. *Negro History in Thirteen Plays.* Wash-
    ington, D.C.: Associated Press, 1935.
Rodman, Selden. *Tongues of Fallen Angels.* New York: New Directions, 1972.
Rodney, Walter. *The Groundings with My Brothers.* London: Bogle–L'Ouverture
    Publications, 1969.
Rohlehr, Gordon. *Pathfinder: Black Awakening in The Arrivants of Edward*

Kamau Brathwaite. Port of Spain, Trinidad and Tobago: College Press, 1981.

Ross, Chambers. "Irony and the Canon." *Profession* (1990): 18–24.

Ross, Andrew, ed. *Universal Abandon? The Politics of Postmodernism.* Minneapolis: U of Minnesota P, 1988.

Ross, Robert, ed. *Racism and Colonialism: Essays on Ideology and Social Structure.* The Hague: Martinus Nijhoff, 1982.

Rotimi, Ola. "The Drama in African Ritual Display." *Drama and Theatre in Nigeria: A Critical Sourcebook.* Ed. Yemi Ogunbiyi. Lagos: Nigeria Magazine, 1981. 77–80.

Rushing, Andrea Benton. "For Colored Girls, Suicide or Struggle." *Massachusetts Review* 22.3 (1981): 539–550.

Ryan, Selyn D. *Race and Nationalism in Trinidad and Tobago: A Study of Decolonization in a Multiracial Society.* Toronto: U of Toronto P, 1973.

Saakana, Amon S. *The Colonial Legacy in Caribbean Literature.* London: Karmak House, 1987.

Said, Edward W. *Orientalism.* New York: Vintage, 1979.

Said, Edward. "Orientalism Reconsidered." *Race and Class.* XXVII.2 (1985): 1–15.

Said, Edward. "Representing the Colonized: Anthropology's Interlocutors." *Critical Inquiry* 15:2 (1989): 202–225.

Sampson, Henry T. *Blacks in Blackface: A Source Book on Early Black Musical Shows.* Metuchen, N.J.: Scarecrow Press, 1980.

Sanders, Leslie C. *The Development of Black Theater in America: From Shadows to Selves.* Baton Rouge: Louisiana State UP, 1988.

Scarry, Elaine. *The Body in Pain: The Making and Unmaking of the World.* New York: Oxford UP, 1985.

Schipper, Mineke. *Theatre and Society in Africa.* Johannesburg: Ravan Press, 1982.

Schoemberger, Nancy. Interview with Derek Walcott. *The Threepenny Review* Fall 1983: 16–17.

Scott, Denis. "Walcott on Walcott." Interview. *Caribbean Quarterly* 14.1–2 (1968): 77–82.

Senghor, Léopold S. *Prose and Poetry.* Selec. and trans. J. Reed and C. Wake. London: Oxford UP, 1965.

Senghor, Léopold S. "The African Apprehension of Reality." *Prose and Poetry.* Selec. and trans. J. Reed and C. Wake. London: Oxford UP, 1965. 29–34.

Senghor, Léopold S. *The Mission of the Poet.* Trans. R. W. Thompson. St. Augustine, Trinidad and Tobago: U.W.I. Extra-Mural Department, 1966.

Senghor, Léopold Sédar. *The Foundation of "Africanite" or "Negritude" and "Arabite".* 1967. Trans. M. Cook. Paris: Presence Africaine, 1971.

Silverman, Kaja. "*Histoire d'O*: The Story of a Disciplined and Punished Body." *Enclitic* 7.2 (1983): 63–81.

Sistren, with Honor Ford-Smith, ed. *Lionheart Gal: Life Stories of Jamaican Women.* London: Women's Press, 1986.

Slemon, Stephen, and Helen Tiffin, eds. *After Europe: Critical Theory and Post-Colonial Writing.* Sydney: Dangaroo Press, 1989.

Smith, Barbara H. *Contingencies of Value: Alternative Perspectives for Critical Theory.* Cambridge, Mass.: Harvard UP, 1988.

Smith, David L. "Amiri Baraka and the Black Arts of Black Art." *Boundary 2* 15.1–2 (Fall 1986–Winter 1987): 235–54.

Smith, M. G. *Culture, Race, and Class in the Commonwealth Caribbean.* Mona, Jamaica: UWI Department of Extra-Mural Studies, 1984.

Smith, Raymond T. "Race and Class in the Post-Emancipation Caribbean." *Racism and Colonialism: Essays on Ideology and Social Structure.* Ed. Robert Ross. The Hague: Martinus Nijhoff, 1982. 93–119.

Smitherman, Geneva. *Talkin and Testifyin: The Language of Black America.* Boston: Houghton Mifflin, 1977.

Sollors, Werner. *Amiri Baraka/LeRoi Jones: The Quest for a "Populist Modernism."* New York: Columbia UP, 1978.

Sotto, Wiveca. *The Rounded Rite: A Study of Wole Soyinka's Play, The Bacchae of Euripides.* Lund: CWK Gleerup, 1985.

Special Issue: The Language Question. *Research in African Literatures* 23.1 (1992).

Special Section on Theatre for Development in Africa. *Research in African Literatures* 22.3 (1991): 7–133.

Spillers, Hortense J. "Cross-Currents, Discontinuities: Black Women's Fiction." *Conjuring: Black Women, Fiction, and Literary Tradition.* Ed. Marjorie Pryse and Hortense J. Spillers. Bloomington: Indiana UP, 1985. 249–61.

Spillers, Hortense J. "Mama's Baby, Papa's Maybe: An American Grammar Book." *Diacritics* 17 (1987): 65–81.

Spivak, Gayatri C. *The Post-Colonial Critic: Interviews, Strategies, Dialogues.* New York: Routledge, 1990.

Stallybrass, Peter, and Allon White. *The Politics and Poetics of Transgression.* Ithaca, N.Y.: Cornell UP, 1986.

Staples, Robert. "The Myth of Black Macho: A Response to Angry Black Feminists." *The Black Scholar* March–April 1979: 24–32.

Stratton, Florence. "Wole Soyinka: A Writer's Social Vision." *Black American Literature Forum* 22.3 (1988): 531–53.

Tate, Claudia, ed. "Ntozake Shange." Interview. *Black Women Writers at Work.* New York: Continuum, 1983. 149–74.

Tate, Greg. "Growing Up in Public: Amiri Baraka Changes His Mind." *Village Voice* 2 October 1984: 41–43.

Taylor, Patrick. *The Narrative of Liberation: Perspectives on Afro-Caribbean Literature, Popular Culture, and Politics.* Ithaca, N.Y.: Cornell UP, 1989.

Terada, Rei. *Derek Walcott's Poetry: American Mimicry.* Boston: Northeastern UP, 1992.

Terdiman, Richard. *Discourse/Counter-Discourse: The Theory and Practice of Symbolic Resistance in Nineteenth-Century France.* Ithaca, N.Y.: Cornell UP, 1985.

"The Black Sexism Debate." *The Black Scholar* 10.8–9 (1979)

The Drama Review 12 (Summer 1968).

Timpane, John. "'The Poetry of a Moment': Politics and the Open Form in the Drama of Ntozake Shange." *Studies in American Drama, 1945–Present* 4 (1989): 91–101.

Toll, Robert C. *Blacking Up: The Minstrel Show in Nineteenth Century America.* New York: Oxford UP, 1974.

Tomlinson, John. *Cultural Imperialism: A Critical Introduction.* Baltimore: Johns Hopkins UP, 1991.

Traore, Bakary. *Black African Theatre and Its Social Functions.* Ibadan, Nigeria: Ibadan UP, 1972.

Turner, Darwin T. "W. E. B. Du Bois and the Theory of a Black Aesthetic." *The Harlem Renaissance Reexamined.* Ed. Victor A. Kramer. New York: AMS Press, 1987. 9–30.

Van Graan, Mike. "International Models of Popular and Political Theatre." *Communications* (Centre for African Studies, U of Capetown) 18 (1990): 71–122.

Viswanathan, Gauri. *Masks of Conquest: Literary Study and British Rule in India.* New York: Columbia UP, 1989.

Wagner, Roy. *The Invention of Culture.* 1971. Chicago: U of Chicago P, 1981.

Wali, Obiajuna. "The Dead-End of African Literature?" *Transition* 10 (1963): 13–15.

Walker, Alice. "In Search of Our Mother's Gardens." *In Search of Our Mother's Gardens,* New York: Harcourt, 1983. 231–43.

Wall, Cheryl A. "Response." In *Afro-American Literary Study in the 1990s.* Ed. Houston A. Baker, Jr., and Patricia Redmond. Chicago: U of Chicago Press, 1989. 185–190.

Wallace, Michele. *Black Macho and the Myth of the Superwoman.* 1978. New York: Verso, 1990.

Wallace, Michele. *Invisibility Blues: From Pop to Theory.* New York: Verso, 1990.

Wauthier, Claude. *The Literature and Thought of Modern Africa.* 1964. Trans. Shirley Kay. Washington, D.C.: Three Continents Press, 1979.

Weiss, Allen S. "Ideology and the problem of Style: The Errant Text." *Enclitic* 7.2 (1983): 17–23.

Wellek, Rene, and Austin Warren. *Theory of Literature.* New York: Harcourt, Brace & World, 1942.

West, Cornel. Interview with Anders Stephanson. In *Universal Abandon? The Politics of Postmodernism.* Ed. Andrew Ross. Minneapolis: U of Minnesota P, 1988. 269–86.

West, Cornel. "Marxist Theory and the Specificity of Afro-American Oppression." *Marxism and the Interpretation of Culture.* Ed. Cary Nelson and Lawrence Grossberg. Urbana: U of Illinois P, 1988. 17–29.

White, E. Frances. "Africa on My Mind: Gender, Counter Discourse and African-American Nationalism." *Journal of Women's History* 2.1 (1990): 73–97.

Whiteside, A., and M. Issacharoff, eds. *On Referring in Literature.* Bloomington: Indiana UP, 1987.

Williams, Adebayo. "Ritual and the Political Unconsciousness: The Case of *Death and the King's Horseman.*" *Research in African Literatures* 24.1 (1993): 67–79.

Williams, Mance. *Black Theatre in the 1960s and 1970s: A Historical-Critical Analysis of the Movement.* Westport, Conn.: Greenwood Press, 1985.

Williams, Raymond. *Marxism and Literature.* Oxford: Oxford UP, 1977.

Williams, Raymond. *Problems in Materialism and Culture.* London: Verso, 1980.

Wittke, Carl. *Tambo and Bones: A History of the American Minstrel Stage.* Durham, N.C.: Duke UP, 1930.

Woodson, Carter G. *The Mis-Education of the Negro*. 1933. New York: AMS
    Press, 1977.
Wright, Richardson. *Revels in Jamaica, 1682–1838*. New York: Benjamin Bom,
    1937.
Wynter, Sylvia. "One Love—Rhetoric or Reality?— Aspects of Afro-
    Jamaicanism." *Caribbean Studies* 12.3 (1972): 64–97.

Index

Achebe, Chinua, 26
Adedeji, Joel, 24
Aeschylus, 48, 113
Africa: African languages in, 39; Afrocentric defense of, 24–25; in Caribbean, 94, 109; cultural forms derived from, 5; English in, 39, 155n. 57; Eurocentric conception of, 31; imaginary, 108, 109; indigenous dramatic forms of, 16–17; post-Afrocentric notion of, 34; and white subjectivity, 143n. 3, 113
African–American: audience, 83; community, 84; condition, 77; cultural automony, 3; difference, 6, 67, 78, 136; experience 84; oppression of, 20; performance forms, 23; theatrical subjectivity, 14
African: cultural identity, 5, 60, 117; essence, 60; festivals, 25; theory of tragic art, 46, 47–49; world as source of epistemologies, 46; worldview, 3, 5, 45–46
Afrocentric discourse: Africa as nodal point of, 37; as anticolonialist, 4, 7;

binary politics of, 26, 39; condition of possibility of, 11; as counterhegemonic practice, 19–20; cultural nationalism of, 32, 40, 82, 107, 116; and culturalism, 32, 34; expressive identity in, 32–34, 116–17; and form, 23; and genre, 37–38, 151n. 37; and language, 38–40; and post-Afrocentric discourse, 27–28; and refusal of subjection, 30; relativism of, 32–33, 151n. 37; and rhetoric of the collective, 144n. 11; theorists, 24, 146n. 38; unevenness of, 20
Alarinjo, 24
Althusser, Louis, 148n. 2
Andrews, W. D. E., 90
Animism, 63
Anticolonialist. See Afrocentric discourse
Apartheid, 3
Apollo, 48, 54
articulation, 5, 34, 35–37, 116, 139, 151n. 32
Ashcroft, Griffiths and Tiffin, 39
Atunda, 47, 61

Baker, Houston A., 127
Baraka, Amiri (LeRoi Jones): and
 African-American cultural identity,
 70; *The Baptism*, 74, 75–76; black
 aesthetics of, 80–81, 82; *A Black
 Mass*, 82; and black music, 77–78,
 160n. 56; and Black Panther, 86;
 black values of 82, 86, 160n. 73;
 Bloodrites, 82; and bohemian
 aesthetics 71, 73, 74–76, 92, 159n.
 43; on color and class 71–82; and
 Cuban Revolution, 76–77; cultural
 nationalism, of, 71, 82, 87, 92; *The
 Dead Lecturer*, 74; and "decrudin,"
 71, 80, 84–85, 81, 92; *Dutchman*,
 82, 109, 78–80; "The Eight Ditch
 Is Drama," 74; and English
 language 74; *Experimental Death
 Unit #1*, 82; and expressive identity,
 85; and Fidel Castro, 76; *Four
 Black Revolutionary Plays: All
 Praises to the Black Man*, 82, *Great
 Goodness of Life: A Coon Show*, 82;
 Hard Facts, 87–88; and Howard
 University, 72; influence of Malcolm
 X on, 82; and Islam, 82;
 J-E-L-L-O, 82; *Junkies Are Full of
 (Shh . . .)*, 82; *Madheart*, 82, 85–
 86, 109, 131; and Marxism, 70,
 87–88, 92, 117; *Motion of History
 and Other Plays*, 88–91, 142; name
 changes of, 82; and "Negro
 literature," 77; and performative
 identity, 69, 92; *Preface to a
 Twenty Volume Suicide Note*, 74; as
 propagandist, 90–91; and protean
 essence, 69–92; radical absolutism,
 117; representation of black women,
 84–86, 161n. 83; representation of
 Harlem, 74, 77; "The
 Revolutionary Theatre," 80–81;
 The Slave, 80; *Slave Ship*, 82–84,
 89; and United States Air Force,
 72–73
Barthes, Roland, 76
Batista, 63
Baxter, Ivy, 16
Baudry, Jean-Louis, 89
Beckett, Samuel, 101
Beckwith, Martha W., 16

Benston, Kimberly W., 23, 71, 160n.
 77
Black Arts Movement, 22, 147n. 49
Black Consciousness Movement, 23,
 147n. 55
Black: activist theater, 3; aesthetic,
 22–23; assertion of subjectivity, 6,
 139; in blackface minstrelsy, 13–14;
 cultural identity against Euro-
 American hegemony, 6; cultural
 identity as articulation, 35–37;
 cultural identity as masculinist, 117;
 cultural nationalism, 32–34;
 difference as relational, 6; dramatic
 practice, 4, 7, 11; dramatic tradition,
 12; dramatic voice, 4; dramaturgic
 forms, 5; and English, 39, 126–27,
 140, 152n. 42; expressive identity,
 32–34; and "folk" form, 21–22;
 historical subjection, 6; performance
 forms, 37; performative identity, 34;
 South African drama, 24; West
 Indian performance forms, 16;
 women's writing, 120–21
Blackface minstrelsy, 13–14
Blau, Herbert, 141, 142
Bourdieu, Pierre, 19, 39,
Brathwaite, Edward K., 94, 98
Brecht, Bertolt, 91, 113
Brecht, Stefan, 83
Brodber, Erna, 34
Brook, Peter, 31, 33
Brown, Lloyd W., 68
Bullins, Ed, 22
Burns, Elizabeth, 141

Cabral, Amilcar, 18, 21
Calyso, 25
Camboulay. *See* Caribbean: carnival
Caribbean: carnival, 13, 14, 15–16,
 25–26, 102, 103, 113, 141; Creole,
 39, 103, 111–12; cultural forms, 5;
 cultural identity, 97, 110, 114;
 dramatists, 3, 5, 140; English in, 39,
 111–12; and history, 94;
 performative aesthetics 103; popular
 theater, 16; slavery and colonialism,
 94
Castro, Fidel, 63, 64, 67, 76
Cesaire, Aime, 100

Childress, Alice, 142
Chinweizu, Jemie, Madubuike, 32
Clifford, James, 30
colonialist. *See* Eurocentric discourse
counterdiscourse. *See* Afrocentric discourse
Creole. *See* Caribbean: Creole
culture, 30, 31, 34, 35
cultural difference, 6; and cultural hierarchy, 34
cultural identity: as articulation, 35–37; and cultural hierarchy, 34; expressive model of, 32–34; paradigms of, 4, 30–32; performative model of, 31, 34, 36
cultural imperialism, 3–4, 5, 35
cultural nationalism, 22, 32, 33, 34, 37, 40, 84–85, 150n. 17
cultural relativism, 32, 33, 34
culturalism, 27, 32, 34, 59

Davies, Carole Boyce, 61
decolonization, 11, 94, 117, 140, 144n. 2
"Decrudin." *See* Baraka: and "decrudin"
DeVeaux, Alexis, 34
Dionysos, 48, 49
discourse: Afrocentric, *see* Afrocentric discourse; definition, 4, 143n. 6; as discursive practice, 4, 143n. 7; Eurocentric, *see* Eurocentric discourse; post-Afrocentric, *see* Post-Afrocentric discourse
Dollimore, Jonathan, 26
DuBois, W. E. B., 21, 22, 146n. 41, 146n. 42
Duvaliers, 37

Elam, Keir, 141
Ellison, Ralph, 3, 6
Enekwe, Ossie, 24
English. *See* Black: English; Afrocentric discourse: and language; Post-Afrocentric discourse: and language
Etherton, Micheal, 34
Eurocentric discourse: on African drama, 16–18; and blackface minstrelsy, 13–14; on Caribbean

carnival, 14–16; epistemology, 20; expressive identity, in, 31–32, 150n. 24; and genre, 37, 151n. 34; as hegemonic and colonialist, 4, 11; institutions of, 139; Manichean terrains of, 108; and realism, 18; and relativism, 31, 32, 150n. 24; and rise of Europe, 11; subjectivist racism of, 12; theatrical norms, 123; universalism, 31, 32, 44, 150n. 12
Ewe, 38
expressive identity: in Afrocentric discourse, *see* Afrocentric discourse: expressive identity in; as coercive and dominative, 31; conception of culture, 30; definition, 30; in Eurocentric discourse, *see* Eurocentric discourse: expressive identity in; mode of representation 30, 149n. 8; as paradigm, 4, 5

Fabre, Genevieve, 28
Fanon, Frantz, 12, 13, 18, 26, 27, 33, 59, 121–22, 148n. 66, 152n. 41, 155n. 64
Finnegan, Ruth, 16, 17, 18, 24, 31, 37
Foucault, Michel, 4, 12, 32, 69, 95, 106, 157n. 2, 163n. 12
Franklin, Benjamin, 59
Freud, Sigmund, 12
Fugard, Athol, 24

gender, 5, 117, 119–20, 167n. 6
genre, 5, 37–38, 68
Ginsberg, Allen, 73
Gobineau, 12
Gotrick, Kacke, 24
Graham-White, Anthony, 24, 33, 37
Greek mythology, 5
Grotowski, Jerzy, 112

Haiti, 37
Hall, Stuart, 35
Harris, Wilson, 34, 101
Harris, W. J., 71
Hay, Samuel, 147n. 45
Hegel, G. W. F., 12
Henderson, Mae G., 116, 121
Henderson, Stephen, 32

Hill, Errol, 15, 25, 26
Hogue, W. L., 69
hooks, bell, 119, 134
Houtondji, Paulin J., 21, 34, 35, 36, 37, 170n. 5
Hughes, Langston, 19, 21
Huges, Ted, 101
Hume, 12

identity. *See* cultural identity
institutions, 68, 139
Irele, Abiola, 139
invention, 6–7, 11

Jefferson, 12
Jeyifo, Biodun, 14, 27, 34, 46, 62, 64, 65, 66, 157n. 93
Joyce, James, 94

Kamiriithu Community Education and Cultural Centre, 120
Kant, 12
Kavanagh, Robert, 24
Kerouac, Jack, 74
Kirby, E. T., 17
Kitchener, Lord, 103
Knight, F. W., 94

Laclau and Mouffe, 35, 36
Leavis, F. R., 110
Levy-Bruhl, 12
Locke, Alain, 21, 22, 32, 147n. 45
Lorde, Audre, 167n. 6
Lyotard, Jean-Francois, 127

Marx, Karl, 148n. 2
Matthews, Victoria Earle, 20–21
McClintock, Anne, 68
McDowell, Deborah E., 134
Mead, Taylor, 75
Merleau-Ponty, Maurice, 114
Milner, Ronald, 38
Mohanty, Satya P., 33
Mthali, Felix, 117
Mudimbe, V. Y., 29, 30, 39, 140
Murphy, Eddie, 91
Murray, Timothy, 89
Muse, Clarence, 19

National Association for the Advancement of Colored People (NAACP), 21
National Black Theatre, 70. *See also* Teer
Neal, Larry, 22
Negritude, 22, 44, 60
Neruda, Pablo, 100
Nietzsche, Friedrich, 5, 48, 52, 54

Obatala, 47, 48, 54, 84
Ogun, 47, 48, 49, 50, 53, 55, 59, 61, 63, 64
Ogunba, Oyin, 24
Ogundele, Wole, 155n. 62
Ogundipe-Leslie, 'Molara, 117, 119
Orunmila, 63
Osofisan, Femi, 34, 62, 63, 64, 65
Other, 30, 31, 32, 36, 79, 137
Owomoyela, Oyekan, 24
Oyo, 49

Palmer, C. A., 94
Parker, Charlie, 79
Patwah 30. *See also* Caribbean: Creole
Pecheux, Michel, 40
performance, 14, 16, 24, 30, 140–41, 142
performative identity: of Afrocentric and Post-Afrocentric discourses, 116; as ceaselessly self-critical, 142; conception of culture, 30–31; and insurgent identity, 36–37; mode of representation, 31; as paradigm, 4, 5; as principle of transgressive and transitional truth, 151n. 31
Perse, Saint-John, 101
popular theater, 6, 144n. 10
post-Afrocentric discourse: and Afrocentric discourse, 27–28; condition of possibility, 11; as emerging, 27–28; and Eurocentric discourse, 27; and Eurocentric institutions, 139; and genre, 38; and language, 39–40; performative identity in, 34; and refusal of subjection, 30; representation of difference, 27; subversion of Manichaeism, 4

Prometheus, 49
Pryor, Richard, 91

racialization of thought, 32
race literature. *See* Matthews
Radhakrishnan, R., 149n. 8, 166n. 91
Ready, Richard M., 54
Reagan, Ronald, 67
Reed, Ishmael, 126
relativism, 20, 32, 33, 34
Rohlehr, Gordon, 98–99
Rushing, Andrea B., 136

Said, Edward W., 11, 18, 30, 31, 32, 144n. 2, 149n. 8
Same, 30, 31
Sango, 59, 64, 84
Scarry, Elaine, 130–31
Schipper, Mineke, 24
Senghor, Leopold Sedar, 22, 32, 33, 147n. 46
Shakespeare, William, 48, 113
Shange, Ntozake: and animism, 135–36, 159n. 74; assumption of African names, 168n. 23; and black women in literature, 122–23; on blackface minstrelsy, 14; *boogie-woogie landscapes*, 136; and combat aesthetics, 124–25; combat breathing, 121; and cultural difference, 123–24; dance and music, 124–25; dramaturgy of the pastiche, 128; and English, 124, 126–27; and expressive identity, 137–38; *for colored girls who have considered suicide/ when the rainbow is enuf*, 120, 124–25, 128–36, 142; gender as nodal point, 136; and performative identity, 128, 136; *a photograph*, 120; representation of blacks and the Vietnam war 134–35; representation of Harlem, 133; and Shakespeare, 123–24; and Soyinka, Baraka, Walcott, 120–21; subversion of transcendental vision, 128; *Spell #7*, 125, 128
Sistren Theatre Collective, 120
Smith, Bessie, 79
Sollors, Werner, 68
Soyinka, Wole: action in Yoruba

tragedy, 53–54; on African festivals 25; and African Marxists, 60–65; African world, 45, 153n. 7; and animism, 63; on Baraka's *Slave Ship* 161n. 82; on class analysis, 61; and "colonial factor," 53–54, 58–59; as a culturalist, 59; *A Dance of the Forests*, 60; *Death and the King's Horseman*, 43, 46, 49–60, 63; deployment of English, 155n. 57; on European worldview 45–46; "The Fourth Stage," 46, 47–49, 50, 62; *From Zia with Love*, 61; and Greek tragedy, 48–49; irony of difference, 153n. 19; *Kongi's Harvest*, 61; *The Lion and the Jewel*, 142; *The Man Died*, 61; *Madman and Specialists*, 61, 62; *Mandela's Earth*, 61; *Myth, Literature and the African World*, 44, 53; and Negritude, 21, 44, 60, 156n. 70; and Nietzsche, 48–49, 52, 154n. 45; nodal point, 45; *Ogun Abibiman*, 60; *Opera Wonyosi*, 61; performative identity, 45, 66; *A Play of Giants*, 61; "race retrieval," 44; representation of death, 62, 154n. 40; representation of gender frictions, 5; and ritual drama, 52–53, 62, 141; *The Road*, 63; *Season of Anomy*, 60–61; self-apprehension, 45; *A Shuttle in the Crypt*, 60; *The Strong Breed*, 63; theory of tragedy, 47–49; and Yoruba mythology, 47–49
Sparrow, Mighty, 103
Spillers, Hortense J., 121, 137
Staples, Robert, 167n. 6, 169n. 73
Stratton, Florence, 61
subjection, 29, 30, 68, 78, 80
subjectivity, 4, 7, 29, 30, 44, 68, 119, 139, 148n. 2, 149n. 3, 149n. 5
Synge, J. M., 102

Tate, Greg, 68
Teer, Barbara Ann, 70, 71, 92
Tempels, 12
Terdiman, Richard, 4
"The Fourth Stage." *See* Soyinka: "The Fourth Stage"

tragedy, 17, 24, 38, 47, 48, 61
Traore, Bakary, 24
Tre, 38
Trin T. Minh-ha, 129
Trinidad Carnival. *See* Caribbean:
  carnival
Trinidad Theatre Workshop, 110

Walcott, Derek: and Adamic poetics,
  100–101; and Africa, 109, 110,
  165n. 63; African phase of, 110;
  Another Life, 97; articulation of
  Caribbean aesthetics, 97–104;
  attitude to Western literary and
  dramatic tradition, 96–97, 109–10,
  115; and Baraka 68; and black
  aesthetic, 98–99, 114–15; and
  calypso, 103; and Caribbean cultural
  identity, 101; carnival as source of
  dramaturgy, 25, 102–3; and Creole
  111–12; as culturalist, 115; criticism
  of Black Power, 98–100, 164n. 30;
  dramatic versus poetic languages,
  166n. 77; *Dream on Monkey
  Mountain*, 104–14; *Drums and
  Colurs*, 103; and expressive identity,
  115; *Flight and Sanctuary*, 110;
  formal eclecticism 114; *Henri
  Christophe*, 102; history as myth, 5,
  115; history as myth as performative
  identity, 98; history as time, 5, 115;
  history as time as expressive identity
  98; hybrid style, 5, 109, 110, 114–
  15; ideal West Indian play of, 103;
  inspiration from Japanese cinema
  and theatre, 102; *Ione*, 102; and
  language, 96–97, 99, 115; *The Last

Carnival, 97; on mulatto style, 103,
  114 (*see also* Walcott: hybrid style);
  Omeros 97; performative practice of,
  115; on poetic form, 99; and Poor
  Theatre, 112–13; and post-
  modernism, 163n. 22; and race,
  165n. 50; representation of women,
  109; *The Sea at Dauphin*, 102; on
  subjection to British Empire, 95–96;
  on Soyinka, 110; *Ti-Jean and His
  Brothers*, 102, 103, 142; and
  Trinidad Theatre Workshop, 102;
  on West Indian history, 94–97; and
  West Indian literature, 98
Wall, Cheryl A., 120, 123
Walker, Alice, 124
Weiss, Allen, 114
Wellek and Warren, 37
West, Cornel, 70
West Indian. *See* Caribbean
West Indies. *See* Caribbean
White, E. Frances, 116, 119
Whitman, Walt, 100
Williams, Adebayo, 156n. 65
Williams, Denis, 101
Williams, Raymond, 38, 69
Wilson, August, 142
Woodson, Carter G., 147n. 45
Wright, Richardson, 16

X, Malcolm, 82

Yoruba, 5, 24, 18, 38, 47, 49, 54,
  58–59, 60, 110,

Zagreus, 48
Zeus, 48